AF304853

accessible page turner, the book provides direct insights that can help anyone realize what they want from their career, their business, their relationships, or their life.

—DAVID FRIEDBERG, Serial Tech Entrepreneur, Host of
All-In Podcast

"Winning is temporary, but principles last. When your life is rooted in the right principles, they guide your decisions, strengthen your character, and impact every area of your life. A principle-driven leader doesn't just chase success—they build people, endure adversity, and leave a legacy that reaches far beyond the game."

—DEMARIO DAVIS, New Orleans Saints Linebacker and
Team Captain

"Improvisation in life, like music, needs a solid foundation. Since my friend Chase shared the book with me, it has become such a useful insight on my journey in business and community service. Having evolved over the years from life experience, *Becoming a Principle-Driven Leader* provides a solid foundation with proven principles that guide how we listen, lead, and create something that endures."

—JON BATISTE, Grammy Award–Winning Musician and
Composer

"Without a college degree or a conventional career path, I found my way by applying principles, learning, and contributing wherever I could. The principles covered in this book helped me grow into leadership roles and support others in their success. *Becoming a Principle-Driven Leader* truly reflects this experience —it's a practical guide for turning challenges into opportunities for growth."

—JARROD BENSON, Chief Information Officer, Koch

BECOMING A
PRINCIPLE
DRIVEN
LEADER

BECOMING A PRINCIPLE DRIVEN LEADER

41 PRINCIPLES TO BUILD AN ENDURING BUSINESS

CHARLES & CHASE KOCH

Becoming a Principle-Driven Leader:
41 Principles to Build an Enduring Business

Copyright © 2026 Koch IP Holdings, LLC.

Principle Based Management, PBM, Principled Entrepreneurship
and related logos are trademarks of Koch IP Holdings, LLC.

Published by StoryBrand Books, an imprint of Forefront Books, Nashville, Tennessee.
Distributed by Simon & Schuster.

Library of Congress Control Number: 2025926712

Print ISBN: 978-1-63763-524-7
E-book ISBN: 978-1-63763-525-4
International Trade Paper Edition: 978-1-63763-616-9

Cover Design by Tony Tharae, Ninth Minute, Inc.
Interior Design by Bill Kersey, KerseyGraphics
Principles table and sidebars designed by Mayra Ocampo, Koch, Inc.

Printed in the United States of America

26 27 28 29 30 31<RR4>10 9 8 7 6 5 4 3 2 1

DEDICATION

We are grateful to the many scholars whose insights led to the Principles of Human Progress. We dedicate this book to all the Koch team members who applied them to build an enduring business and transform our lives and the lives of many others.

ALSO BY CHARLES KOCH

The Science of Success

Good Profit

Continually Transforming Koch Industries Through
Virtuous Cycles of Mutual Benefit

With Brian Hooks
Believe in People: Bottom-Up Solutions for a Top-Down World
America's 250th anniversary edition

CONTENTS

PART I
HOW YOU CAN TRANSFORM YOURSELF

PART II
HOW YOU CAN TRANSFORM YOUR BUSINESS

PART III
HOW YOU CAN TRANSFORM SOCIETY

START YOUR JOURNEY OF
BECOMING A PRINCIPLE-DRIVEN LEADER

Ready to dive in? *Becoming a Principle-Driven Leader* offers a practical, story-driven, lifelong-learning platform that helps anyone apply principles to solve problems and build an enduring business and life.

Scan the QR code or head to www.principledrivenleader.com to find a multi-media destination filled with videos, ideas for application, and a generative AI book companion.

We look forward to hearing how people around the world are using these principles to make better decisions, empower people, build capabilities, and create lasting progress in every area of life.

PREFACE

never imagined I'd write a book with my father.

Don't get me wrong. I love Pop. I am who I am because of his and Mom's teaching and influence. But *he's* the one who writes the books and consumes dozens at a time in his quest to keep learning. While I'm also a lifelong learner, I prefer to be on the road, building partnerships and finding the next opportunity. The idea of working with him to further develop his ideas instead of just applying them never crossed my mind.

But then Brian Hooks, CEO of Stand Together (an organization Pop founded), suggested that I coauthor this book with Pop. He thought I could add a new perspective, increase the effectiveness of my business development role at Koch, and deepen my understanding of the principles that guide everything we do.

I knew this was the chance of a lifetime. And I especially liked the idea of focusing on the importance of applying principles to overcome failure. I have plenty of stories to share on that front. The lessons I've learned from those failures have created the framework for my life.

Throughout my career, many people have asked me, "How does Koch do it?" How did Koch build such an enduring business? They've read Pop's previous books, but they want more specifics—a full list and clearer explanation of the principles behind our success. They want stories that show how these principles work in practice—a how-to book.

You're likely reading this book for the same reason. You are wondering, "What are the Principles of Human Progress and how were they applied to build an enduring business?" It's a great question. It's a question that I've been learning the answer to from childhood. You see, I was a guinea pig for what you're about to read, so perhaps I can help translate some of the concepts we'll discuss and provide a few lessons and stories of my own.

As Pop was learning how to apply Principles of Human Progress, he experimented with his children. Every Sunday, my sister, Elizabeth, and I were required to listen to books on tape from the thinkers, doers, and dreamers who were shaping his understanding of the world.

It was, in a word, painful! What ten-year-old wants to listen to lectures from Friedrich Hayek, Abraham Maslow, Thomas Sowell, and Milton Friedman? Ugh. But when I came back to work at Koch in my mid-twenties, the principles from these lectures started coming to life for me.

I am now grateful for these lessons. After two decades of experience applying these principles, I understand their power. They enable us to better solve problems and capture opportunities. But even more amazing is what they enable beyond business. For me, they apply to everything—family, business, philanthropy, and even my other passion, creating music.

I am confident this book will speak to you, no matter where you are in your career or life. Maybe you feel stuck in a job that doesn't fit you. Maybe you aren't getting the results you think you could. Maybe you're struggling to keep up with today's rapid pace of change. No matter what challenges you face, Principles of Human Progress, the very principles that can transform you into a principle-driven leader, will help you overcome the obstacles holding you back.

These principles have led to Koch's success for the past sixty-plus years. For it to continue, we have learned the necessity both of understanding them and of continually improving their application. This may surprise you, but succession at Koch isn't based on our family's name; it's based on these principles.

I also hope this book will help you spread these principles to broader audiences: business leaders, entrepreneurs, philanthropists, influencers, and, ultimately, anyone who seeks a life of meaning. These are the CliffsNotes from a lifetime of learning—both Pop's and mine.

Applying these principles has transformed my life. So I've joined my father in writing this book to help you experience your own transformation. I believe you will find principles that will enable you to improve your life. And if you help others do the same, you will achieve something even better—a life of meaning.

Chase Koch

CHAPTER 1

HOW THESE PRINCIPLES CAN TRANSFORM EVERYTHING

Failure is success in progress.
—ALBERT EINSTEIN[1]

This book is about applying principles to succeed by overcoming failure. As the two of us have found from painful experience, failures are inevitable.

Our goal is to help you move from failure to lasting success in your work and life—the kind of success that comes from achieving your potential and helping others improve their lives.

We're attempting to give you an effective how-to book. We say "attempting" because overcoming failure and achieving success requires ongoing effort and trial and error. The thing about failure is that we tend to experience a lot of it before it teaches us the lessons necessary to succeed. Just ask Thomas Edison, who, after five months and more than nine thousand failed attempts to develop a battery, said, "I know several thousand things that won't work!"[2]

We've learned these lessons at Koch the hard way, having stumbled more times than we can count. For us, the redemptive aspect of failure is that you can learn from it. When you do, failure can be a blessing in disguise. If you don't, you have missed a valuable opportunity. Despite their great value, though, our many failures tend to surprise people.

Koch is generally known as an American success story. The numbers reflect this, at least over the long term. Between 1960 and the end of 2024, the company's value increased more than nine-thousandfold.

But getting there has been anything but smooth. Our long-term growth hides a rocky road. We haven't just had *difficult* times—there were years when it looked like Koch might not survive.

Consider a few of our corporate lowlights.

Our success in building our petroleum and tanker trading business in the early 1970s led us to take reckless financial risks and get into situations beyond our capabilities. When the Arab oil embargo and production cuts hit in 1973 and 1974, we suffered massive losses, causing overall earnings to drop by 81 percent. These losses, combined with enormous potential liabilities stemming from price controls, could have forced us into bankruptcy.

To solve these company-threatening problems, we changed leadership and vision, greatly tightened trading authorities, and improved compliance. These changes righted the ship, and by 1975, earnings were growing again.

Fast-forward two decades. By the 1990s, growth had slowed. In our attempt to recapture it, we set in motion a chain of events that led to a series of failures, most notably in our agriculture (Ag) and oil refining businesses.

In Ag, we hired leaders who took us into markets in which we didn't have the capabilities to succeed. The list included grain trading, milling and baking, feed lots, meat processing, and animal feed. Our largest Ag investment was the acquisition of Purina Mills, which went bankrupt. We even attempted to create a business making shelf-stable pizza crusts. As our failures compounded, it became clear we needed to radically limit ourselves to what we did well.

Meanwhile, in refining, we put people in charge who turned out to be unprincipled. Rather than working to create value for customers and the business, they focused on maximizing their control by keeping Koch leadership in the dark. They also pushed out good, long-term employees who were trying to do the right things. In addition, they misrepresented their performance to increase their compensation.

These problems contributed to Koch's overall earnings decline of 73 percent in 1998. The situation was exacerbated by a long-simmering lawsuit by former shareholders that went to trial that same year. It created a major distraction for Koch leadership, especially Charles.

After winning that lawsuit in 1998, we quickly began dealing with our many problems. In our refining business, we replaced unprincipled leaders and made other changes to get the organization back on track. Crucially, we adopted a bottom-up approach, with solutions recommended and implemented by committed employees. No more top-down command and control. As for agriculture, we exited the segments that were failing, refocusing on our core fertilizer business.

Finally, consider what happened in the mid-2010s. Between 2013 and 2016, our earnings declined 25 percent, with worse declines on the horizon. At a gathering of our two hundred most senior leaders, we learned from various specialists that many of our core industries were on the brink of profound disruption. Electric vehicles, alternative energy, advances in automation, artificial intelligence, and other developments were reshaping our world. We realized that **Creative Destruction** was happening faster than ever, threatening the entire company.

That realization led to a plan of action: We would transform ourselves more fundamentally and quickly. We embraced continual transformation and reorganized the company, helping our leaders find roles where they could make the biggest contribution. In 2017, we returned to healthy growth, and by 2021, earnings had more than doubled.

These are only a few of the tough times we faced, reflected in the following chart. In fact, you will notice that we've had almost as many bad years as we've had exceptional ones. Management guru W. E. Deming said it well, "You never get out of this hospital."[3]

So much for the idea that Koch's story is one of continual success!

Koch Inc. Earnings Variation 1960–2025 (1960=1)

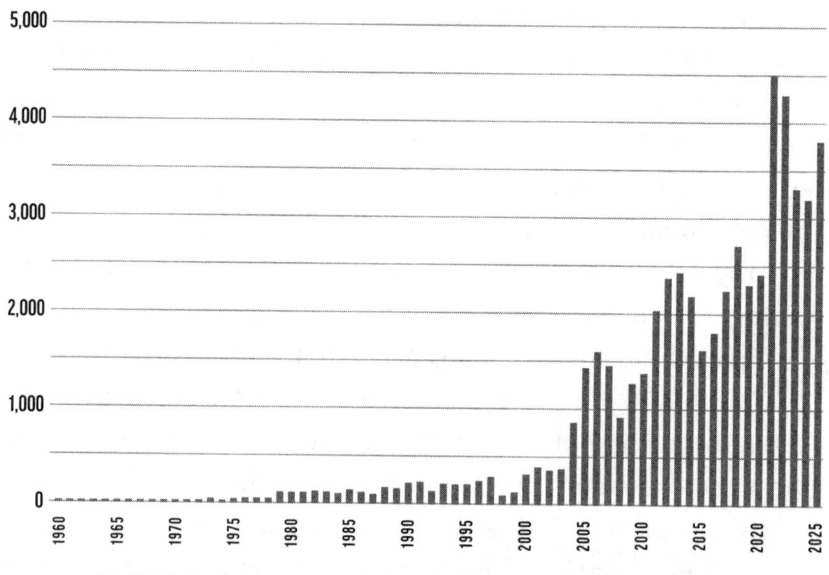

Note: While this chart shows earnings have increased as much as 4,500-fold, Koch's valuation has increased 9,000-fold.

And yet, we have succeeded over the long haul, precisely because we've learned from our failures and acted to address them. While we've made many mistakes, once we recognized them, we used principles as our tools to correct them.

This is the primary characteristic of a principle-driven leader: a person who applies principles of human progress to solve problems, especially when those problems were caused by mistakes made by the leaders themselves.

Principles of Human Progress have been core to Koch ever since the mid-1960s. We have continually worked to better understand, apply, and add to them. We do so in every aspect of our company—from the biggest business decisions to the seemingly smallest actions. We say "seemingly" because the more we all apply principles, the better we do.

Whenever we've ignored or misapplied principles, we've brought hard times upon ourselves. In fact, it's fair to say that almost every business failure we've had ultimately stemmed from a failure to put these principles into practice. Conversely, when we've correctly applied principles, we've moved from failure to success, often rapidly. You can see this in our earnings chart.

Applying principles starts with leaders who have the responsibility of recognizing when we are failing and taking action. Both of us feel that responsibility intensely, as do other leaders.

But applying principles is important for everyone in the company. We strive to empower Koch's more than 120,000 global employees with the tools to identify gaps between what we *are* and what we *could be*. We empower employees to close those gaps, in continual cycles of analysis, improvement, and transformation—individually and as a company.

Our focus on principles sets Koch apart from many companies. History is littered with the names of those that have been overtaken by events or competitors. Like bankruptcy, a business collapse tends to happen gradually, then suddenly. Applying principles is the proven way to minimize the risk of failure and succeed long term.

But what, exactly, are these principles? While the company has tried to answer this question for sixty years, this book is our most comprehensive attempt to date. It's also our most expansive effort to introduce these principles to the world—starting with you.

In our experience, a business is only as good as its people, and people are only as effective as their implementation of principles. You can achieve incredible success—and overcome any failure—by applying them in your life and work.

Once you are committed to the principles—that is, committed to a never-ending journey of discovering and applying them—you become a principle-driven leader.

For proof, let's review history—that's what makes the importance of principles the clearest.

PRINCIPLES OF HUMAN PROGRESS

The principles that guide us aren't uniquely Koch principles. Rather, they're what we call Principles of Human Progress.

These actionable concepts have been proven over time to promote peace, civility, opportunity, and fulfillment. In the context of business, they enable us to deal with failure and find the success that comes from creating value for others—what we call good profit.

Think about our nine-thousandfold growth. It's the result of our attempt to emulate humanity's ascent by applying the underlying principles in ways that enable a business to succeed long term.

We've often heard people compare Koch's growth to a hockey stick, with continuous growth that's only picked up speed. That's a false picture, given our many failures to apply these principles that contributed to the large fluctuations in year-to-year earnings.

To see a real hockey stick, consider the next chart. It shows what economist Deirdre McCloskey calls the hockey stick of human history. She also calls it the "Great Enrichment."[4] But even it has been smoothed out. The reality is that entire countries have also had large fluctuations in the quality of life due to a failure to apply Principles of Human Progress. This resulted in wars, dictatorships, and depressions.

Global Average GDP Per Capita over the Long Run[5]

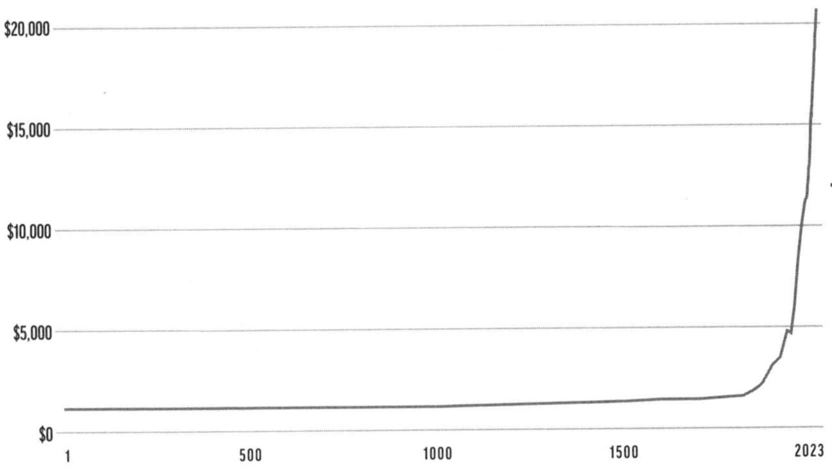

Look at the low, flat line that runs across nearly the entire chart. It depicts the reality that, for countless millennia, humanity trudged along in what can best be described as a miserable existence. Until the world began to haltingly apply these principles, there was virtually no sustainable progress.

Prior to 1800, almost half the children died before age fifteen. Average life expectancy hovered between thirty and forty years. The vast majority of the population lived and died poor.[6]

Up to that point, even the greatest civilizations hadn't shifted humanity's trajectory. The ancient Egyptians, Greeks, Romans, and Chinese at best delivered modest improvements that disappeared quickly. Moreover, even the wealthiest and most powerful had profoundly unpleasant lives, compared to the standards of the twenty-first century.

History, it seemed, was destined to regress toward the mean, in both senses of the word. The seventeenth-century philosopher Thomas Hobbes described life without society as "solitary, poore, nasty, brutish, and short," but in fact, he was describing life as it was for essentially everyone.[7]

Then humanity's fate changed abruptly. Since the late 1700s, poverty plummeted, life expectancy soared, and virtually every measure of human well-being rose dramatically. You see it on the right side of the preceding chart, in the shape of the hockey stick.

In the past 250 years, humanity has powered the world with electricity, cured diseases that once ran riot, and discovered ways to instantaneously communicate over the farthest distances. For thousands of years, the wheel was the cutting edge of transportation. Then, in the historical blink of an eye, we developed steam engines, cars, and airplanes. In just over a hundred years, we went from horses to rockets that took us to the moon, and soon even to Mars.

This is an illustration of the power of principles. The economic philosopher F. A. Hayek summed this up well: "The possibility of men living together in peace and to their mutual advantage . . . bound only by abstract rules of conduct, was perhaps the greatest discovery mankind ever made."[8] Those "abstract rules of conduct" are Principles of Human Progress.

Because each principle is important in its own right, and because these principles work together—not unlike the way the laws of nature work to create the ecosystem that allows human life to flourish—we have not numbered the principles as though they were rules or a step-by-step plan. The numbering does not indicate relative importance. Rather, we will weave in and out of them, showing you how they reinforce each other. As you internalize and apply them, you'll be better equipped to build an enduring business and live a meaningful life.

Some societies began to identify and apply principles that enable human flourishing—to move away from top-down control. That's a large part of what impoverished humanity throughout history prior to the late eighteenth century. Rulers dictated how people lived their lives, causing stagnation at best and suffering at worst. Instead, for the first time, ordinary people were empowered through Property Rights to drive progress from the bottom up, improving lives by working together for their mutual benefit. All kinds of people quickly proved capable of accomplishing extraordinary things.

> **1**
>
> PRINCIPLE:
> # PROPERTY RIGHTS
>
> Although property rights have been around for centuries, only recently have they been considered essential to a civil, peaceful, and prosperous society. When they are protected, property rights flow to those who produce the products, services, and innovations that people value, and away from those who do not. This is a requirement for human flourishing.

This process was not seamless or without serious shortcomings. Even societies that began applying *some* principles violated others. Still, as they slowly improved their selection of principles, they demonstrated what's possible when people begin to be empowered. This set in motion a chain of empowerment that broke ever more barriers that block human potential.

More barrier-breaking is urgently needed today. Poverty still ruins billions of lives. Disease still causes millions of deaths. Injustices both large and small still hold back huge numbers of people in our country and throughout the world. Imagine if humanity had discovered and started applying the right principles a thousand years ago. We could have already reached a much better future, with the hockey stick rising to even greater heights.

If people, organizations, and societies more fully applied the principles that have transformed human progress, the possibilities would be unlimited. In the same way that today's progress was unimaginable to people in the 1700s, tomorrow's progress is unimaginable to us. Principles give you the ability to get there!

By now, you're surely asking yourself: "What, exactly, are those principles?"

There are many more than we can adequately cover here, but we've identified forty-one that are particularly important to business. We will focus on them.

HOW WE'LL SHARE THESE PRINCIPLES

Only a few of the principles in this book are original to us. Rather, we primarily drew them from the lessons of history, conveyed in a number of disciplines and by hundreds of authors, thinkers, and doers. Because of our dedication to principles, we've come to understand the importance of "standing on the shoulders of giants."

We also acknowledge that not all principles are beneficial. Some are very destructive, as evidenced by the top-down principles applied by Lenin, Hitler, and Mao, which led to the death of hundreds of millions and the immiseration of billions.

We've framed the beneficial Principles of Human Progress in ways that we've found to be most helpful to starting, running, and transforming businesses of all kinds. There are other ways to describe and organize them, but we hope our language and framework help clarify exactly what we're talking about.

We'll never claim to have a complete list of principles.

Charles has spent the last sixty-plus years identifying and learning to apply Principles of Human Progress. Chase was introduced to these principles early on, but it was only when he began working at Koch twenty years ago that they truly came to life for him.

There are now employees throughout Koch devoted to understanding, explaining, and helping others apply those Principles of Human Progress that we have identified so far. Our forty-one principles are listed on the next two pages. They are an endless spring of knowledge, worthy of a lifetime of learning.

Each one is covered in the book and numbered in order of appearance, not in order of importance, and explained in the appendix (alphabetically).

Of course, the number of principles isn't set in stone. By the time you read this, we'll be debating better ways to explain and apply principles and even discovering and adding more.

You may find forty-one principles intimidating, but by the time you finish this book, they won't be. The stories of Koch's experiences will accelerate your ability to apply these principles to get results.

While principles are mentioned on almost every page, you'll also find principle sidebars throughout the book. These brief, focused explanations provide helpful insight. All principles are interrelated, often closely. It is rare to find a problem or failure that hinges on a single principle. This is why they are best understood as a collection. They are much more likely to help produce superior results when applied holistically rather than separately.

PRINCIPLE: (in order of appearance)	Sidebar on page…
1 Property Rights	25
2 Transformation	30
3 Experimental Discovery	38
4 Talents	40
5 Self-Actualize	41
6 Life of Meaning and Synergy	42
7 Empowerment	45
8 Bottom-Up vs. Top-Down	46
9 Virtuous Cycles of Mutual Benefit	48
10 Integrity	49
11 Division of Labor by Comparative Advantage	50
12 Knowledge	67
13 Mutual Benefit	69
14 Humility	70
15 Creative Destruction	73
16 Scientific Method and Challenge	89
17 Republic of Science	91
18 Requirements for Human Action	94
19 Motivation	95
20 Measures	100
21 Principled Entrepreneurship™	105

PRINCIPLE: (in order of appearance)	Sidebar on page…
22 Our Values	108
23 Principle-Based vs. Rule-Based	111
24 Personal Knowledge	115
25 Closing Gaps	118
26 Headwinds and Tailwinds	127
27 Accountability	131
28 Changing Paradigms	133
29 Marginal Analysis	135
30 Options	139
31 Overcoming Entropy and Bureaucracy	143
32 Contribution Motivated	155
33 Stewardship and Compliance	165
34 Risk	167
35 Respect	170
36 Capabilities	188
37 Time Preference	209
38 Alignment of Incentives	213
39 Economic Thinking	217
40 Partnerships	221
41 Openness	222

The principle of Transformation conveys how applying principles can help you overcome failure and succeed.

At Koch, we prioritize transformation because the world is not only rapidly changing, but the rate of change is accelerating. We used to emphasize "continuous improvement." Then we shifted to "periodic transformation," before moving to "continual transformation" after realizing we needed something more urgent. If we don't continually transform, we will fail.

> **2**
>
> PRINCIPLE:
> # TRANSFORMATION
>
> Transformation means fundamentally improving what you do and how you do it. It's both the driver and result of progress for companies and individuals alike.
>
> Transformation doesn't mean doing what you've been doing a little better or a little faster. It means finding ways to do things much better or much faster, or doing entirely new things. Transformation requires relentlessly seeking knowledge of methods, technologies, and trends from anywhere in the world that might improve, disrupt, or revolutionize what we do today.

As for the structure of the book, there are three parts. All are focused on business, each with a different emphasis.

In the first part, we tell our individual stories. We show how we came to recognize and respect principles and how they've shaped our lives and careers. We especially focus on how we've used principles to deal with failure.

The second part is about the ongoing application of these principles in Koch. They've helped us overcome our failures and learn how to succeed long term. We show how they can help transform your business or organization too. If you're interested in how a company like Koch tackles hot-button issues such as Diversity, Equity, and Inclusion (DEI), and Environmental, Social, and Governance (ESG), you'll find the principle-based answers here.

The book's third and final part is about how our company approaches social change—something many businesses struggle to do effectively.

Business has a powerful role to play in improving society. Many companies fail to make a difference and even make things worse. Whether supplying products and services or engaging in corporate philanthropy, businesses can drive the most progress by applying principles. We'll also share our failures here, along with what we've learned from them.

We view this book as the beginning of a conversation with you, not the final word. Principle Based Management™ (PBM™) is the framework we developed to help everyone at Koch understand and apply principles to get results. Many companies and organizations use this framework to improve their results. It's our hope PBM can also help you succeed.

A PRINCIPLED FUTURE

Koch is destined to experience more failures.

In fact, we think failure is becoming more likely given the rapid pace of economic, technological, and political change. When applying principles, we must continually up our game given the stakes.

That is why we've spent the last few years going to unprecedented lengths to help our employees understand and apply principles. We've never listed them so clearly and consistently, nor explained them so fully. While we will always have more work to do, Koch is now better positioned to handle failure than at any point since the company's founding.

We wrote this book to empower you to overcome failures, whatever your business or individual role.

We want to help you achieve continual transformation. By applying principles, you won't just find success in your own work; you'll find a **Life of Meaning**, and your contributions will help make the hockey stick of human history move ever upward.

We believe in such a future and in your ability to help reach it. And we know from experience that applying principles will enable you to become a principle-driven leader and accomplish more than you ever could otherwise.

As a family, we often talk about a letter written by Fred Koch, the cofounder of our company. The letter was found in his safe deposit box after his death in 1967. In it, he wrote to his sons that he would "regret very much to have you miss the glorious feeling of accomplishment." He quickly followed that uplifting note with a reminder that "often adversity is a blessing in disguise and is certainly the greatest character builder."

Those words have powerfully shaped our lives. In our experience, "the glorious feeling of accomplishment" can only be found in the continual application of principles as you strive to make a difference. It's never simple, and we're always prone to make mistakes. But the resulting adversity can truly be a blessing in disguise.

As you encounter failure, remember that principles can guide you back to success. Failure isn't final as long as you learn enough from it. And remember that however much you've achieved, these principles can help you accomplish still more, not only in business, but in all aspects of your life.

This is the story of our lives and our company. May applying principles to succeed become part of your story too.

PART I

HOW YOU CAN TRANSFORM YOURSELF

CHAPTER 2

HOW PRINCIPLES TRANSFORMED CHARLES' LIFE AND OUR BUSINESS

What one can be, one must be.
—ABRAHAM MASLOW[9]

BIG IDEAS TO WATCH FOR

- Discover your gifts and apply them to create value for others.
- Progress comes from empowering all people to realize their potential.
- Well-designed experiments allow you to learn from failure, leading to better solutions.

'm often asked a simple question: "Charles, how did you become so successful?"

My answer is equally simple: by applying principles and being willing to make mistakes.

Much of my life has been a combination of wandering in the wilderness and trial and error. I freely acknowledge that I won the birth lottery. My parents worked hard to give me and my brothers a head start in life. But I nearly squandered my blessings many times. I spent twenty years lost, narrowly avoiding catastrophes.

3

PRINCIPLE:
EXPERIMENTAL DISCOVERY

Progress in business, science, and life comes through experimentation and failure. Experimentation helps you find what works—and what doesn't. As attributed to Einstein, "Someone who has never made a mistake has never tried anything new."[10] Any attempt to eliminate failure only ensures greater failure.

A successful business must apply Experimental Discovery to its vision, strategies, products, services, and methods. When well designed, it leads to new knowledge that brings about change, even if our assumptions or hypotheses are disproven. We learn even more when we explore a range of possibilities that includes the areas of greatest uncertainty and potential.

To encourage Experimental Discovery, well-planned experiments that fail shouldn't be penalized since they generate discovery and learnings. This is vital to innovation, growth, and long-term profitability. It also empowers employees: Experimenting to discover new ways to create value makes their work more interesting and exciting.

My early life was defined by a search for meaning. Like most kids, I learned that I was better at some things than others. I vividly remember my third-grade teacher writing math problems on the blackboard. The answers were obvious to me, but not to others.

That realization was my first clue that I had a gift. Of course, I didn't fully understand it. It took many years before I realized that my gift went beyond solving basic math problems; rather, I had a talent for understanding and applying abstract concepts.

As a child, however, I had no time for the abstract. I was too busy getting in trouble. My father, Fred, had no intention of allowing me and my brothers to grow up to be "country club bums." I bore the brunt of his intensity, likely because he saw how rebellious I could be. His solution was a daily regimen of manual labor. Years later, I asked him why he had been so much tougher on me than my younger brothers. His answer: "Son, you plumb wore me out!"

Starting at age six, I spent my afternoons and weekends feeding animals, shoveling manure, and milking cows on the family farm, graduating to harder work as I grew older. At age fifteen, my father shipped me off to our Montana ranch for the summer, where I worked fourteen hours a day at a line camp. My bunkmate, Bitterroot Bob, was an ornery cuss. After being bucked off his horse, he threatened to beat it to death with a two-by-four. He didn't, but rather than riding him, he spent the afternoon shooting holes in the roof of our cabin to scare me. Most of his other bully pranks aren't fit for print.

I didn't respond well to my father's hard-nosed approach; it left me feeling like I had little value. Despite my third-grade epiphany about math, I put no effort into my education, so my grades were less than stellar. My parents sent me to three different elementary schools, with little improvement. For my seventh and eighth grades, they shipped me off to a school in Arizona. When that didn't go well, they tried one in Colorado. Those boarding schools were straight out of *Lord of the Flies*, with the stronger kids tormenting the weaker ones. My pleading and tears finally swayed my parents to let me attend a public high school in Wichita, Kansas, my sophomore year.

My best buddies were the wildest kids—because they were the most exciting! Starting at age fourteen, I snuck out at night on the weekends. My friends would pick me up on the road, then we would head for bars and strip clubs. My mother complained that my friends were a bad influence. My father replied, "Maybe *he's* the bad influence."

To save me from myself, they searched for a boarding school that might help me. Deerfield Academy in Massachusetts agreed to accept me, but only if they held me back a grade. My father refused.

He then discovered Culver Military Academy in Indiana, which he believed would provide the discipline I needed. My grades improved, but during my junior year, I was caught drinking with other cadets on the train returning from spring break. We were all expelled.

When I arrived home the next morning, after an all-nighter on the train, I was terrified in anticipation of my father's wrath. His greeting was, "I see you made it, boy. I've been trying to decide what to do with you." His decision was to send me to Quanah, Texas, where he grew up, to live with his brother. Once again, I befriended the wildest kids. We would sneak across the Oklahoma border to buy beer. Once discovered, my uncle stopped it and got me a job shoveling wheat in the local grain elevator—a fate I richly deserved.

Despite my antics, my grades in Quanah were very good. I got a perfect score on the math final, but I was shocked when my friends criticized me for doing more than the seven out of the ten problems needed to pass. That seemed to me, even then, to be a recipe for failure. I was also beginning to see that I needed to associate with people I could learn from, rather than those who brought out the worst in me.

Years later, I started reading psychologists who helped me understand the challenges and realizations I was experiencing.

One was Howard Gardner, who developed the theory of multiple intelligences. He helped me see that no one is *either* smart or dumb. Rather, we're *all* smart and dumb in different ways. Based on Gardner's classification system, I excel at logical-mathematical thinking, but I'm mediocre, at best, at almost everything else. He identified eight kinds of intelligence, which

---

4

PRINCIPLE:
TALENTS

A key factor when selecting and retaining employees is whether they have a talent they use to help us succeed long term. This requires employees who work to fully develop their talents and apply them in roles where they can maximize their contribution.

I believe is a major underestimation of our variations, but his insight still holds. The idea that everyone has a talent and can contribute played a big role in my later principle-based attempts to transform the family business.

Psychologist Abraham Maslow became one of the biggest influences in my life. I found his insights so helpful that in the 1970s I requested permission from his widow to print several thousand copies of his out-of-print book *Eupsychian Management* for distribution to our employees. Maslow clarified what I had been experiencing: "If you deliberately plan to be less than you are capable of being … you'll be deeply unhappy for the rest of your life. You will be evading your own capacities, your own potential."[11] You avoid this fate by self-actualizing, by becoming everything you are capable of.

We most fully self-actualize when we achieve what Maslow called "synergy" by resolving "the dichotomy between selfishness and unselfishness."[12]

I was tiptoeing toward this principle during my days in Quanah. Thankfully, my good grades got me readmitted to

5

PRINCIPLE:
SELF-ACTUALIZE

To self-actualize is a deeply personal journey of discovering your aptitudes, developing skills, and using them in productive ways. Self-actualizing is not about reaching the peak of a mountain, but rather, navigating a series of peaks that you continue to climb that give your life meaning.

Self-actualizing requires deliberately and persistently striving to improve and develop your gifts in ways that are beneficial to others. This journey involves experimenting to discover the work in which you can make the greatest contribution and be fulfilled. It also requires being a lifelong learner. As Maslow put it, "We learn also about our own strengths and limits and extend them by overcoming difficulties … by meeting challenge and hardship, even by failing."[13]

Culver, although I still had to repeat the spring semester in summer school. I spent that summer and my senior year working as never before. My turnaround paid off as I neared graduation. Thanks to my grades and gift for math and science, I was accepted at the Massachusetts Institute of Technology.

I liked MIT because it spoke my language: math. But when I arrived in the fall of 1953, I didn't have a good sense of what major best fit me. So I followed my father's example in experimentation, not in trying to be as tough as he was. (When he was at MIT, he was captain of the boxing team. I played rugby, which I loved because of its fellowship, not its toughness, and became vice captain.)

My father was a quintessential innovator. As a kid, I watched him continually search for new and better ways of doing things—in business, family, and every facet of his life. One of his experiments was with "Tiger's Milk," an abominable combination of buttermilk, orange juice, and yeast that he made me drink because he believed it was healthy. My way of experimentation was to try several different majors and take as many math and concept-oriented courses as I could.

I should have known from my father's experiences that I'd have more misses than hits. I disliked chemical engineering, mainly because of the required memorization of chemicals and their reactions. The same went for geology; I had no desire to memorize the scientific name for every rock on

---

6

PRINCIPLE:
LIFE OF MEANING AND SYNERGY

We live a life of meaning when we succeed in our own life by helping others succeed. We can live such a life "by pursuing [our] own self-interest, automatically benefitting everyone else, whether we mean to or not."[14]

earth. Finally, I tried mechanical engineering, but that didn't fit either. By the start of my junior year, I had tried so many different majors that I hadn't built up enough credits for any one specific discipline. So I defaulted to an undergraduate degree in general engineering.

My appetite for learning was whetted, and I began to realize that I needed to focus where I could apply my gift for abstractions. I signed up for a master's degree in nuclear engineering on the assumption that nuclear energy was the perfect combination of abstraction and application. It quickly became clear that in the nuclear industry I would be stifled by top-down regulation, which didn't appeal to me. I wanted a career where I could experiment and innovate.

So I felt compelled to pursue a second master's degree in chemical engineering, which I earned the next year, in 1959. While I considered going a step further with a doctorate, my department head explained that my advisors would have me working on things that benefited *their* careers, not mine. He said that if I wanted to go into business, I should get out of there as quickly as possible. He was absolutely right.

I went to work at Arthur D. Little, a broad-based Boston consulting firm. I chose the firm because it gave me the chance to try out many different fields. I started in product development but wasn't very good at laboratory work. To motivate me to improve my safety practices, they made me safety chairman. I arranged to get transferred to process development, which fit me a little better, but something was still missing. So I tried management services, which gave me the opportunity at age twenty-five to consult on strategy and innovation.

The experience confirmed that I should become an entrepreneur. Fortunately, I was about to get that opportunity and start my transformation.

A STRUGGLING BUSINESS

In 1961, my father called me with an ultimatum: "My health is poor, and I don't have long to live, so either you come home to run the company, or I'll have to sell it."

He had asked me to come to work for him before, but I had politely declined. I believed he would be too controlling for me to succeed. But this time, he promised that I could run Koch Engineering without his interference. Since he had made my brothers and me the only shareholders, I didn't believe I would get a better entrepreneurial opportunity. And, as always, my father kept his promise.

I knew coming home wouldn't be a walk in the park. Koch Engineering was small and barely breaking even. Plus, I had no experience running a business; I'd only advised up to that point. But, from the moment I started, I asked myself, "How do I ensure this business can succeed and grow?"

Koch Engineering was such a mess that, even with my lack of experience, I was able to make significant improvements. But I was motivated to do more—much more.

I turned to my gift for abstractions. From my studies and consulting work, I knew that entrepreneurs succeed by building the capabilities to create value for others. So I needed to understand the principles that made that possible.

To find them, I read everything I could from history and every relevant discipline—from Abraham Maslow and Viktor Frankl to Sigmund Freud; from Friedrich Hayek to John Maynard Keynes; from John Locke to Karl Marx; and thousands of others from a vast array of fields and perspectives. To this day, no topic is off-limits. No authors are out-of-bounds. Even when I don't agree with them, it broadens my perspective. As the philosopher John Stuart Mill put it, "He who knows only his own side of the case, knows little of that."[15]

A world of knowledge opened before me. The more I read, the more captivated I became with the story of human progress—the story you briefly encountered earlier, and which I've detailed more fully in another book, *Believe in People*. I became convinced that certain principles had enabled humanity to rise from the darkness of the cave into the light of progress.

Since I was running a business, I was intrigued by the central role of innovation and entrepreneurship in changing humanity's fortunes. I was especially keen to understand why innovation suddenly took off in the eighteenth and nineteenth centuries. The answer was **Empowerment**—one of the earliest principles I discovered.

The environment I found at Koch Engineering denied empowerment. It was controlling and stifling. No one was allowed to contribute or innovate. Consequently, employees were prevented from moving forward and reaching their potential.

I quickly found that many employees had excellent ideas—ideas that would never have occurred to me. But instead of engaging and

7

PRINCIPLE:
EMPOWERMENT

When we believe we have gifts that can be developed and are free to determine and control our own lives, we are empowered to contribute, make a difference, and realize our potential. A contribution mindset and a supportive, inclusive environment facilitate Empowerment, while internal barriers hinder Empowerment. These include doubts and limiting beliefs. If someone feels incapable of contributing or afraid of making mistakes, they will fail. By contrast, those who believe in themselves are more likely to realize what they can become and then succeed.

External barriers exist when the key institutions of society hinder or impede an individual's progress. When a business erects such barriers, its employees tend to fail, causing the business to fail. People become empowered when they are enabled to discover, develop, and apply their gifts.

8

PRINCIPLE:
BOTTOM-UP VS. TOP-DOWN

A top-down approach presumes those in control know what's best for everyone else. Those who apply it typically seek power, impose their decisions, and use detailed rules and coercion that stifle others.

A bottom-up approach respects the inherent worth of each person and unleashes their creativity, initiative, and talents. When behavior is governed by this principle, the outcome exceeds what anyone could have planned or predicted.

This approach does not mean decentralizing all decisions or equally distributing authorities. Leaders should only make those decisions for which they have the demonstrated capability, while seeking and using the input and challenge of those who can improve those decisions.

listening to them, company leaders had only tried to control them—the opposite of Empowerment.

For instance, the company's president would send weekly questionnaires to his subordinates, making them explain each expense item, no matter how small. As a result, they had no motivation and little time to apply their skills doing productive work. This lack of empowerment helped explain why the office equipment was obsolete and the bookkeeping was always six months behind.

As bad as things were, I knew they'd get even worse if not quickly addressed. Koch Engineering was on a destructive downward spiral. When employees know that no one will listen to them, they keep their ideas to themselves. Worse, they stop looking for ways to improve.

There's a name for that: stagnation. A stagnant business will soon be a failed business, just as a person who doesn't learn and improve will fail to realize their potential.

I set out to create a culture of Empowerment in which employees would offer suggestions and solve problems. While I didn't use this exact language at the time, I was trying to apply a closely related principle—**Bottom-Up vs. Top-Down**. As the human story shows, progress isn't imposed from on high. Rather, it results from individuals spontaneously applying their talents to benefit others. The Wright brothers, for example—bicycle mechanics who had no college education—invented the airplane and reached the skies long before the "experts" who had gotten the federal government's support and funding. The persistent upstarts with a dream did what the "best and brightest" could not.

My goal was to give Koch Engineering a new lease on life. In the early 1960s, the company made only one product: a fractionating tray that separates and purifies liquids.

Listening to our customers and employees helped us find a path forward. We put a new emphasis on serving our customers, brought in new leadership who modernized our systems, and consolidated our European operations into a single facility in Bergamo, Italy. Until then, multiple contractors in various countries were used to make the different parts. Although intended to protect our designs, the resulting complexity made the business uncompetitive in every way.

That same facility later provided a case study in top-down mentality. Its union leaders told us that our philosophy was no good because in Italy, "managers think, workers work, and you're asking us to do the manager's job." That philosophy, of course, is antithetical to Empowerment, holding back business success and economic progress.

In true experimental fashion, we launched a host of initiatives in the 1960s, many of which failed. Among them was attempting to make activated carbon out of petroleum coke, thus creating a premium product with near zero raw material costs. Another was scaling up chromatography to perform commercial separations, which we hoped would give us a big cost advantage. Despite those failures, the overdue combination of much-needed changes quickly turned the business around. We doubled sales and added products that fit our capabilities. By 1965, Koch Engineering was solidly profitable. This success was brought about by creating **Virtuous Cycles of Mutual Benefit** (a principle I formalized many years later).

Our family's main business, Rock Island Oil, which gathered crude oil by pipeline in southern Oklahoma, was also transformed by creating a Virtuous Cycle of Mutual Benefit. My father began involving me in that business in 1962.

Once again, I found that leaders hadn't been listening to employees or pursuing opportunities. Rock Island's leadership was afraid the major oil companies wouldn't do business with them if they competed in gathering new fields. That's a protectionist mindset, and as you'll see in future chapters, it directly conflicts with the principle of Creative Destruction.

PRINCIPLE:
VIRTUOUS CYCLES OF MUTUAL BENEFIT

9

A Virtuous Cycle of Mutual Benefit is the process by which we continually build capabilities that create value for others, a never-ending, mutually beneficial process of opportunity generation.

Just as I learned by taking Koch Engineering's business beyond fractionating trays, I learned from Sterling Varner, the assistant to Rock Island's president, to extend our oil gathering business beyond Oklahoma. Sterling was a kindred spirit. We began building the capabilities to compete for new fields in the US and Canada. We hired crude oil purchasing representatives and bought trucking companies that were gathering oil in new areas. Independent producers selected us to build pipelines into new fields because we moved quickly and without the demands the major oil companies were making. We created a trading capability so we could always move the producers' oil, even when there was a surplus. In short, we provided what the independent producers valued.

I was feeling euphoric. As I applied the principles I was learning outside of work, I was developing my primary aptitude—that is, understanding and implementing abstract concepts. Better put, I was self-actualizing, enjoying ever more fulfillment by making an ever-bigger contribution. As a result, my father got all the other stockholders to agree to create a parent company and make me the president to ensure that I would be his successor.

> **10**
>
> PRINCIPLE:
> ## INTEGRITY
>
> Integrity means being committed to and living by a beneficial moral code, which requires courage, because doing the right thing is often difficult or even threatening. Fred Koch never flinched.

But while I was having the time of my life, my father was facing imminent death. His health problems mounted, leading to three heart attacks in 1967. The last one was fatal.

Upon my father's death, I was made chairman and CEO of our company at age thirty-two. I wanted to honor my father, who had taught me so much—especially the value of hard work, the importance of **Experimental Discovery,** and the nonnegotiability of **Integrity**. In his memory, we renamed the parent company Koch Industries, Inc. (now Koch Inc.).

But I didn't just want to honor his name. I wanted to take the business he cofounded as far as possible by contributing to human progress.

PRINCIPLES PROVE THEIR POWER

Those early years were a whirlwind. The more I read, the more principles I learned. The more principles I learned, the more I tried to apply them in the business and inspire coworkers and others to do the same. The more we tried to apply principles, the more we found what didn't work. And the more we experimented, even when we failed, the more paths to success we found.

From the start, I focused a lot on an essential principle first identified by economist David Ricardo, the **Division of Labor by Comparative Advantage**. While the phrase sounds wonky, it is one of the most important Principles of Human Progress. We have found that a beneficial division of labor by comparative advantage requires a diversity of employees who are contribution-motivated and have a variety of aptitudes or skills. That's key to solving problems and seizing opportunities.

Throughout human history, hardly anyone discovered their own gift, much less developed or applied it. They couldn't, because they weren't allowed. Daily life was controlled from the top down, making it a struggle to survive.

Everyone has a gift or gifts. My third-grade realization about math hinted at my own gift for understanding and applying abstract concepts. By focusing on our gifts and by collaborating with other people who are focused on theirs, we achieve significantly more. Focus leads to specialization, and that specialization has been a key to human progress over the past 250 years.

11

PRINCIPLE:
DIVISION OF LABOR BY COMPARATIVE ADVANTAGE

Progress occurs when people specialize based on their gifts and cooperate with others who have different gifts. The resulting teamwork is much more effective at satisfying people's needs than any other form of organization. This occurs when every employee is in the role where they can make the greatest contribution relative to what else they could be doing and what other employees could do.

It's equally essential to business success. Companies do better when their employees realize their potential while working together, leveraging one another's skills most effectively. We began partially implementing this insight in the 1960s and '70s by doing a little better at getting people in the best roles. When we got that right, we tended to succeed. When we didn't, our results suffered.

One of the best in the company's history at applying his gifts to get results was Sterling Varner, whom I mentioned earlier.

Sterling was a quiet person who was often overlooked by people at first. He was born in an oilfield tent with no doctor present, which may have contributed to his lifelong health problems. He also stuttered, which dogged him throughout his life. He never graduated from college and joined us as a clerk in a 1946 acquisition. As a result, people rarely recognized Sterling's incredible potential. But I thought he was exactly what we needed.

Sterling was everything I'm not. He was excellent at implementing strategies; I'm better at designing them. We combined our strengths, which enabled us to accomplish far more together than we could have alone.

Sterling was the one most responsible for the aggressive expansion of our crude oil gathering business in the 1960s and well beyond. In 1969, we made him a vice president overseeing that entire division, and in 1974, we named him president and COO of Koch Industries—a job he held until 1987. After retiring, he stayed on as a valuable member of our board of directors until his death in 2009.

Suffice it to say, if we had never discovered Sterling Varner's gifts and comparative advantage, Koch Industries would have been much less successful!

To put a finer point on it, Sterling was one of the best partners I've ever had. My absolute best partner, the one who has done the most to transform my life, is Liz, my wife of more than fifty-three years. We share vision and values and have complementary capabilities. She has compensated for my many flaws and has frequently helped me in business, especially with people issues. Had I searched throughout my life, I could not have found a better mate.

Koch's success is the result of our employees, both past and present, who discover, develop, and apply their gifts to achieve much more than they otherwise would have. Finding your comparative advantage is essential for self-actualizing. And as more people do so and cooperate based on a beneficial division of labor, they begin to contribute to virtuous cycles of mutual benefit.

We create these cycles when, and only when, we become a preferred partner of those important to our success. This is achieved when someone prefers working with us rather than their alternatives. This requires employees who create their own virtuous cycles, who focus on creating superior value for our customers and other partners, such as investors, suppliers, communities, and lawmakers and regulators.

These cycles are at the heart of human progress over the last 250 years. Life today is exponentially better than it was in the 1700s because people have been increasingly empowered to discover and apply their gifts to succeed by benefiting others.

For a real-world example, consider the evolution of communications. For more than a thousand years, humans had only handwritten books. Then, in relatively short order, we've gone from the printing press, to typewriters, to the telegraph, to the telephone, to television, to computers, to the Internet, and to the smartphone, with further progress on the horizon. At each stage, people built on what came before, while enormously improving more lives.

It's no exaggeration to say that all progress—from the advance of equal rights to artificial intelligence—has resulted from Virtuous Cycles of Mutual Benefit. It is up to us to keep them going.

At Koch, we've worked hard to empower our team to do just that. We recognize that virtuous cycles start with employees before spreading to the business. We want to help our employees find their greatest opportunity to contribute and succeed. As they seize it, they open the door to even more opportunities, individually and as a company. Progress begets progress, in a never-ending cycle.

Koch has created widely diverse virtuous cycles—not just once, but five times.

You've already read about the start of two. Koch Engineering transformed from a small company making a single tray design into the world leader in numerous areas: other distillation equipment and services, process burners and flares, process plant design and construction, chemical process development, and solar plant engineering and construction. Koch Engineered Solutions, as we now call it, has grown two-thousandfold since 1960.

Our second cycle started with Rock Island's crude oil gathering business. In the 1960s, we gathered and purchased about sixty thousand barrels a day. By 1990, we'd grown to more than a million barrels a day, transforming America's oil supply chain as the largest gatherer in the country. That's a virtuous cycle in its own right, but the overall cycle has extended much further since it enabled us to move into gathering, trading, and distribution of gas liquids, natural gas, asphalt, refined products, metals, fertilizers, and many other commodities.

As you read in chapter 1, we tried to move into fields where we didn't have the capabilities, dampening the virtuous cycle in the late 1990s. Off-loading those businesses put the cycle back in motion by enabling us to focus where we have the capabilities to create the most value for others.

On that note, exiting businesses is essential to creating virtuous cycles. Our crude oil gathering capability is proof. Oil gathering was foundational to Koch's early success, yet by 1999, onshore US crude production was declining, dragging down our return on the entire cycle. So we sold that business.

All told, a company that had only two significant businesses in 1961 has now exited more than sixty. Meanwhile, we're engaged in dozens more, illustrating the rapid compounding that virtuous cycles can bring.

None of this is to imply we have only gone from strength to strength. Far from it. Our first foray into ammonia production, a key component in fertilizer, was a plant purchase in 1992. It failed, but it taught us valuable lessons. We made the opposite mistake by exiting our successful gas liquids business in 2005, believing that gas liquids production would decline. Instead, the subsequent invention of fracking technology supercharged it. Those mistakes point to the importance of another principle that you'll encounter soon: **Humility**. We all need to recognize how little we know.

Koch's other virtuous cycles have been in chemical processes (our largest), investments, and electronic and data technology. For a fuller explanation of our transformation in each area, I wrote a book in 2020 titled *Continually Transforming Koch Industries*, which is available on Koch's website.

A key point: None of our cycles are focused on specific industries. Instead, we're capability-focused. In the same way that individuals have abilities they can apply in many circumstances, we have capabilities that we apply in many industries—from forest products to software and electronics. If there's an industry where we think we can create value, we enter it. Hence, our company, which is often associated with energy, now deploys just 5 percent of its capital in fossil fuels businesses.

We aren't focused on specific business practices or processes. Rather, we're guided by principles, applying overarching concepts to guide our decisions and become increasingly effective at solving problems.

As F. A. Hayek said, progress happens when people are "bound only by abstract rules of conduct," instead of being wedded to concrete prescriptive rules.[16] My goal, from the 1960s onward, has been to instill those abstract rules—principles—across Koch, so that all of us can transform ourselves, our company, and our communities. While all of Koch's capabilities are important, our Principle Based Management capability is essential to our success—past, present, and future.

EVALUATING MY LIFE

In chapter 1, you read that Koch's nine-thousandfold growth has been incredibly rocky, despite the overall upward trend. The same is true for everything you read in this chapter, which is an admittedly short synopsis of my life.

My early struggles to find how to contribute and believe in myself gave way to new struggles to transform the business. I've failed more times than I can count. But the failures have helped me and the company move forward.

That's especially true about applying principles. That, too, has been uneven with many failures. Yet it is principles that have made our success possible. The ones you've encountered in this chapter are just a few of those that have guided us. There are dozens more in the pages ahead. They aren't just words on a page; they reflect the wisdom of history and are worthy of becoming life guides.

When I tell people that my success is the result of trial and error—with an emphasis on error—I often get a follow-up question: Do I regret my mistakes?

The answer is generally no. Most of my mistakes have led to more value than harm. They have given me and our company a better understanding of principles and how to apply them. It's not accurate to say that I look forward to failure—failure is painful, both in the business and my personal life—but it's true that I look forward to *learning* from failure. Even at the age of ninety, if I keep failing in ways that keep me learning, I'll find even more ways to contribute.

HOW YOU CAN APPLY THESE PRINCIPLES

- Reflect on a past failure. What did you learn about your aptitudes and limitations?
- Identify someone who complements your strengths. How might you collaborate with them more intentionally?
- Do you tend to penalize well-designed experiments or celebrate the lessons they reveal?
- Which areas in your personal or work life could be done better by someone else—and vice versa? What could you be doing instead?·

CHAPTER 3

HOW TO SURVIVE AS THE BOSS' SON

*If you deliberately plan to be less than you are
capable of being, then I warn you that you'll be
deeply unhappy for the rest of your life.*
—ABRAHAM MASLOW[17]

BIG IDEAS TO WATCH FOR

- Choose contribution over comfort. You will unlock opportunities for purpose and growth.
- You win when you help others win. Be the partner people want to work with.
- Growth requires risk. It is essential for learning, innovation, and long-term success.
- Choose principles as opposed to pedigree when succession planning. Run a meritocracy, not a "family business."

My pop is often asked how he became so successful. But I usually get a different question: "What's it like being Charles Koch's son?"

Given the advantages that come from being part of this family, most people think my life's all fun and games. There certainly are a lot of upsides to "being born on third base," but the truth is, being Charles Koch's son also means struggling to meet daunting expectations.

Pop (and Mom) were relentless in their efforts to help me make my own way in life. Thanks to their influence, I've been able to navigate a rocky road in finding my purpose and a path to self-actualization.

Pop isn't the stereotypical billionaire. He's also not what you've possibly seen portrayed in the media. He's warm, funny, and totally dedicated to his family. Like his own father, he was determined not to let his children squander their potential. Pop wanted me and my sister, Elizabeth, to experience what my grandfather called "the glorious feeling of accomplishment."

This is my earliest memory of where it all began: The dinner table—be in your seat at 6:00 p.m. sharp. Pop's opening question: "How did you exemplify one of our values today?" (We had to choose from Love, Courage, Faith, Honor, and Loyalty.) I was a nervous wreck trying to figure out how to answer that question night after night. It was an early example of his never-ending focus on principles.

Pop also had a laser focus on helping us discover and develop our aptitudes. This started with sports. My parents believed that sports taught valuable lessons, especially the benefits of teamwork, competition, and self-development. They encouraged us to try everything. Poor Elizabeth bore the brunt—she was good at track (the last thing I would have wanted, because it seemed like torture).

Starting at age seven, I played Biddy Basketball through the local Salvation Army's program. I was one of only two white kids on the team—a great experience in my otherwise homogeneous existence. As the team's worst player, I would have never left the bench except for the rule that every kid play at least one quarter.

When I was ten, I was invited to join an all-star team that qualified for the national playoffs in Puerto Rico. There wasn't much joy in knowing I only made the cut because my mom was on the national Salvation Army board and was willing to fly the team to the tournament. This was an early lesson in reality-based thinking. The feeling of getting something you didn't earn is just plain empty.

I did excel at tennis, however. After my first few lessons, it was clear I had good hand-eye coordination, so my parents encouraged me to drop all other sports. I made nationals in San Diego at age twelve and ended up ranked in the top one hundred in the country. In high school, I was runner-up in the Kansas state singles championship all four years.

Tennis dominated my early life. But I didn't love it. (More on that later.)

As for school, I wasn't destined to be valedictorian, that's for sure. I had average grades—some A's, more B's, the occasional C. I did well in classes that were more collaborative and project-based, reflecting an aptitude for teamwork. In classes that relied on textbooks and memorizing content, I struggled to stay motivated and apply myself . . . so I didn't!

The same applied to the education I received in Pop's library. Starting when I was ten, he held weekly sessions with Elizabeth and me, every Sunday afternoon, for two hours. We listened to books on tape from some of the big thinkers who had influenced him: Friedrich Hayek, Abraham Maslow, Joseph Schumpeter, Aristotle. You know, all the stuff a ten-year-old would find riveting.

Every few minutes, he'd pause the tape and ask us to tell him what we'd learned. Elizabeth crushed it. I don't think she ever gave a bad answer. But I rarely had much of any answer at all. After playing us a passage from Milton Friedman's *Free to Choose*, he had to wake me up. I had pulled my hat low enough to cover my eyes so I could sleep.

When I was ten, he took us to dinner with Mr. Friedman, who worked with Pop for thirty years. I was still lost. It was only when I was older and dealing with many of the problems Friedman warned about, such as bureaucracy and overregulation, that I found myself connecting my experiences back to those sessions.

Then there were my extracurricular activities. Like my father had done in his youth, I started hanging out with risk-takers once I got to high school—the kind of guys your parents wouldn't like. I even figured out how to beat our home's alarm system by rigging a door to prevent the alarm from going off. After my parents were asleep, I'd sneak out.

My record was twenty nights in a row. I would "borrow" our Ford Explorer and meet up with my friends for late-night trouble. Nights one through nineteen were a blast. Night twenty, however, didn't go as planned.

At about four in the morning, way past curfew, a police officer noticed me and my friends getting into my car in a very rough part of town. When he turned his lights on, we knew we were done. Thankfully, he gave us a choice—jail or give him my parents' phone number. In what I thought was a clever move, I gave him my *sister's* phone number. I naively hoped she would cover for me, but like any scared sibling would, she woke my parents.

Mom and Pop soon showed up to take all ten of us home. The kids in Mom's car were lucky. She dropped each one off quietly, allowing them to sneak back into their homes. Those of us in Pop's car were . . . less fortunate. Pop read us the riot act from the second we got into his car, and he personally marched each one to their front door, rang the bell, and made sure each gave their parents a full account of how they'd spent their night.

As for me, Pop let me know I'd breached his trust, and he wasn't sure what would earn it back.

I later realized that pushing boundaries and taking risks has always been a part of me. Luckily, it's part of my job. **Risk is a principle.** While it's tempting to think of risk as something to avoid, risk should be embraced, as long as it's prudent. "No risk, no reward" may sound trite, but it's key to progress of every kind.

My next escapade ended about the same. But instead of climbing out of the hole, I dug deeper.

FINDING MYSELF... AT A FEEDYARD

By age fifteen, I was fed up with tennis. I wanted to stay home and hang out with my friends instead of practicing six hours a day and spending my weekends at tournaments. So during the regional tournament in Kansas City, I intentionally threw my matches.

My mom was on to me immediately. She sat there, stifling angry tears. We drove home in silence and went straight to Pop's office. He told me that if I wasn't willing to give 100 percent effort to tennis, he would get me a job. I said I was sick of tennis and would prefer to work, thinking he would get me a comfy job in Wichita where I could still party with my friends.

But that wasn't what he had in mind. I had no idea what I was in for or how it would transform my life.

Pop woke me the next day at 6:00 a.m. I stumbled out of bed, bewildered. He handed me a duffel bag that Mom had packed the night before. Outside, an old beater pickup truck was waiting for me.

I didn't know the driver, nor did I know where we were headed. I looked out the window to see my parents wave goodbye.

Over the next six hours, I slowly began to put the pieces together. The driver was the manager of our company's cattle feedyard in Syracuse, Kansas, near the Colorado border, and that was our destination. The feedyard was like nothing I had ever seen ... or smelled. I was hit by the stench of cattle miles before we got there. All fifty-five thousand of them.

Around midday, we pulled up to a small single-wide trailer. The manager, Kelly, said: "This is my home, and now it's your home too." He had one bed, so he told me I could sleep on the couch or the floor. Either way, he was taking $350 a month out of my paycheck for rent. When I asked what I'd be doing, he just told me that work starts at 5:00 a.m., so I should be up by 4:30 a.m. every day. I didn't get much sleep on the couch that night. That was partly due to physical discomfort, but mainly due to my brain trying to comprehend this new reality.

At five the next morning, I was in a stall shoveling a mountain of manure. Two days earlier, I had been playing tennis at a country club. What just happened?

The shoveling lasted a few weeks. Then I was moved up to digging postholes. Eventually, I was given a horse and sent out to find sick cattle and bring them back to the sick pen. Sometimes it was my job to help the vet treat them. That meant lancing massive boils and wearing an armpit-length glove to fish inside for kidney stones.

For the next two and a half months, I worked from 5:00 a.m. until at least 7:30 p.m. for minimum wage. We had only one day off the entire summer—the Fourth of July.

At first, I cursed my father to everyone who'd listen, and I didn't care if they told him. I couldn't believe I was stuck shoveling manure while my friends were partying the summer away and hanging out at the country club. But as the days turned to weeks, my mindset changed from being a victim to wanting to genuinely do the work.

Was it better to focus on resentment or make the best of this and treat the job as a growth opportunity? That reframe flipped my attitude like a light switch.

About a month in, I realized something incredible. *I was happier than I'd ever been.*

Even now, I vividly remember the sense of accomplishment I felt after a long day of hard work. For the first time, I felt like I was actually contributing to something important. It didn't matter that the job was dirty and difficult; it was fulfilling. My first paycheck wasn't much for an eighty-hour workweek, but I valued every penny because I'd earned it.

This was my first experience with the principle of **Contribution Motivated**. The feedyard taught me the difference between two types of mindsets an individual can have. During my first several weeks at the feedyard, I was negatively motivated. This meant I had a bad attitude, acted like a victim, and wasn't a productive team member. Thankfully, I changed my attitude and started to become contribution motivated. I began to want to help the team and earn new opportunities across the feedyard.

The feedyard helped me realize why I lost my passion for tennis—playing mostly singles, I wasn't part of a team. At the feedyard I was. I worked with everyone from a pen rider to the veterinarian to the feedyard manager. We all had different roles but worked together to get the job done. When I started contributing, I was accepted as a member of the team. We achieved a lot together and the work became fulfilling and even enjoyable.

Later in life, I realized this was the experience that helped me discover that I have a gift for working with all kinds of people from different backgrounds and perspectives. I was learning from them and loved it. I shouldn't be surprised that this is now a key part of my job.

When the summer ended, I came home a changed person. I took pride that I had not only survived but thrived. I'd accomplished something meaningful, and it gave me a sense of confidence and purpose. Looking back, I wonder where my life would be if Pop hadn't shipped me off to Syracuse for the summer. I'd probably be just another entitled, unhappy, unmotivated rich kid.

Shortly after I came back, Pop told me he had another job for the next summer too. I didn't complain. I knew it was the best thing for me.

The following summer, at age sixteen, I went to Medford, Oklahoma, where Koch owned a gas liquids plant. I worked as a pump mechanic and electrician's assistant. The next two summers, I worked at our oil refinery in Corpus Christi, Texas, mostly doing manual labor and learning from employees throughout the plant. I drew on the lessons learned at the feedyard of working with others to contribute to the team's success. I had a great experience at all those summer jobs despite having to wear full-body, fire-retardant Nomex coveralls and a hard hat on which my teammates wrote "This is Charlie's boy."

I also worked for Koch during my first few summers of college. My last summer job was at Pine Bend, Minnesota, at the refinery where my grandfather, Fred Chase Koch, made a minority investment in 1959. I was placed with the sales team. They helped me learn even more about **Mutual Benefit** and how to develop customer relationships.

The wide variety of summer jobs exposed me to many different types of work. The more I worked, the more obvious it was where I excelled and where I didn't. As Pop already explained, Experimental Discovery is crucial to learning. I'm no exception. My deliberate failure in tennis unlocked the opportunity to grow and learn about myself, starting in the feedyard.

Truly identifying my passion and purpose was still a long way off. First, I had to survive the obligatory college experience.

I set my sights on Texas A&M because I liked the culture and wanted to get out of Kansas and meet new people. I decided to major in marketing since I thought that would best match my aptitudes. My mindset was unchanged from high school—do the minimum to get acceptable grades. I excelled in the smaller classes with group projects but was bored to tears in the large classroom "teach to test" model.

The biggest thing I gained during my college years was an obsession for music. I got involved in the local music scene and began learning to play guitar. I quickly saw the power of music to unite people and build community. This insight has fueled my philanthropic efforts, as I will explain toward the end of the book.

Like my father and his father before him, I had no intention of going back to the family business after I graduated. Instead, I moved to Austin, Texas, where I took a job at a marketing firm. The city was electric, but the work wasn't a fit for me. After three years, I was bored and feeling guilty for not fully applying myself. Now what?

The answer came from one of my father's closest friends, Wichita-based entrepreneur Leslie Rudd. Leslie, Pop, and I went to New York in 2002 for the US Open. After a few days, Leslie pulled me aside and simply said, "You haven't earned the right to say no."

Leslie explained that through my actions, I'd said no to the idea of coming back to Koch. He was challenging my life of "goofing around in Austin." I respected Leslie very much, but how did he know I wasn't living up to my potential in Austin?

Leslie's comments struck a nerve and triggered my insecurities about not unlocking my potential. I knew I was stalling to get my life on track. It was the nudge I needed to make a decision. A week later, I quit my job, left Austin, and headed to Wichita.

WHY I FIRED MYSELF

I'll never forget that sinking feeling my first day back, staring at the tower entrance of Koch's headquarters. I immediately had serious impostor syndrome. It got worse every day until it owned me. Did I really belong here? Could I understand such a complicated business? Was this really going to be my life?

A few months in, I asked Pop how many good days and bad days he had a week. Pop, in his usual way, turned the question back on me. I said that in the average week, I had three good days and four bad ones. Pop smiled and said, "Sounds like you're doing pretty well!" He helped me realize that feeling comfortable in my job wasn't instant pudding.

My first job was in accounting, where I helped analyze Koch's overhead expenses. That was not fun. Imagine the boss' son asking business leaders why their costs are so high! Another "welcome to Koch" moment. From there, I was sent to the tax department, followed by risk management. I also did a turn on the team that specializes in helping our employees understand and apply our management framework, which we now call Principle Based Management. I enjoyed trading, mostly because I got to work on a risk-taking team. After rotating through a few of the capabilities, I landed in Koch Equity Development. It handled Koch's mergers and acquisitions activity.

Along the way, I had many screwups. One of the most memorable was when I was assigned to analyze selling our crude oil storage and blending business in St. James, Louisiana. I was in charge of analyzing the market and running the numbers. At one point, I led a presentation to my father and the rest of senior management.

It was my first experience in the management conference room, and I was very nervous. In a room with twelve Koch leaders, my father directed the first question to me. He asked how much capital would be consumed if we leased back the terminal after we sold it. I completely dropped the ball for the team, stammering all over the place as I tried to answer the question.

My father was polite, only saying, "I think we should reschedule this meeting when you boys are ready." I left the boardroom beet-red and embarrassed.

My supervisor pulled me aside and asked in frustration, "What happened? I thought you had this." I told him I was struggling to understand the capital consumption framework and the complexity of the sale structure. My boss gave me three weeks to learn it cold, then I had to present again. I knew I couldn't fail, so I spent the next twenty-one days basically pulling all-nighters.

I'm grateful my boss gave me those three weeks. I learned it inside and out. I presented the framework to the Koch Equity Development team with flying colors and then followed it up with a successful meeting with senior management. That failure proved to be a blessing because it taught me about the

12

PRINCIPLE:
KNOWLEDGE

Knowledge is more than data, facts, or information; it's about understanding and know-how to profitably improve results. It comes from Openness, Challenge, free speech, and market signals.

principles of Humility and **Knowledge.** I learned to have the humility to admit what I didn't know and to seek the best knowledge from others to help close my knowledge gaps. My other learning was that we don't truly understand something unless we can teach it.

After three years that felt like three decades, I'd worked in six roles across the company. In 2006, I asked for an opportunity to learn one of our businesses from the ground up. Fortunately, Koch Fertilizer had an opening I could fill. I spent the next nine years there.

Pop has often said, "Sometimes it's better to be lucky than smart." I landed in the right business at the right time. The late 2000s and early 2010s were a golden age of agriculture, and thanks to smart decisions made before my time, our fertilizer business was in a great position to meet the growing demand.

What a learning journey it was. My first role was on the sales team, and my first business trip was unforgettable. I joined one of our top sales leaders on a trip to Iowa, where he introduced me to one of our biggest customers. When we arrived, that customer called us into his office and pulled out his accounting books. They were covered in red ink.

The client turned his ire on us: "Last year, you sold me fertilizer at the peak price. The market crashed, and I lost my ass!" Instead of answering, my colleague broke some more bad news. He was leaving for another job. I was now the client's new sales rep. The client turned to me and barked, "Who the hell are you?"

I didn't mention my last name, instead focusing on how I'd been with Koch for a while and that my first job was in agri-culture, at a feedyard. The client rolled his eyes. "So, you don't know s— about fertilizer?" I immediately responded with, "No sir, but I'm a quick study." I had a long way to go to earn his respect, but after learning his business and what he valued, we developed a great long-term relationship.

Next, I moved into fertilizer trading. We had recently leased a new terminal in France that allowed us to move product outside the US. One of our trading partners needed to sell a large cargo of fertilizer but couldn't find a domestic market, so I offered to take it off his hands. I knew he was out of options, so I struck a hard bargain, buying it at a deep discount and then selling it in France at a high price. I felt like I'd won the lottery, so I was high-fiving the team on the trading floor.

Turns out, I lost more than I gained. A lot more. A few months later, I called the client and asked if he wanted to sell us any more product. He surprised me by saying he had created his own terminal position in France, seeing how much money we made off him. That was the direct result of my shortsighted actions and flawed trading mindset. If I had thought "win-win," and let him capture a reasonable margin, I would have earned a great long-term partner. Instead, by taking him to the mat, I created a direct competitor.

When the dust settled, everyone lost. Our trading business in France was impaired. He became distracted from his core US business to build a terminal in France. The overall market

> **13**
>
> PRINCIPLE:
> ## MUTUAL BENEFIT
>
> In 1776, Scottish economist and philosopher Adam Smith observed that people in a civilized society always require the cooperation and assistance of others. We obtain what we value by providing others with what they value. This simple idea, which we call mutually beneficial exchange, has, where practiced, helped lift people throughout the world out of poverty and subsistence. Mutual Benefit is foundational to the role of business in society.

became oversupplied, shrinking returns for the entire industry. This was a painful lesson in the consequences of maximizing short-term profit versus long-term mutual benefit. I violated several principles all at once, especially Mutual Benefit.

Ever since, I always ask myself: "Do all parties win in this transaction? What will create the most long-term value in this partnership?"

Despite some of these early missteps, I learned a lot about the various segments of the fertilizer business. In 2014, the president of Koch Ag & Energy Solutions asked me to be the leader of its fertilizer business. It was an incredible opportunity—a chance to prove myself as the head of Koch's third-largest operating business.

Things didn't go as planned. Less than a year into the role, the business was performing well, but I was struggling. I had discovered that leading and running a large operating business in thirty countries was not a fit for me. My instincts were to focus on the next big thing—a new product line, the next innovation, or building a new capability. I didn't enjoy running the day-to-day business. I also wanted to be out in the market building relationships and sourcing new opportunities, not

---

14

PRINCIPLE:
HUMILITY

Humility is being intellectually honest and dealing with reality constructively. It is having an accurate sense of self-worth based on your strengths, limitations, and contributions. Humility is admitting when you need help, can't do something well, or need to improve. It is sincerely seeking constructive feedback and striving to see things as they really are, instead of only looking for evidence to support your ideas and views. Humility requires dedication to the truth, even when painful.

The minute we believe our success is inevitable, becoming entitled or arrogant, we are headed for failure.

stuck in meetings in the office. I learned I was a builder, not an operator. I also knew that if I stayed in an operator role, I was destined to fail.

So I made one of the best decisions of my life—I fired myself. No joke. I walked into my boss' office and told him that I wasn't cut out to lead the business, and someone else would do much better. My recommendation reflected the application of one of the most transformational principles of my life—Comparative Advantage—which Pop covered in chapter 2. My colleague had the skills and desire to lead the business. I did not.

It's true that firing myself didn't leave me out on the street with no prospects, but the next few months were absolutely humbling, to put it mildly. Many at Koch thought the boss' son had failed. In a way, I had. I've had to learn the importance of Humility many times.

People also didn't understand my next move. I asked to be sent to Koch Agronomic Services (a division of Koch Fertilizer), where I could focus on innovation. KAS was losing money, whereas Koch Fertilizer was making huge profits. Was I as crazy as everyone thought?

TURNING TRANSFORMATION INTO A CAREER

I joined KAS shortly after we had acquired Agrotain™, an innovative product that enables more efficient delivery of nitrogen, a key crop nutrient. To many in the ag industry, acquiring Agrotain made no sense. Koch was one of America's largest nitrogen producers. We were challenged from across the industry, our customers, and even members of our own team. Why on earth would we buy a company that reduced the use of nitrogen? Weren't we just hurting ourselves?

Not at all. The reason points to one of the most important principles in my life—a principle Pop had tried to teach me during those dreadful Sunday sessions: Creative Destruction. The economist who coined that term, Joseph Schumpeter, turned out to be much cooler than I thought! I came to understand the power of a principle by practicing it.

At Koch, we apply Creative Destruction in everything to create a wide range of opportunities. This requires continual experimentation leading to disruptive innovations, as well as shedding products, assets, and businesses that are unprofitable or worth more to others.

Businesses must continually innovate if they hope to survive, including disrupting the things they do best. If they don't, they're practicing protectionism, which ultimately leads to failure because someone else will always innovate. If Koch Fertilizer wanted to grow and succeed long term, it had to experiment with many different types of products—including those that used nitrogen more efficiently and were better for the environment.

Since acquiring Agrotain, KAS has continued to invest in these capabilities and its team, creating a profitable and growing business. Equally important, it has improved our knowledge and origination networks of new ag technologies and products that enable farmers to grow more with less and provide them with a broader product offering.

Agronomic Services was the spark that lit my fire for disruptive innovation. I spent the next two years looking for more potentially transformative opportunities, including product acquisitions and expanding our R&D efforts. I loved it, especially in comparison to running Koch Fertilizer.

My new role put me in contact with a variety of disruptive entrepreneurs across other industries. I started spending time with tech leaders in Silicon Valley, New York, and Boston. Creative Destruction is central to the tech industry, and the more time I spent with these entrepreneurs, the more I realized we had an opportunity to build new knowledge and opportunity networks that could apply to all of Koch.

So, in 2017, I led the launch of a new business and capability for the company: Koch Disruptive Technologies (KDT).

KDT filled a critical gap for Koch. While we believe in Creative Destruction, we never had a network that could source early-stage disruptive technologies. KDT addresses that by finding, funding, and scaling transformative companies in a way that helps them unlock their growth potential and enables Koch to transform faster. Given technology's accelerating pace of change, we needed a dedicated capability to disrupt rather than be disrupted.

In early 2024, I realized there was an opportunity to more fully apply my comparative advantage to create more value for Koch. At a business leader summit, I ran into an owner I had previously worked with during my time in the fertilizer business. He was selling his company's best fertilizer plant. After talking with

15

PRINCIPLE:
CREATIVE DESTRUCTION

Businesses stand on "ground that is crumbling beneath their feet,"[18] wrote economist Joseph Schumpeter. This is Creative Destruction—one of the most powerful and important drivers of progress. As people create new businesses, products, services, processes, methods, or types of organizations, less effective ones become obsolete.

Over the long term, Creative Destruction makes most everyone better off. It not only creates better products and services, but it also creates better, safer jobs for more people. Unfortunately, in the short run, those whose jobs or businesses are threatened by Creative Destruction often try to stop it. When they do, progress is stifled. The real solution is to help those affected learn new skills, enabling them to find better jobs or businesses.

him, it was clear he wanted to sell to someone who had a long-term focus.

My friendship and history with him ultimately helped Koch win the deal. This stimulated me to brainstorm with Koch leadership to determine whether I could create more value if my role focused on building trusted relationships with other business leaders—not just in fertilizer or disruptive technology but across all of Koch's businesses.

So we created a new role: executive vice president—Origination and Partnerships. In this role, I'm continuing to apply the principles and lessons that led me here. Listen to your customers. Create virtuous cycles of mutual benefit to enter new areas where you have the capability to succeed long term. Scale up as you learn and demonstrate capability in the new area. Apply your comparative advantage to make the biggest contribution and find the most fulfillment.

Given my role in the company, people often incorrectly assume that Pop is grooming me to become the next CEO. But that would go against every principle we apply. While our name may be on the building, Koch is not a family company. It's a meritocracy.

The assumption that a son or daughter should become the next CEO—that leadership is inherited, not earned—is a recipe for disaster. Succession by pedigree, not principle, can doom a family business.

Why is this? Too many family companies avoid the hard conversations. They prioritize legacy over logic, handing over the reins based on bloodline, not ability.

I've heard leaders of family companies say, "I built this company—my son or daughter should carry the torch," or "I just didn't want to have that conversation." This is rooted in human nature. But without the right principles, it can lead to misaligned leadership, family conflict, stalled growth—or worse, collapse.

Growing up, I witnessed firsthand how our own family struggled with these questions. My father faced intense challenges navigating succession, as he candidly shares in his books *Good Profit* and *Believe in People*.

One incident left a lasting mark on me and my sister. In 1998, while I was on a college trip in Europe, my father called. "Son, I need you in Topeka next week. I'll be on the stand defending myself and the company in federal court."

He wanted us there not just for moral support but to understand what happens when a family doesn't align on principles. To this day, when Elizabeth and I have disagreements, we come to the table and ask each other: What principles should we be following to avoid these situations?

These emotionally charged experiences have taught me several critical lessons:

1. Separate Voting Rights from Financial Benefits

Everyone in the family can share in the economic success of a business. Voting control, however, should go to the person who has demonstrated he or she is most aligned with the company's vision and values and has the knowledge and integrity to vote in a way that will enable the company to succeed long term.

In keeping with the principle of Comparative Advantage, not every family member needs to play a role in the company. Families often confuse giving board seats with sharing financial participation in the company. By separating voting rights from stock ownership, you can give decision-making to the most qualified person while still allowing others to share in the economic benefits.

2. Appoint Leaders Based on Merit, Not Lineage

At Koch, it doesn't matter if the next CEO is named Koch. What matters is who's best equipped to lead. This approach shows our 120,000 coworkers that leadership is earned, not inherited. If one of my kids rises to a top role on merit, great. If their comparative advantage is something different, that's where I will encourage them to focus.

3. Live Your Purpose, Not Others' Expectations

The principles of Comparative Advantage and **Self-Actualize** have led Elizabeth and me down paths that align with our purpose. Elizabeth decided to build an organization based on her own North Star of helping individuals and communities with self-investigation and self-understanding, and not being distracted by involvement in Koch details.

4. When Visions Misalign, Find a Mutually Beneficial Exit

If your values or vision are not shared by others in your family, uncover and address it early. If alignment is not possible, pursue a mutually beneficial exit instead of mutual destruction. A productive departure can benefit everyone involved.

There is no formula for succession—only principles to guide you. If you want your business to last generations, applying these principles isn't just wise—it's essential. It's one of the hardest and most important things you'll ever do.

I'm especially mindful of the decades of failing, learning, and pivoting that brought me here. Whether it was sleeping through Pop's Sunday sessions, getting shipped off to the feed-yard, or firing myself from Koch Fertilizer, these experiences have led me to realize my purpose in life. All those experiences helped me discover that my North Star is uniting with others to create disruptive solutions that can transform lives.

Now to answer the question, What's it like to be Charles Koch's son? It means continually learning and applying the principles that enable me to grow, self-actualize, and transform my life.

But the greatest gift he gave me is permission to be me, instead of pushing me to be someone I am not. I'm excited to see where these principles take me next.

HOW YOU CAN APPLY THESE PRINCIPLES

- See critical feedback as a blessing—seek to understand how it could help you grow. Who should give you feedback? What's one change you should make based on that feedback?
- Are you in a role that doesn't fit? Write a new job description that better fits your comparative advantage.
- Think of a time you took a risk. What did you learn? What risks should you take this week?
- What is your business succession plan? What principles is that plan based on?

Scan to go deeper into the stories behind these principles. Explore personal reflections from Charles, Chase, and other leaders—including written stories, short videos, and guided prompts—on how they discovered these principles, where they struggled to apply them, and what failure taught them.

HOW YOU CAN TRANSFORM YOUR BUSINESS

CHAPTER 4

HOW TO STAY AHEAD OF RAPID CHANGE

*It is not . . . [price and output] competition which counts,
but competition from the new commodity, the new
technology, the new source of supply [and distribution],
the new type of organization . . . which strikes not at the
margins of the profits and the outputs of the existing
firms but at their foundations and their very lives.*
—JOSEPH SCHUMPETER[19]

BIG IDEAS TO WATCH FOR

- Creative Destruction is always with us. A culture that embraces change—even when it threatens what you've already built—is required for long-term success. Those who resist it are likely to be left behind.
- The five dimensions of Principle Based Management—Vision, Virtue and Talents, Knowledge, Comparative Advantage, and Motivation—can help you create an organization that thrives amid rapid change.

Creative Destruction affects us all. However good your business may be, at some point—probably sooner than later—it will no longer be good enough. We must recognize this before someone else comes up with a better solution. (As Jeff Bezos said, "Your margin is my opportunity."[20]) As the rate of change increases, how we address Creative Destruction will determine whether our business endures or not.

In 1942, economist Joseph Schumpeter described Creative Destruction as "the process of industrial mutation" that "incessantly revolutionizes the economic structure from within, incessantly destroying the old one, incessantly creating a new one."[21]

The process is always with us, from cars and trains replacing horses and buggies, to smartphones and the Internet replacing older forms of communication. At Koch, we recognize that change in the economy is more rapid than ever, with the new and better replacing the old. This is why our Vision is open-ended and embraces Creative Destruction. It focuses on building the capabilities that enable us to continually create new opportunities and transform. We strive not to just withstand Creative Destruction but to drive it faster than our best competitor.

In the US, many businesses try to protect themselves from Creative Destruction by lobbying federal, state, or local governments for favors that stifle competition and innovation. They include import tariffs and other trade restrictions, onerous permitting, occupational licensure, certificates of need, subsidies, and mandates. These destructive practices increase prices, decrease innovation, hurt the poor, and undermine progress.

The alternative to this harmful approach is to not only embrace change but also lead it. It's not enough to just become more efficient or incrementally improve; we need to think in terms of new, transformative ways of doing things. To deal with today's rapid rate of change requires a willingness to transform ourselves at every level—as businesses, as teams, and as individuals. This is what Koch strives to do, even though we have often failed and will again.

Our approach to Creative Destruction has been shaped by Joseph Schumpeter. As he pointed out at the beginning of this chapter, progress comes largely through four different categories of innovations: new commodities (products and services), new technologies, new sources of supply and distribution, and new types of organizations.[22]

We strive to apply Creative Destruction in all four areas, but with an unusual focus. Most major companies succeed primarily from a new technology, product, service, or source of supply (or distribution). Koch's success has come primarily from creating a new kind of organization—one based on Principles of Human Progress. We've found that a principle-based approach enables us to better avoid failures, learn from failures, and achieve greater long-term success.

THE NEW TYPE OF ORGANIZATION: PRINCIPLE BASED MANAGEMENT AND ITS FIVE DIMENSIONS

To us, Schumpeter's "new type of organization" has nothing to do with a company's structure or org charts. Our "new organization" resulted from our principle-based framework, which determines our approach to everything—from which opportunities we pursue to how we empower and motivate employees.

Our organization used to be small enough that these principles could be communicated firsthand. As early as 1965, Charles was stressing the need to "first think through the principles involved, and then act logically to promote those principles."[23] Helping employees understand principles was easy compared to applying them. After years of trial and error—mostly error— we learned that many of the mechanisms that enable free societies to prosper don't work in an organization.

For example, we knew that in well-functioning societies, the pricing mechanism was critical to efficiently allocating resources. So we began trying to price internal transactions. The result: arguments over very small items such as the price of pencils. There were also wasteful philosophical debates rather than a focus on getting results. Other pitfalls included employees reducing concepts to buzzwords or claiming that whatever they were doing was consistent with our principles. Also, as we added principles, their application became more complex.

A key to overcoming these obstacles was to organize the principles into five dimensions:

- Vision
- Virtue and Talents
- Knowledge
- Comparative Advantage
- Motivation

This framework helped employees better understand how the principles fit together and how to apply them in their work. When applied holistically, these dimensions enable us to transform ourselves and our organizations through Creative Destruction. To stay ahead of the increasingly rapid rate of change, we never stop creatively destroying our framework.

Let's briefly look at each of these dimensions and the vital role they play in defining and directing our "new organization."

Vision

Our Vision is to succeed long term by profitably applying Principles of Human Progress to help people improve their lives.

We accomplish this by creating Virtuous Cycles of Mutual Benefit. As Charles explained in chapter 2, virtuous cycles begin when we develop capabilities through which we can create superior value for others and ourselves. We apply these capabilities to serve the customers for whom we can create the most value, and who will reward us accordingly.

As we improve and add to our capabilities, new opportunities open, which point to the need for additional capabilities. This leads to never-ending cycles of improvement, opportunity, failure, and success.

Since 1961, we have created five major cycles: engineered solutions; gathering, trading, and distribution; chemical process industries; investments; and technology. These cycles are interrelated and mutually reinforcing. What they have in common, besides shared foundational principles, is a history of experimentation and risk-taking that has built our company while resulting in many failures.

Koch's Virtuous Cycles of Mutual Benefit

	Successes	Failures
1. Engineered Solutions	distillation trays, tower packing, process burners and flares, gas plant engineering and construction, chemical process licensing, solar plant systems	fiberglass products, chromatography, cooling towers, membrane separation systems, activated carbon, heat exchangers, cryogenic systems, dredge manufacturing, electric motor actuation
2. Gathering, Trading, and Distribution	crude oil gathering, commodity trading, gas liquids gathering and processing, gas pipelines, ammonia- and phosphate-based fertilizers, gas trading, methanol, asphalt, petroleum coke and sulfur distribution	feedlots, ammonia pipelines, grain milling and trading, animal feed, Purina Mills, meat processing, weather derivatives, slag cement, Performance Roads, telecommunications, drilling rigs
3. Chemical Process Industries	oil refining, aromatic chemicals, nylon polymers and fibers, spandex fibers, polypropylene, Georgia-Pacific, Guardian glass	polyesters, sulfuric acid, Alaska and Rotterdam refineries, European tissue, specialty chemicals, Guardian SRG, ethanol
4. Investments	pensions, Koch Equity Development, Koch Investment Management, Koch Real Estate	Koch Genesis (venture capital), Koch Strategic Platforms, Koch Equity Development Europe
5. Technology	i360, Molex, Phillips-Medisize, Infor, Koch Labs (Koch Disruptive Technologies), Transaction Network Services	Koch Internet Business Strategies, PF.Net (fiber optics)

In general, we've failed whenever we have overestimated an opportunity or our capability to create superior value; had a poor strategy, culture, or leadership; or failed to innovate as fast as others.

Our most glaring example of a bad vision was the 1990s "gas-to-bread spread." Trying to do their part in contributing to Koch's overall growth goal, Koch Ag set out to "own" many links in the chain between natural gas production and finished products on the dinner table. This included turning natural gas into fertilizer, buying and storing grain, milling flour, feeding cattle, and producing premium steaks and microwave dinners. On paper, it sounded great; in practice, it was a disaster.

We plunged first and paid dearly later. Koch Ag's leaders were recklessly pursuing growth with the hope that more assets and products would be the path to profitability. We bought unprofitable feedyards in Texas and Kansas (as you'll recall, Chase spent a delightful summer at one of those feedyards), built a pizza-crust plant that produced products no one wanted, and acquired Jet-Pro, a start-up that vowed to turn french-fry peelings and other food waste into animal feed, but the chemistry never worked. Simply put, we did not have the capabilities to succeed in most of the segments we were buying or building. And we did it at a scale that violated our principle of Experimental Discovery.

The biggest blunder was the Purina Mills acquisition. Koch Ag's leaders desperately wanted Purina Mills, but they failed to understand the magnitude of the associated obligations and liabilities. Even worse, they didn't disclose these risks to Koch Industries' leaders in getting the deal approved. Further, Koch's leaders failed to apply the **Scientific Method and Challenge** principle by not digging into the downside risks. After owning Purina for less than two years, it filed for bankruptcy.

Koch Ag was losing money in almost every link of the value chain, so we sold its marketable assets and closed the doors.

It would be easy to conclude that this enormous failure was simply the result of having the wrong leaders who made bad decisions. While that certainly was a contributing factor, the magnitude of the loss was driven by the failure to apply many other principles. At the top of this list was a vision that wasn't supported by the necessary capabilities. Rather, it was driven by the desire to match Koch's overall growth goal. (One of the Ag leaders told Charles, "We were just doing what you wanted us to do.") When it becomes the justification to do whatever you want to do, even when you don't have the necessary capabilities, you will fail. In hindsight, at the very least, we should have required small-scale experiments throughout, which would have prevented the failure from being so costly.

> **16**
>
> PRINCIPLE:
> ## SCIENTIFIC METHOD AND CHALLENGE
>
> Karl Popper called his view of the scientific method "Science as Falsification." After developing a theory, he taught that you should strive to disprove or find flaws in it, rather than trying to defend or justify it.
>
> "Every genuine test of a theory is an attempt to falsify it, or to refute it," said Popper. "It is easy to obtain confirmations, or verifications, for nearly every theory—if we look for confirmations."[24]
>
> Truth is not what an expert or the person doing the work declares is true. Truth is what stands the tests of evidence and criticism. To discover the truth requires challenge through continual questioning and brainstorming to find a better way.

Virtue and Talents

The Virtue and Talents dimension focuses on the culture and personal attributes necessary for long-term success.

Koch seeks employees who are contribution motivated, have a talent that will help us succeed, and are committed to our framework. These employees seek growth and challenge, and they find meaning in work that utilizes their abilities, enabling them to realize their potential by creating value. They are fulfilled by their work, which they perform well in a spontaneous and creative way. Such employees use a principle-based approach to help others succeed.

Unfortunately, during the 1990s, we failed to follow our own advice in applying this dimension. A big source of the failure was that senior management was distracted by stockholder lawsuits that persisted throughout the decade. Another is that we put people in senior roles who lacked the necessary talent, and still others who were simply unprincipled.

We were also slow to deal with the unprincipled leaders we had put in charge of several of our largest businesses. They were in place for years before we fully realized their mismanagement and repeated violations of our principles.

After we won the stockholder lawsuit in 1998, we began cleaning up our mess. We refocused on principles, such as prioritizing values when hiring.

The punishing lessons we learned during that decade still serve as powerful reminders of the importance of having the right people in the right roles—people who exemplify **Our Values**, including welcoming and seeking challenge. As you'll see in the next chapter, this type of leader is vital for building a principled culture that gets results.

Knowledge

We strive to continually learn, innovate, and transform at an ever-increasing rate to succeed in a rapidly changing world. We learn and innovate through broad knowledge networks, well-designed experiments, and reality-based measures. These increase our rate of transformation in an environment where Challenge is essential and innovation is rewarded.

We are guided by the **Republic of Science** principle to continually build internal and external knowledge networks. We seek to understand emerging trends from anywhere in the world that might improve, disrupt, or destroy what we do today.

Many entrepreneurs have great ideas but need a real-world environment to test and develop them. Koch can provide them with that opportunity. It's what led to the creation of our Koch Labs model—a powerful example of the Republic of Science in action. Koch Labs isn't a physical place for building new technology on a benchtop. It is a capability with resources we offer to help disruptive entrepreneurs with whom we invest. It lets them benefit from the full talent, capability, and portfolio of Koch assets as they build, test, iterate, and ultimately commercialize and scale their technology.

17

PRINCIPLE:
REPUBLIC OF SCIENCE

Superior knowledge and a culture that empowers everyone to realize their potential and fully contribute are essential for long-term business success.

The Republic of Science is a valuable guide for organizing to ensure knowledge is generated and shared freely, leading to beneficial innovations. When people are free to work on problems that fit their abilities and interests and are well-informed about the work of others, they learn, adjust their efforts, and make discoveries.

For example, Koch Disruptive Technologies is working with the entrepreneurs at Outrider (a company we have invested in) to commercialize autonomous trucks for moving trailers around warehouse yards. In a traditional setup, when an eighteen-wheeler pulls into a yard, the driver manually unhitches the trailer, which is then moved by another truck to a dock for loading or unloading and then returned to a designated parking spot to be re-hitched and hauled off. Outrider has designed an autonomous power unit to pull trailers to and from docks and optimize the full process flow of a yard. It was able to test the concept initially with Georgia-Pacific, a Koch company. Thanks in part to the success of that Koch Labs testing phase, Outrider is preparing to offer the product commercially.

The Koch Labs model isn't just for supply chain and logistics use cases like Outrider. Koch has successfully helped all kinds of entrepreneurs improve their businesses with this model across life sciences, semiconductors, cybersecurity, and energy.

These and other Koch Labs experiments have been mutually beneficial for both entrepreneurs and Koch. Some of the entrepreneurs who partner with Koch to improve and validate their concepts also have Koch as an early customer.

Koch Labs is another way we can drive Creative Destruction faster while empowering employees to practice Experimental Discovery with cutting-edge technologies—in other words, the Republic of Science. This enhances our capabilities and our culture. When we do this well and consistently over time, our employees see a broader range of opportunities, and Koch attracts the most talented entrepreneurs.

Comparative Advantage

This principle guides the division of labor so that everyone can succeed by contributing the most to long-term success. This success results from the fullest utilization of individual abilities, along with the best cooperation and teamwork.

It's no surprise that our degree of success closely parallels the extent to which we apply Division of Labor by Comparative

Advantage. This is why we work so hard to ensure that employees at every level are focused on where they can make the greatest contribution relative to what else they and other employees could do.

For example, each of our refineries employs about forty to fifty engineers. We used to expect all of them to perform the same wide range of tasks, such as process design, competitive analysis, monitoring, process control, and data management. While variety might be the spice of life, not all engineers have the same interests or gifts. If a chemical engineer is great at math, why have her run a processing unit or fix valves and leaks? She should do analysis. Generally, you create an advantage when you allow her to focus on what interests her and where she can best contribute. Then, the whole business and everyone on the team can benefit from this specialization.

This principle of Comparative Advantage applies to any organization—or society for that matter. If you're a football coach, for example, you wouldn't put your team's best passer on defense. A restaurant's best chef shouldn't wait tables. You would want everyone in the role where they can best contribute.

At Koch, we apply this principle everywhere—in every business and capability, and from the shop floor to the executive level. Everyone's comparative advantage can change over time as conditions and their skills change. Both of us have continually changed our own roles in order to better contribute to Koch.

We strive to design roles and responsibilities not only to fit each employee's talents and interests but in relation to the roles and capabilities of other employees in a way that optimizes the group's overall performance. When an employee leaves, is added, or changes roles, responsibilities throughout should be reevaluated.

Motivation

We strive to motivate employees to apply their abilities and interests to maximize their contributions to Koch's long-term success. This requires employees who are empowered and believe they will benefit. The **Requirements for Human Action** principle provides essential guidance for us in this regard and can do the same for you as well.

When organizations don't satisfy all three of these conditions, they don't get the full benefit of employees' abilities.

> **18**
>
> PRINCIPLE:
> ## REQUIREMENTS FOR HUMAN ACTION
>
> In his book *Human Action*, economist and philosopher Ludwig von Mises describes the three requirements for individuals to act:
> - Unease or dissatisfaction with the current state
> - A vision of a better state
> - A belief they can reach the better state[25]

We intentionally create dissatisfaction by helping employees recognize that no matter how well they and the company are doing, unless they continually improve and transform themselves, Creative Destruction will ultimately cause us to become obsolete.

We help employees develop a vision of a better state, first by understanding their organization's and Koch's vision and our principle-based framework, then by demonstrating they will be better off if they fully apply these principles.

The most difficult requirement is helping employees believe they have a path to a better state. For many companies, satisfying this requirement is impossible because they have a bureaucratic framework and a culture that stifles employees' ability to contribute. To overcome this tendency, we strive for a bottom-up approach that empowers our employees to reach that better state.

This includes avoiding compensation formulas. Instead, we provide rewards that motivate greater contributions and reinforce performance feedback. We recognize contributions that have built capabilities and have or will generate positive results.

Plus, we don't penalize well-designed experiments that fail, because they create knowledge that leads to better decisions in the future. For example, in Koch Disruptive Technologies, we have made investments that have been written down or completely written off. In those cases, we have not penalized the team members as long as the investment was appropriately risk-adjusted and sized for an experiment. And we identify the key reasons for failure so we don't make the same mistake again. We do, however, penalize failed experiments that are not well-designed.

So, basically, failure is okay—as long as the value of the lesson outweighs the loss.

For many years, we referred to this dimension as Incentives. Unfortunately, too many people equate an incentive with money (and only money) when it is so much more than that! Given that we all have subjective values (*this* person would prefer a change in role to a pay raise; *that* person would prefer to exercise his talents more fully rather than supervise),

19
PRINCIPLE:
MOTIVATION

Motivation (from Latin: *to move*) is what prompts us to act. A person's motivation comes from a combination of what is within them (intrinsic) and their environment (extrinsic). Thus, to have an organization of contribution-motivated people requires employees who define success as creating value for others and supervisors who reward them accordingly. Essential rewards, in addition to pay, include providing meaningful work that the employee is good at and cares about, some control over their own activities, and the opportunity to be creative and develop.

we saw the need to rename this dimension. We chose **Motivation** so people can more fully understand its purpose.

We're not naïve. We know that financial incentives are important. They reinforce beneficial attributes by rewarding contributions to the long-term success of Koch. But we should never assume that everyone values the same things in the same way. Individuals are much more likely to be motivated when they are involved in crafting their own role, focusing on work they are good at and care about, and that is valuable to the company.

OTHER TYPES OF INNOVATIONS

Our type of organization has greatly contributed to Koch's long-term success. It has led to breakthroughs in the other three aspects of Creative Destruction noted by Schumpeter:

- New commodities
- New sources of supply (and distribution)
- New technologies

It's worth noting that we have an even broader definition of these aspects than Schumpeter did in 1942. We look beyond commodities to include all types of products and services. We recognize that getting the right employees is our most important supply challenge. What's more, we consider innovations that make our employees more effective to be our most valuable technologies. We have, in a sense, creatively destroyed a portion of Schumpeter's definition of Creative Destruction. No one and nothing are exempt.

New Commodities (Products and Services)

We have broadened Schumpeter's commodities category to include unique products and services, because all of them, not just commodities, can drive Creative Destruction.

Consider how Koch has done this in engineering, procurement, and construction. The major customers for EPC businesses tend to be large companies with rigid, bureaucratic rules that make projects more expensive and time-consuming.

Our EPC business, Optimized Process Designs, has avoided these problems by working with customers in the hydrocarbon industry who value OPD's ability to operate flexibly and efficiently.

OPD integrates all the dimensions of building a plant, including consulting, engineering, design, fabrication, and construction. It does this *well* by empowering its employees to work seamlessly as teams. This enables it to complete projects, such as building gas processing plants, faster and more efficiently than traditional alternatives, regardless of scale. Through a bottom-up culture of mutual benefit, OPD is able to create more value for its customers.

Another example is enterprise software, which tends to be expensive and requires years to implement, since it must be extensively customized to each user's needs. Infor, a company Koch acquired in 2020, developed an innovative approach to specialize in a few industries. It can pre-configure deep, industry-specific knowledge into its software. This allows customers to buy simpler, less costly solutions and take advantage of automation, advanced analytics, and AI capabilities more quickly.

Or consider Georgia-Pacific's touchless paper towel dispensers. (Chances are, you've used one of GP's enMotion® dispensers at a US restaurant, airport, hospital, or office building.) Many paper companies went to market with something similar but lacked GP's capabilities to succeed. GP not only produced paper towels, but it also built capabilities in motors, circuit boards, batteries, and more. After proving its capabilities with paper towel dispensers, GP discovered new opportunities for sanitary, portion-controlled dispensing of other products, such as liquid soap and plastic cutlery—all of which became essential during the COVID-19 pandemic.

New Sources of Supply and Distribution

Regardless of where you work, you likely depend on having effective forms of supply and distribution. No matter how good those sources of supply are, you should continually ask yourself how you can develop better ones. The same is true for distribution—you need to continually evaluate where and how you can better sell your products and services.

Many companies try to improve their value chains through an integrated model. Major oil companies, for example, explore to find new crude oil supplies for their refineries, which convert the crude into refined products, which are then distributed through their company gas stations. Instead of trying to do everything ourselves, Koch relies on a trading model. We trade for parts of our value chains that we can't do as well as others. This lets us focus on those aspects of the value chain where we are advantaged.

Our feedstock supplies—crude oil, natural gas, timber, metals, plant nutrients, chemicals—come from trading partnerships. We own no oil or gas fields. We have chosen to become preferred partners with suppliers who have a competitive advantage in those supplies. For example, Suncor has provided FHR with Canadian crude for our Minnesota refinery for decades, a mutually beneficial arrangement that got us into a very friendly disagreement over who benefits most from the partnership—them or us. (We both thought we were getting the better end of the deal, which is ideal.)

The same is true for product distribution. We own no gas stations or convenience stores and instead move our product through a variety of preferred partners. One partner, Holiday Stationstores, a convenience store chain, said, "Koch was the best partner we could have ever had."

Similarly, Georgia-Pacific, which makes paper and building products, does not own or harvest trees. Instead, it relies on partnerships with those willing to participate in sustainable forestry initiatives. Given its wide range of products, GP distributes through diverse channels, including preferred partnerships with giant innovators such as Walmart, Costco, and Amazon.

The supply that is most important to us is not crude oil or timber or even water. Our priority is attracting a sufficient supply of employees who are contribution motivated. This requires continually searching for new sources of talent, such as the innovative apprenticeship programs we recently developed. These have enabled us to identify people with good values and the right aptitudes who couldn't afford to attend college but are capable of helping us satisfy our need for high-quality accountants and IT professionals. We plan to develop similar programs for other disciplines.

The shortage and high cost of IT professionals in the US was so severe that we began searching beyond the US to find other sources. Rather than recruiting foreign students to come here, we found the best solution was to build a technology center in Bangalore, India. That nation has more than a million students enrolled in computer science, and more than two thousand professionals have joined us there without ever having to leave home.

We also engage in second-chance hiring, giving contribution-motivated individuals who have been incarcerated for nonviolent crimes an opportunity to enter the workforce and contribute. Richard McMichael is a great example of this: He earned an accounting degree while in prison and joined Koch in 2021.

20

PRINCIPLE:
MEASURES

As Einstein observed: "Not every-thing that counts can be counted, and not everything that can be counted counts."[26] That is why we strive to measure things that matter—things that lead to prof-itable action—even when it is difficult to do so. And it is why we avoid relying on measures that do not provide insights leading to improvements and innovations.

Many of these measures are largely subjective and qual-itative rather than quantitative. Important measures include:

- Net income and return on capital
- Marginal analysis
- Culture
- Opportunity cost
- Stewardship and compliance
- What customers value
- Price-setting mechanisms
- Competitive position
- The value and cost of activities

New Technologies (Innovations)

Since 1933, corporate accounting in the US has been governed by a framework called GAAP (Generally Accepted Accounting Principles). Koch is required to use this frame-work despite how unhelpful and unrealistic it can be. For example, GAAP can require you to book profits that you haven't yet realized, including revaluing what you paid for a minority interest if you later acquire the controlling interest for a higher price. It also prevents you from writing down assets that you know are overvalued. All these faulty measures can lead to bad decisions.

To address these problems, we developed what we call economic accounting, which equips us with financial statements that provide much more accurate estimates of asset values, profitability, and future possibilities. We now use economic accounting for our internal decision making, while continuing to use GAAP to satisfy our counterparties' requirements. Our economic-based financials have resulted in much better measures, greatly improving our decisions.

We strive to ensure that every business, capability, facility, unit, and team continually evaluate its measures. All employees need to know which parts of their work are profitable, based on measures that help them understand what to start, stop, change, or improve.

Another Koch technology that is contributing to Creative Destruction is EverLearn, which helps us leverage the knowledge of our 120,000 global employees. Launched in 2020, EverLearn lets employees apply the Republic of Science principle by finding the information they need from other employees quickly and efficiently. This platform searches through employee profiles and other internal content sources. Type in a word such as "Basque" or a phrase such as "blockchain technology," and EverLearn will provide a list of potential subject matter experts and their contact information.

When an employee at one of our chemical plants needed to do an internal audit but those who typically helped him weren't available, he used EverLearn. He quickly found other Koch employees with audit experience and soon created a diverse and effective audit team. Every day, thousands of Koch employees use EverLearn to search for others who have needed knowledge, contacts, or experience.

———

Whether we're dealing with organizational issues, commodities, supply, or technology, we apply all five dimensions of Principle Based Management to stay ahead of change. Since Charles has already written a *New York Times* bestseller on that subject (*Good Profit*), let's end this chapter with a practical insight you can use immediately.

There's a natural tendency to focus on one dimension at a time: "What is my business strategy?" "How do I hire the right people?" "How do I create the right motivation for my team?" But getting the full power of the five dimensions of PBM requires applying them all in a mutually reinforcing way.

If you have a great vision but hire talented people without virtue, you're headed for trouble. If the right people are in the right roles but you segregate those roles in ways that prevent knowledge from being shared, you're in trouble. If you encourage employees to do whatever is best for them rather than for the organization as a whole . . . well, you know what happens.

Most people look at Creative Destruction as a troublemaker that wants to write you out of the story. They fail to imagine how much more fulfilling and exciting it is to author some creative destruction of your own.

HOW YOU CAN APPLY THESE PRINCIPLES

- Use the five dimensions to assess which capabilities your team needs to build or strengthen to stay competitive.
- What needs to change to make your organization more innovative?
- Identify one area in your work that's ripe for disruption. What are you doing to stay ahead? What could you start doing?
- Invite someone outside your usual circle to challenge your assumptions. What new possibilities emerge?

CHAPTER 5

HOW TO CREATE A PRINCIPLED CULTURE

*It's really important to come up with core values that
you can commit to. And by commit, we mean that you're
willing to hire and fire based on them. If you're willing to do
that, then you're well on your way to building a company
culture that is in line with the brand you want to build.*

—TONY HSIEH[27]

BIG IDEAS TO WATCH FOR

- Use principles, not prescriptive rules, to empower employees and encourage improvement and innovation.
- Culture is a choice. A principled culture is built through intentional actions, not vague aspirations or slogans.
- Leaders are the stewards of culture. Their actions determine whether principles are taken seriously or dismissed as corporate jargon.

At Koch, we strive for a culture that empowers employees to find meaning in their work—to contribute and grow using their gifts, helping them realize their potential and self-actualize. Regardless of role, we want them to be entrepreneurial, striving to solve problems and capture opportunities. That way the business will endure and our people will transform into principle-driven leaders.

But creating this culture is anything but easy. It requires a relentless focus on cultivating shared attitudes, values, goals, practices, and paradigms across our organizations.

Culture tends to be shaped by supervisors at all levels. It can be intentional or accidental, beneficial or destructive. Succeeding long term requires a culture that embraces both dedication to principles as well as the freedom to dissent and rebel against particular practices—a tricky balancing act. Only cultures that embody this "internal tension" (as philosopher of science Michael Polanyi called it) can drive Creative Destruction.[28] Such cultures overcome the tendencies to rely on rules and a top-down approach, to be tribal or territorial, to reward efforts or intentions rather than results, and to expect things of employees that we don't expect of ourselves. These problems are universal; they are present in all bureaucracies.

When it comes to culture, it's a mistake to assume that whatever you communicate is enough. Employees can only improve culture by embracing and developing personal knowledge of beneficial principles.

We have dealt with flawed cultures repeatedly. Some we inherited through acquisition. Others were monsters of our own making. Shaping beneficial cultures has been a continual struggle since the company's early days.

In 1946, Koch acquired a small refinery and gathering system in south-central Oklahoma. We later sold the refinery but kept the gathering system, which was our biggest and most profitable business throughout the 1950s and early 1960s. Unfortunately, its leaders did little to innovate or expand in any meaningful way. Their culture was overly cautious and stagnant, the opposite of entrepreneurial. They ignored the principles of Creative Destruction, Transformation, and **Principled Entrepreneurship**, among others.

That culture began to transform when we started putting the right people (such as Sterling Varner, whom you met in chapter 2) with the right vision in the right roles. That allowed us to build the right capabilities, such as adding sales reps, trucks, and trading. As a result, we became the biggest crude oil gathering operation in North America. Although we didn't know it at the time, we were applying the principle of Virtuous Cycles of Mutual Benefit.

The culture at Koch Engineering in the 1960s was highly protectionist. In Europe, manufacturing was parceled out to multiple vendors to prevent them from learning all our know-how. This was tremendously inefficient and costly, hindering our ability to supply equipment competitively.

These shortcomings were echoed at the sales office in Wichita. Fearing the loss of intellectual property, they refused to share fractionating tray designs, even when required by large potential customers. This cost us countless orders. Consequently, Koch Engineering had sales of less than $2 million and was unprofitable.

Overcoming that stagnant culture began with replacing rule-bound, risk-averse, and protectionist leaders with people who were contribution motivated and entrepreneurial. They expanded product lines, introduced innovations, streamlined supply chains, marketed aggressively, thought globally, and worked much harder at meeting our customers' needs. During

> **21**
>
> PRINCIPLE:
> ## PRINCIPLED ENTREPRENEURSHIP
>
> Principled Entrepreneurship is the discipline of always practicing entrepreneurship in a principled manner. It is creating good profit long term by providing products, services, and innovations that customers value more than their alternatives, while consuming fewer resources and always acting lawfully and with integrity.

David Koch's (Charles' younger brother) decades leading this business, it grew several hundredfold.

Other cultural issues have popped up repeatedly. In 1998, we entered into a fifty-fifty joint venture to acquire one of the world's biggest polyester producers. The venture's culture was toxic. Our partner's representatives would intentionally show up an hour late for board meetings, just to prove that they were in control. They also took actions without our approval that hurt the business.

The lesson here was clear: No matter how big a financial opportunity may be, if the principles of Integrity, Respect, Knowledge, and Mutual Benefit are missing from your culture, the consequences are predictably dire. Success requires partnerships that have shared visions and values, with both parties bringing complementary capabilities.

The Farmland fertilizer assets we acquired at a bankruptcy auction in 2003 came with a collectivist mindset. As employees put it, the culture was employment for life. They were under-challenged and entire plants seemed complacent. If you just did as you were told, you were fine. Everyone shared equally in the financial rewards, regardless of who really created the value. If one division made a profit and another had a loss, bonuses for both divisions were the same. Individuals were not rewarded based on their contribution.

Our biggest-ever transaction, the 2005 acquisition of Georgia-Pacific for $21 billion, brought some enormous cultural headaches—especially at GP's fifty-one-story corporate head-quarters in Atlanta. Senior leaders there had essentially created a caste system, which included having their offices on the top floor. Other employees were only allowed to visit when invited, and even with an invitation, they had to put on a coat and tie or equivalent before they were allowed onto the floor. We signaled that the culture needed to change by relocating the pampered executives to other floors and converting their precious offices into conference rooms open to all.

Meanwhile, in the real world, GP was struggling with several major issues derived from its bad culture. It was content to be a fast follower rather than an innovator, which caused it to fall further behind. It also had less-than-stellar safety performance. Operations employees had a misguided paradigm that shutting down equipment to address a mechanical problem would make the company uncompetitive, so it was better to try to fix a machine while it was running, regardless of the risk. GP seemed complacent about its incident rates, comparing itself to others in the forest products industry: "We're as good or better than they are." It should have strived for no incidents or injuries at all.

There are many more examples we could give, but you're probably already wondering how one would go about practically creating a principled culture. We'd like to share four of the most important culture-building lessons we've learned over the years.

PRINCIPLED CULTURES BEGIN WITH LEADERS

The first and perhaps most important lesson is that principled cultures begin with leaders at every level. We must insist that all leaders emphasize and exemplify Our Values.

At Koch, Our Values are a set of eight principles that focus on several especially important principles for culture.

Our Values matter to leaders because leaders, more than anyone, are responsible for creating an environment where individuals and the company flourish by living beneficial principles. They cannot just talk the talk. They must also walk the walk.

Of the many leaders we have met, one of the most impressive is Jack Clark, rugby coach of the University of California at

Berkeley. Jack has won more championships than any coach in NCAA history: twenty-nine national titles in forty years. What sets him apart is not only his winning record but his approach to culture. As one sportswriter observed: "They drill culture above all else."[29]

> **22**
>
> PRINCIPLE:
> ## OUR VALUES
>
> Of all the proven Principles of Human Progress, these eight are the foundational values of our culture and thus are among the most important for all of us to exemplify daily. They define who we are as an organization and are necessary for the long-term success of Koch and each of us.
>
> 1. Integrity
> 2. Stewardship and Compliance
> 3. Principled Entrepreneurship
> 4. Transformation
> 5. Knowledge
> 6. Humility
> 7. Respect
> 8. Self-actualize

Much like the eight principles that we call Our Values, Clark identified areas that he considered essential for the team's culture. They include being thoroughly accountable, improving relentlessly, having a shared vocabulary, and valuing the team. Players are reminded they should be "grateful for everything" and feel "entitled to nothing." Everyone is expected to lead. In fact, Clark has one of the best definitions of leadership we've ever heard. He defines true leadership as "the ability to make those around you better and more productive."[30]

Abraham Maslow stressed the importance of merging the goals of an individual with those of the organization—the true definition of synergy.[31] This is a primary role of leaders. The degree to which they can make that happen will determine the effectiveness of the culture as well as the degree of motivation and success of employees.

After Charles started working at Koch, he began to see that some employees already had a gift for leading in this way. They were contribution motivated, thought like entrepreneurs, and worked to build preferred partnerships. Chief among these employees was Sterling Varner.

Early on, when Sterling and a group of salespeople returned from an industry meeting, the salespeople began boasting about how they had taken advantage of a customer. Sterling was outraged and let them have it with both barrels. "Our customers are our friends! They are the ones who keep us in business. We have to build trust by treating them with respect!" No one ever created more friendships for our company than Sterling Varner.

Another great leader was Shelby O'Dell, the head of our gas liquids business. Shelby consistently coached his team to get to know their partners better. "You don't know your customer," he said, "until you know what's on their refrigerator door." Shelby preached subjective value—the realization that every customer values things differently. Some of our customers, such as refineries or chemical plants that have had an equipment breakdown, prefer speed and quality over price and are willing to reward us accordingly. That's because their priority is to get back up and running as quickly as possible. Knowing these differences opens the door to creating mutually beneficial outcomes.

We've also had plenty of leaders who didn't practice these principles. In fact, some of the leaders we relied on most to develop our culture and run our biggest businesses did some of the worst damage. They thought their own intelligence gave them the freedom to do whatever they wanted. They were top-down and sought to profit at the expense of others. This is the opposite of a Contribution-Motivated, Mutual-Benefit mindset, which is essential for a principled culture.

As difficult as it is for individuals to contribute when they're not contribution motivated, it is almost impossible when negatively or destructively motivated. They can be driven by tribalism; narcissism; the will to power; jealousy; a lack of integrity, humility, or respect for others; or the desire for vengeance for real or imaginary injustices.

Embarrassingly, when we discovered the shortcomings of our negatively motivated leaders, we were often slow to act, which only compounded our problems. These and other self-inflicted failures taught us that we need supervisors at all levels who are committed to Our Values—leaders who can mentor employees in the application of principles to get real results. They are essential for creating an environment that is bottom-up, empowering, and transformative. Hiring decisions—whether for supervisors or anyone else—must be based on values first, and performance assessments should include contributions to culture.

DON'T TURN PRINCIPLES INTO RULES

The second lesson for building a principled culture comes with an important warning: Don't turn principles into rules.

Principles are wonderful, powerful things, but the minute you allow them to become a checklist or set of buzzwords, or reduce them to rigid formulas, that's when you can be certain that you have squeezed the life out of them. It doesn't really matter if that was your intention—it's the natural course of things. This speaks to the principle of **Principle-Based vs. Rule-Based**.

At Koch, Principles of Human Progress guide everything, including visions, strategies, policies, practices, partnerships, investments, and performance evaluations. These principles encourage entrepreneurship, discovery, and transformation. They apply universally, whereas detailed rules and methods only work in specific applications under certain conditions, and even then, they tend to stifle motivation and creativity.

We've learned these lessons over many years. As a young man just barely out of college, Charles' goal became discovering and productively applying principles to make our employees and Koch much more successful. Since Koch was a small company at the time, those ideas could be effectively transmitted in meetings or one-on-ones.

However, as the company grew and Charles discovered more principles, it became impossible for him to instill them personally, even for a fraction of employees. We needed a codified framework that could be implemented everywhere, but we also wanted to avoid reinventing the wheel if possible.

So, starting in the early 1980s, we attempted to integrate the principles we were applying with frameworks created by others, such as W. Edwards Deming, Michael Porter, and Dale Carnegie. While each of these had something of value to offer, none was sufficient for our needs, and some of their rule-focused aspects even caused confusion and misplaced

---

23

PRINCIPLE:
PRINCIPLE-BASED VS. RULE-BASED

It was only when Principles of Human Progress began to be applied around 1800 that people's lives dramatically improved. As millions of people gained the opportunity to more fully live as they saw fit, they began applying their abilities and knowledge to improve their lives by helping others improve theirs. While there will always be room for improvement, most people are healthier, wealthier, and happier than ever before.

Setting expectations according to general principles without prescribed, detailed directives or rules is core to building a beneficial culture and long-term success. It frees everyone to think and innovate—to develop different methods and solutions—rather than mindlessly follow instructions. It creates an environment where every employee has the opportunity to find the right role, knows what to do to maximize value creation, and is motivated to do it without being told. This needs to be a primary responsibility of every supervisor at every level.

priorities. If focusing on saving $1 million through continuous improvement (one of Deming's areas of emphasis) keeps us from developing a capability that could make $100 million, we've become less successful.

The minute we melded our principles with the frameworks of others, our tendency became to apply them through detailed rules. Deming's fourteen points for management and Porter's five forces became prescriptive lists, stifling innovation and entrepreneurship. Employees began assuming that creating data tables or charts for leadership was more important than actual work. They referred to Deming's statistical methods for improving quality (what he called statistical process control) as "charts for Charles." Checklists and templates are tempting, but they often result in employees "turning off their brains," going through the motions instead of thoughtful application. Never forget that the goal is results, not charts.

Chastened by these developments, we began creating our own framework and tools in 1983. We had a significant breakthrough in 1990 when we began to organize our principles into a five-dimensional framework, which helps employees understand our principles as well as how to apply them.

The challenge of implementing this culture is ongoing. We routinely see well-intentioned leaders create "culture checklists" in an effort to "score" employees on their PBM knowledge. Some teams have even devised quizzes to test how well employees can regurgitate dimensions, values, and descriptions of principles—in proper order, as if that matters.

This same sort of misguided mentality is at work when organizations try to use rules, formulas, or checklists in hopes of greater efficiency or fairness. For example, companies often overlook great talent by focusing on resumes rather than individual skills. Or take the widely used Hay System, which evaluates your job (and ultimately determines your pay) based on factors ranging from your physical environment, overall know-how, and number of direct reports to stress levels and something called "sensory attention" requirements. Bonuses, raises, and salaries are based on complex formulas rather than contributions to long-term results. All of this undermines your ability to apply principles to get results.

Similarly, most US companies and manufacturing sites have a safety paradigm that's all about rules. This is not surprising, given that the Occupational Safety and Health Administration has devised nearly one hundred so-called standards for manufacturers. "OSHA standards," says that agency, "are rules that describe the methods that employers must use to protect their employees from hazards."

At Koch, we comply with all OSHA rules and regulations. We also take a more effective approach. When we have conversations about safety at our plants, we stress principles as the best way to improve safety. Yes, rules and policies are intended to keep people safe, but rules and policies can't cover every situation. Principles can help people make wise decisions in circumstances not specifically addressed by a rule. That's why we work so hard to help employees understand and apply principles.

Asking yourself (and your leaders) a couple of simple questions will quickly determine if you are overreliant on rules versus principles:

Does your organization spend more time telling people what to do, rather than empowering them to come up with better ways to do things?

The second approach opens their thinking and provides superior results. To discover better ways, employees need to continually experiment.

Do your supervisors spend more time on vision, principles, roles, and expectations, or rules and procedures?

If principles are being applied bureaucratically as a rigid formula or a prescriptive process, they have ceased to be principles. Instead, they have become stifling obstacles.

There's a simple way to tell a rule from a principle. Ask yourself if the principle you're focused on leads to improvements and is applicable to a wide variety of situations. If it's not, it's probably a rule.

PRINCIPLED CULTURES REQUIRE GENUINE UNDERSTANDING

A successful culture requires that individuals have a genuine understanding of principles. When first exposed to a company's principles, it's human nature to minimize any differences and rationalize your actions as if they align with those principles. We often hear employees of acquired companies say, "Our cultures are similar," or "We're already doing that." This is almost never true.

Thinking this way prevents the necessary effort to understand what is different about a principle-based approach. All too often, people tend to adopt new language without changing their beliefs and behaviors, turning them into buzzwords instead.

For instance, after we acquired Georgia-Pacific, its leaders were surprised that under our culture, employees could make more than their supervisors. They were also surprised to learn we're comfortable absorbing a short-term loss in exchange for a longer-term gain. They were shocked that we empower first-line employees to halt a production line for the sake of safety. And they didn't see how it's better to hire someone without a college degree who embodies Our Values than a highly educated candidate who doesn't.

Admittedly, principles take time to understand, much less put into practice and develop into a culture. They require frequent, regular, and correct practice. To motivate employees to do this, we communicate and celebrate the results of principle-based behaviors. Not surprisingly, when employees are rewarded for the results they get from applying our principles, they're motivated to keep applying them.

Such **Personal Knowledge** is a crucial principle for building culture. As Michael Polanyi taught, we only truly know something when we can apply it to get results. This is why we work so hard to help employees internalize our principles.

We recognize—largely based on past failures—that it's not enough to just know theory. It only takes a few minutes to learn the basic principles

24

PRINCIPLE:
PERSONAL KNOWLEDGE

Developing personal knowledge involves a personal transformation—what philosopher of science Michael Polanyi called "a self-modifying act of conversion."[32] Reading a book or watching a video on how to ride a bike can be helpful, but developing personal knowledge requires actually riding one. Because practice makes permanent, not perfect, you must engage in correct, frequent, and prolonged practice.

When you're just learning how to do something, a template or operating procedure can be necessary and useful. As you study and practice in a particular field, you absorb increasing amounts of specific knowledge, including rules, facts, and relationships. This encourages a type of conformity, but at some point, you know these details well enough that you can begin to focus on the whole and innovate, recognizing the limitations of templates and processes.

of chess, but learning to play it well can take years. What counts in business is not just knowing principles but also how to apply them to achieve results.

Of course, we haven't always followed our own advice in this regard. We made the mistake of relying on professors to teach our employees. They were excellent communicators, capable of talking about theory for hours, but they weren't helping employees put those theories to practical use.

We also failed to apply Personal Knowledge when we started making large acquisitions and needed to introduce principles to tens of thousands of new employees. We call that mistake our "sheep-dipping" phase because we relied on high-volume, one-size-fits-all training—like sheep ranchers who dunk their herds in vats of insecticide and fungicide. In. Out. Done.

We used to be proud of the fact that we once "trained" five thousand GP employees in just ninety days. However, that hurried, premature strategy backfired when feedback revealed that most attendees quickly became cynical about our principles. Why? Because there were supervisors at several levels who weren't practicing the principles taught in the class. We had not realized how committed they were to a top-down approach. Even more destructive was when we selected leaders who pretended to be principled but were not.

Organizing our principles into a five-dimensional framework proved incredibly useful. Employees have found that using this organizing structure is a valuable and effective way to apply principles to solve problems. In most cases, it works best to start by challenging the group's Vision, then the application of Virtue and Talents, and so on. Utilizing the five dimensions not only makes it easier to identify and solve problems but also helps improve the user's personal knowledge of the relevant principles.

As counterintuitive as it may sound, new technologies have helped us make knowledge more personal. Generative AI has improved our ability to meet each learner where they are. For example, AskFred is a generative AI tool (inspired by Khan Academy's Khanmigo) that assists employees in understanding principles, rehearsing employee development conversations, and learning how they might better apply principles in their work.

Because effective learning is deeply individual, it requires personalized conversations and intentional practice. Practice does not make perfect; it makes permanent. You tend to get worse rather than better if you endlessly practice the wrong golf swing or an incorrect way of playing an instrument. Personal knowledge of principles means understanding how to apply them in ways that get results.

PRINCIPLED ORGANIZATIONS CONTINUALLY TRANSFORM

Here's our final important lesson about building a principle-based culture: If you genuinely want a principled organization, you must be willing to transform continually.

For nearly thirty years, we underwent periodic (rather than continual) transformations. Every few years or maybe once a decade, we'd change or refine our Vision, redefine our Guiding Principles, reinvent our methods for developing personal knowledge, and so on. Although we stayed profitable, we were still falling behind competitors. We weren't building new capabilities fast enough, and many of our investments—including some huge and costly acquisitions—weren't performing as we hoped. We had an inadequate sense of urgency in every aspect of our businesses, not just our financial results.

As we began to address these problems, our efforts brought only minor improvements. This shouldn't have surprised us, given that we continued to operate in much the same way as we had in the past. (The definition of insanity.) We concluded that, to improve our performance, we had to transform ourselves—starting with those of us at the top of the org chart.

In 2018, we began making significant senior management changes, dividing and resetting responsibilities based on Division of Labor by Comparative Advantage. Our example encouraged our leaders to do the same at all levels of the organization. (You'll hear from some employees who benefited from this transformation in chapter 7.) This was a crucial first step in creating a new type of organization.

> **PRINCIPLE:**
> ## CLOSING GAPS
> **25**
>
> Successful entrepreneurs are never satisfied with the status quo. Those who become satisfied are soon no longer successful. To continue to succeed, entrepreneurs need to envision the gap between the value they are creating today and what is possible. Successful entrepreneurs are always driving Creative Destruction.

We also had to take our application of principles to a whole new level. We significantly changed Koch's Vision and Our Values. For most employees, this was their first exposure to concepts such as virtuous cycles, continual transformation (as opposed to continuous improvement), preferred partnerships, and stewardship.

In keeping with our principles, we believe that no matter how well we are doing today, we can and must do better tomorrow. There will always be gaps, but a culture continually focused on growth and opportunity can close them—that's the principle of **Closing Gaps**. This kind of culture empowers contribution-motivated employees to improve themselves and the company, in a never-ending cycle of success.

At Koch, we seek to close the gap between what we are doing, however good, and what we could be doing if we were fully applying our principle-based framework. The application of these principles enables us to continually see additional opportunities for improvement and growth for ourselves and Koch.

A restless discontent, fueled by a vision of a better state and a belief that such a state can be realized, spurs never-ending cycles of improvement and transformation for employees and the company.

———

There is no rigid, top-down approach that will beneficially transform a company's culture, nor is there any secret sauce. No memo, class, checklist, or poster is sufficient. Building a principled culture takes effort and commitment. If you ignore culture, it won't matter how good your strategy is.

One of the easiest ways to assess a culture is to look at who gets recognized and rewarded. Is it the person who gets results at all costs, never mind the collateral damage? Or is it the one who improves overall results by making those around her better? Do leaders practice what they preach? Is the organization bureaucratic and top-down, or empowering and bottom-up? Do supervisors live by and apply principles in ways that motivate employees to do the same?

Whenever we've done a better job of creating a principle-based culture, we've gotten better results. This is a never-ending journey. We will always have new gaps to close, new virtuous cycles to create, new lessons to learn, new principles to discover and apply, and new employees to develop and empower. At Koch, our culture continues to evolve—because it has to.

HOW YOU CAN APPLY THESE PRINCIPLES

- How does your workplace hold leaders accountable for living by the organization's values?
- What positive or negative contributions have you personally made to your organization's culture? How can you improve?
- How do you recognize individuals who demonstrate principles through their actions?
- Identify one rule or policy that stifles creativity. How could you replace it with a principle that empowers innovation?

CHAPTER 6

HOW TO BUILD A SUCCESSFUL BUSINESS

The great businessman . . . produces more, better, and cheaper goods . . . his initiative and activity force his competitors either to emulate his achievements or to go out of business.
—LUDWIG VON MISES[33]

BIG IDEAS TO WATCH FOR

- Successful organizations focus on improving, building, and acquiring capabilities. And when those capabilities open the door to new opportunities, progress accelerates.
- Learn from failure and adjust quickly by applying principles. Every setback is an opportunity to rethink strategy, clarify roles, and realign incentives for better results.
- Think on the margin. Averages and sunk costs distort decision-making; profitable decision-making hinges on understanding the marginal benefits and costs of an activity.

Principles of Human Progress are the key to building an enduring business, regardless of its size, age, purpose, or industry. In this chapter, we share four different examples of Koch companies that have learned this lesson through failure.

Their industries vary from refining and agriculture to technology and finance. One has tens of thousands of employees worldwide; another has fewer than thirty and is only in the US. One has been a Koch company for more than half a century and another for barely a decade. They all had failures before transforming themselves through the application of principles.

There's an old saying that success has many fathers, while failure is an orphan. Everyone likes to take credit for a winner. At Koch, we strive for the opposite—to recognize that our numerous failures have usually been our own fault. From the chairman to the newest intern, we've all experienced failure and will continue to do so. Our successes, by contrast, have sprung from just one source: applying principles.

The same can be true for you. It doesn't matter whether you work in a startup or a stalwart, a tiny nonprofit or a global enterprise. Principles can work for you. As you read these stories, keep the principle of Transformation foremost in your mind. If there's one main takeaway, it's that businesses that are successful long term continually transform.

REFINING OUR REFINERIES

Flint Hills Resources (FHR) looks to most people like a nonstop success story. That hasn't been the case, to put it mildly.

It began when we acquired control and a 100 percent interest in the Great Northern Oil Company that owned a small refinery (Pine Bend) near St. Paul, Minnesota, in 1969. We made the acquisition despite its very destructive culture and obsolete facilities. We believed that by changing the leadership and vision and applying our principles, we could overcome these problems and succeed.

After a difficult struggle, we were able to turn the business around, making Pine Bend one of America's most efficient refineries. It has greatly contributed to FHR's profitability, which has increased a thousandfold since 1969. But its and FHR's earnings have always been volatile, as the following chart shows.

FHR Earnings Variation 1969–2024 (1969=1)

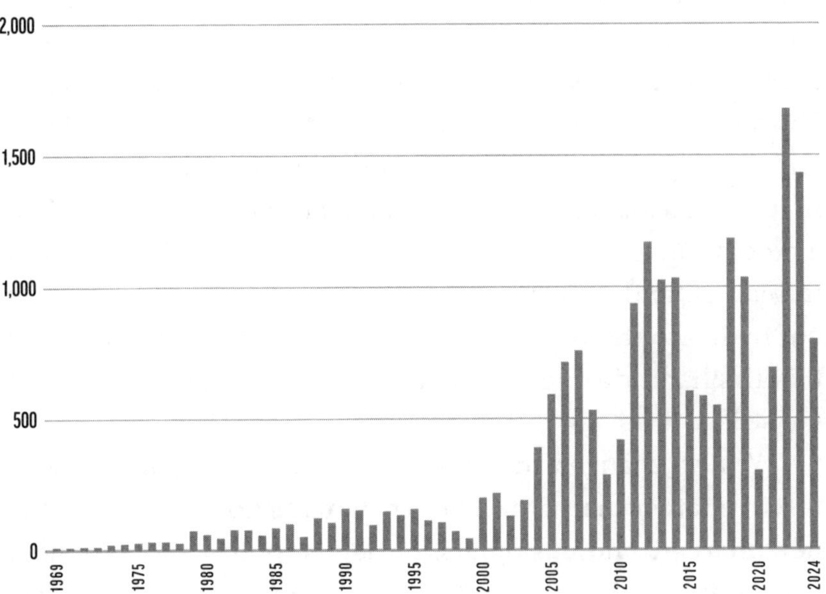

Having owned a minority interest in Pine Bend since 1959, we recognized that the business needed to be transformed. The plant was being run by the union with detailed work rules that made it impossible to operate efficiently, and prohibitively expensive to make improvements or additions. Great Northern was only profitable because it had a favorable market for its products and a competitively advantaged crude supply. These made its management protectionist. Both its leaders and employees resisted any risk to the status quo—no Creative Destruction for them.

Our vision went beyond investments to improve and expand Pine Bend. It included beginning to change the culture from protectionist to entrepreneurial, leading to Virtuous Cycles of Mutual Benefit. This required replacing management and being able to terminate destructive employees.

We recruited a fearless refinery manager from the outside who was committed to making needed changes, regardless of the opposition. This meant getting the union to agree to major changes in the work rules to enable the plant to be run efficiently. The response was a bitter nine-month strike that led to violence and sabotage that could have resulted in fatalities. Shots were fired into the plant, and saboteurs tried to run a locomotive into a processing unit. Tires were slashed on trucks taking products to market, and replacement workers had to be flown in and out by helicopter due to threats. Charles experienced much of this firsthand during frequent visits to the plant throughout the strike.

We also changed the sales and supply teams, which were reactive rather than proactive. They made no effort to identify new markets and customers, or new supplies and suppliers. The Minneapolis sales staff would take two-martini lunches, after which they would go into their offices and probably take a nap. We moved the sales office to Wichita and staffed it with employees who lacked experience in refined products but who were entrepreneurial.

These changes to vision and leadership quickly began to transform the business. Reliability and efficiencies improved, and construction time and costs dropped. We eventually developed a good relationship with the union by applying the principles of Empowerment and Mutual Benefit. It was slow going as we needed to build trust on both sides. This started by having better supervisors, which required retraining or replacing them and being able to reward individual performers.

We also added new products, such as asphalt, and became preferred partners with important retailers and crude oil suppliers. With the employees becoming more empowered and entrepreneurial, Pine Bend's results improved more than fiftyfold over the next ten years.

FHR's 1981 acquisition of Sun Oil's refinery and chemical complex in Corpus Christi, Texas, also got off to a miserable start. Corpus runs high-gravity, low-sulfur domestic crude. In addition to fuels, it produces the basic aromatic chemicals used to make apparel, automotive components, and construction materials.

Sun had treated the plant as an orphan, totally neglecting its employees and stifling any initiative or entrepreneurship. Immediately after Koch's acquisition, senior management from Wichita began visiting the plant monthly. When we asked why we were getting no investment requests, we were told that when proposals were sent to Sun's headquarters, not only were they never approved, but there were no responses at all.

To change that culture, we began asking for improvement ideas during our visits. When plant employees suggested they could get more throughput on the crude unit if we replaced the heat exchangers, Charles requested a proposal and approved it on the spot. Employees began speaking up, drawing on their knowledge to offer better and bigger improvements. When results improved, those who contributed to them were recognized and rewarded and earned additional authority. Transformation accelerated at Corpus as the culture became more entrepreneurial.

What happens when you foster a culture of Principled Entrepreneurship? The answer is innovation and progress created from the bottom up by a diversity of employees. The changes we made at Pine Bend and Corpus Christi, combined with our investments, enabled their earnings to set a series of records.

Principled entrepreneurs pursue good profit, providing products and services customers value more than their alternatives, while consuming fewer resources and always acting lawfully and with integrity. Good profit is earned by making a contribution to society—not from corporate welfare or other ways of profiting by taking advantage of people.

Unfortunately, refining is a highly cyclical business, and earnings soon declined as the industry's margins dropped substantially. That decline accelerated when we began hiring and promoting the wrong leadership in 1996. It was only after replacing these unprincipled leaders in 1999 and making other major organizational and strategic changes (such as simplifying the organization, establishing clear accountability and decision rights, eliminating bogus measures, and only rewarding real value creation) that earnings quickly rebounded, increasing four-fold to a record the next year.

These successes tempted FHR to invest outside its expertise. In the early 2000s, it made major acquisitions in other chemical process businesses, such as ethanol, ethylene, propylene, and polypropylene. We believed its management, technical, operational, trading, and commercial capabilities could significantly increase profitability. But the returns for these non-refining businesses fell far short of expectations due to low barriers to entry and greater than anticipated operating, environmental, and regulatory issues.

At the same time, our refining business was facing a set of circumstances that threatened the industry's very existence. This experience gave us an appreciation for a new principle: **Headwinds and Tailwinds.**

FHR's headwinds were numerous and serious. They included the harsh political and regulatory environment regarding fossil fuels that emerged in the early 2000s, coupled with oversupply, a severe recession, and mandates that reduced demand for refined products. During the second half of 2008, prices for FHR's products dropped by half.

In response to these headwinds, FHR adjusted its vision and began more fully applying principles such as Comparative Advantage, Empowerment, and **Capabilities**. The focus was shifted to improving the competitive position of its core refining business. This included making improvements that boosted refining utilization, yields, product flexibility, and distribution. Meanwhile, we sold most of the underperforming non-refining assets to allow us to better focus our capabilities.

Other transformational changes included helping employees move into roles that better empowered them to self-actualize and motivated them to contribute more. This improved the division of labor by comparative advantage, brought greater transparency, improved prioritization and challenge, and eliminated silos that stifled knowledge sharing.

FHR created business teams—cross-functional groups that included operations, maintenance, engineering, economics and

---

26

PRINCIPLE:
HEADWINDS AND TAILWINDS

Headwinds exist for a business or product where its long-term opportunities and profitability are being seriously eroded by declining demand or a reduction in barriers to entry. These can be generated by, among other things, competition from new technologies or products, unfavorable changes in consumer preferences, or government interventions.

Wherever a headwind exists, it can create short-term tailwinds or new opportunities in the market. Headwinds are lessened as they deter new entrants, investments, and innovations.

Tailwinds, while creating short-term opportunities, tend to create long-term headwinds by attracting rather than deterring new entrants, investments, and innovations.

planning, and sales; eliminated silos; and focused on the application of our five dimensions framework. This greatly improved results. For example, one Pine Bend team was able to capture 80 percent of the benefit of a new refinery unit at 15 percent of the cost.

We also used technology to transform work processes, increasing safety and job fulfillment. Additionally, the principle of **Stewardship** helped FHR improve its environmental performance, which enhanced its community relationships. (See chapter 8.)

Today's Pine Bend has earned EPA ENERGY STAR® status (the US EPA award for improved energy efficiency) five years in a row and has been named an EPA ENERGY STAR Partner of the Year for four consecutive years. Recently, the facility installed a three-hundred-acre solar array that can generate up to forty-five megawatts of electricity to help power the refinery. This is the largest direct use of solar power in the US.[34] Corpus Christi, which has an exceptional safety record, is in the process of installing a twenty-seven-megawatt solar farm.

Our application of principles enabled these successes. When we acquired our Minnesota and Texas refineries, their combined capacity was 100,000 barrels per day. Today, they have a combined capacity of 725,000 barrels per day. That's an impressive example of continual transformation.

Those actions proved timely. When demand for refined products collapsed in 2020 due to the COVID-19 lockdowns, many refineries shut down permanently, and those that stayed open suffered losses. We believe FHR was the only profitable US refiner that year—barely so, but profitable nonetheless. When the market roared back in 2021, FHR enjoyed record earnings, even as it continued reducing emissions. Once again, applying principles helped turn failure into success.

FIXING FERTILIZER

Today's Koch Ag & Energy Solutions (KAES) began in 2003 with the acquisition of Farmland's US fertilizer assets, including four plants and twelve terminals. We immediately repeated an old mistake: decreasing headcount to reduce costs. In doing so, we failed to apply the principles of Capabilities and Knowledge. This was a mistake we would repeat with INVISTA and a large portion of Georgia-Pacific. This misguided strategy, called Rapid Transformation, focused on reducing the number of employees without considering (1) the capabilities needed to run the business and (2) why the business wasn't successful.

Farmland employees who had the best knowledge of how to run the assets were let go. Without them, reliability cratered and risks increased as the remaining employees were overworked, causing many of them to quit. Also, there was little knowledge sharing between the plants, and employees tended to wait to be told what to do—decision-making was top-down.

The next decade brought improvement in fits and starts. We saw the need for new leaders and made changes. Our largest plant at the time, in Enid, Oklahoma, primarily produced ammonia, which was once the most popular form of nitrogen fertilizer in the Midwest.

However, as farmers began switching to other forms, and as the cost of transporting ammonia from Enid to the Corn Belt dramatically increased, Enid's competitive position deteriorated.

Solving this problem required a transformation. Enid needed to be upgraded so we could add the capability to convert most of its ammonia production to urea. It also needed an improved transportation capability—a switch from pipelines to railcars, since urea is a solid, granular product. The price tag for those changes added up to what was, at the time, Koch's largest-ever construction project.

Enid's physical transformation was complete two years and $1.3 billion later. But when the new equipment started up, we stumbled again. Old and new units either limped along or sat idle as employees struggled to understand how to operate the new configuration. Unplanned shutdowns and other operational issues drove up Enid's production costs until they became the highest in the industry. Unreliable production left the sales teams with no idea of what product, if any, could ship the next day. Meanwhile, plant leaders wasted time seeking consensus in endless meetings rather than seeking the knowledge necessary to address ongoing technical problems. By 2017, Enid was losing money and employee turnover was soaring.

Unexpectedly, it was the former Enid plant manager who became instrumental in fixing the problems in Enid. He had left before the expansion to run a much smaller plant in Iowa and eventually took a senior management role with the company. His experience in quietly transforming our plant in Fort Dodge, Iowa, had given him the confidence that he could make a difference at a larger site. When he asked for the opportunity to return to Enid as plant manager, we realized he was the obvious candidate to lead a much-needed cultural transformation.

He started by engaging with every employee, publishing "leadership expectations" in town hall meetings. These let employees know exactly how leaders were expected to act and encouraged employees to hold those leaders accountable—himself included. Instead of finger-pointing and blaming others, leaders started to demonstrate **Accountability**, thinking and talking about "Who owns this?"

Among the new expectations was that leaders would spend time listening and seeking to understand their workers' challenges and problems. Those closest to a problem often have the best ideas. A maintenance employee, working with a steady stream of contractors, suggested Enid buy its own crane—a $100,000 investment that paid for itself in less than eighteen months. That maintenance employee is now a licensed crane operator and is finding even more ways to contribute.

Employees' roles and responsibilities were adjusted based on the Division of Labor by Comparative Advantage. Supervisors worked with team members to help them use their talent and knowledge to make the greatest contribution. This made a huge difference, especially for the plant manager, who gave up being a top-down boss and instead focused his efforts on the areas in which he had a comparative advantage.

Applying the Republic of Science principle, Enid's leaders began reaching out across Koch, seeking ideas and knowledge to improve the business. As they did,

> **27**
>
> PRINCIPLE:
> ## ACCOUNTABILITY
>
> Accountability occurs when a person bears the consequences (good or bad) of a decision or action. It starts by establishing clear decision rights and building a culture of Principled Entrepreneurship. This helps avoid inaction, abdication, plunging, or finger-pointing.

they discovered FHR was willing and able to help. FHR had valuable knowledge about advanced process control, wireless technology, and even how to use drones for plant monitoring. However, perhaps the most valuable knowledge had nothing to do with technology.

FHR's success in applying the Human Action principle helped Enid's leaders realize that sustained improvement requires more than just dissatisfaction with the current state. It also requires a better vision and a plan to realize it. FHR's practical advice about building a shared vision and how to achieve it became essential to Enid's transformation.

Early wins were celebrated and shared, no matter how small or incremental. Over time, those individual improvements began to add up as employees bought in. Urea output climbed, costs fell, and Enid became profitable again. Further improvements between 2018 and 2023, plus a stronger fertilizer market, pushed Koch Fertilizer's results to record levels. In addition, Enid has earned ENERGY STAR® status for five straight years and was the first Oklahoma facility to win the Water for 2060 Excellence Award.

Enid's transformation has reestablished it as a flagship facility. It has also become a talent exporter to other parts of Koch. Its success has led KAES's overall growth, creating a new Virtuous Cycle of Mutual Benefit, including a world-scale

KAES Earnings Variation 2003–2024 (2003=1)

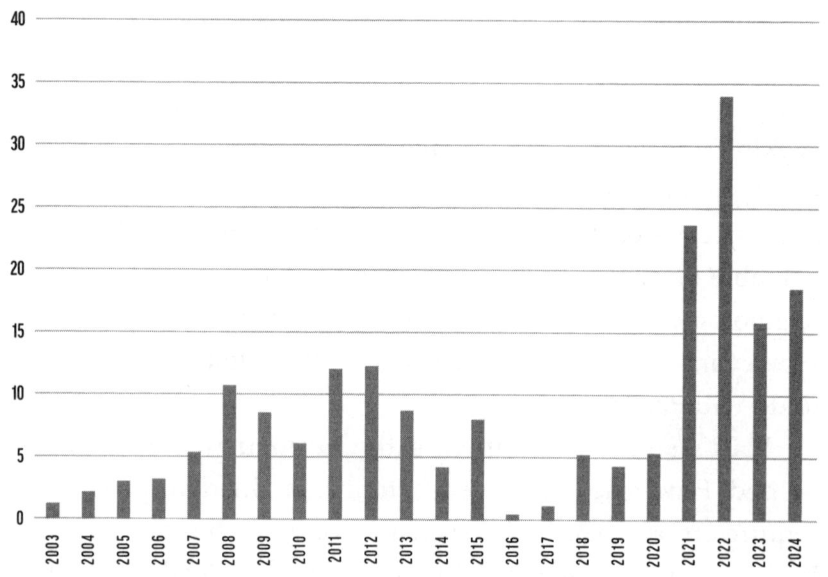

methanol plant, a leading natural gas supply and trading business, a phosphate joint venture in Morocco, and KAES's largest acquisition, the Wever, Iowa, nitrogen complex.

As the previous chart shows, earnings have increased eighteen-fold since 2003, making KAES one of our largest businesses. Its employees continually find more opportunities to grow and contribute. KAES would not be making this kind of progress if its employees weren't using principles to overcome failures.

CHANGING PARADIGMS

Molex, which became a Koch company in 2013, was our first big technology acquisition. It had a long history of innovation, owned thousands of patents, and was an industry leader in many areas. Its profitability and returns, however, were stagnant, lagging those of its peers.

We believed those shortfalls could be overcome by combining our principle-based framework, private ownership, strong capital resources, and long-term focus with Molex's innovation, customer relationships, global presence, and emphasis on technology. Together, we believed we could transform the business in a mutually beneficial way. Even so, we had our work cut out for us.

> **28**
>
> PRINCIPLE:
> ## CHANGING PARADIGMS
>
> A paradigm is the shared set of assumptions, theories, and methods that guides the work of individuals and groups. When most people are faced with a new paradigm, they tend to ignore, deny, or even attack the new way of thinking rather than being open to giving it a chance.

Molex had a strong top-down paradigm, characterized by a paternalistic approach. Managers made decisions they believed were in the employees' best interests. In reality, those decisions undermined employee empowerment and diminished Molex's success. Tough decisions were avoided, especially if it meant changing people's roles or letting them go, shutting down plants, or discontinuing product lines. Consequently, poor performers were kept in the wrong roles, and unprofitable plants and products weren't addressed. Since managers weren't allowed to make the tough decisions required to address unprofitable activities, they rationalized that a one-dimensional focus on revenue was their only path to success.

Molex manufactured more than a hundred thousand products, everything from cables and antennas to toys and automotive components. But it was best known for its electrical connectors, which sold for an average price of twenty cents.

In 2014, we urged Molex to change its vision, expand its focus, and seek more value from its innovation capability. Molex responded by developing more complex "solutions" for customers, often made by combining its core interconnect technology with other purchased components. Although these solutions were more expensive (and thus expected to raise revenue), the non-Molex content lacked any competitive advantage, resulting in poor margins and returns. Chasing less-profitable solutions also distracted them from selling their higher-margin connector products.

As Molex's owner, Koch made plenty of mistakes as well. We believed our principle of **Economic Thinking**—with its focus on **Marginal Analysis**, profit and loss, and return on capital— had the power to transform Molex and had obvious appeal. We were slow to recognize how Molex's paradigm hindered its ability and desire to adopt our principle-based approach.

It finally occurred to us that the best way to get Molex to change its paradigm was to help its leadership understand and apply the principle of Economic Thinking. They had never focused on the profits and returns of specific products or assets. Without that information, they were blind to the cost of perpetuating their top-down, paternalistic culture. Unfortunately, it took several years and many changes in personnel, especially among senior leadership, before Molex changed its paradigm.

In 2019, a new CEO, who had spent his entire career at Molex, clearly saw that the status quo could not be maintained. Working with his leadership team, they began to make a concerted effort to apply the five dimensions of PBM, starting with Vision. Molex's old vision, which focused on providing "electronic solutions," was replaced with a new one calling for investments where Molex had advantaged capabilities. This became the new path for creating superior value for customers and generating attractive returns.

Guided by this new vision, each division was challenged to develop a business improvement plan that would achieve acceptable returns. When those plans were turned in, the new leadership team realized what had become apparent: that Molex relied on growing revenue rather than dealing with difficult issues.

> **29**
>
> PRINCIPLE:
> ## MARGINAL ANALYSIS
>
> ---
>
> Marginal Analysis involves evaluating the benefits and costs associated with a specific change—it's what occurs "at the margin." It helps us improve business decisions, eliminate waste, and discover profitable opportunities. Applying Marginal Analysis requires understanding the difference between incremental costs and benefits, and those that are not, such as sunk costs.

To break Molex's old paradigm, its CEO asked the leaders of each business division to redo their plans, this time without assuming any growth in revenues. This required them to focus on identifying and eliminating unprofitable activities, products, and plants, and to ensure they had the right people in the right roles based on Comparative Advantage.

For the first time, Molex began analyzing its profitability and associated investments at the most granular level, by applying Marginal Analysis, which they call de-averaging. Given the complexity involved—its 100,000 products were made by 48,000 employees working at seventy-five plants in forty countries—significant effort was required to determine which products and plants were genuinely profitable and which had unacceptable returns. Armed with this knowledge and realizing that earnings were barely covering the cost of capital, Molex had a new sense of urgency.

As a result of this highly focused look at every product, plant, and process to determine their profitability, Molex stopped subsidizing unprofitable product lines, exited losing businesses, and closed underperforming plants. It began mapping R&D expenses to individual products, helping highlight what was and was not profitable. This revealed the true economics of the business.

To the surprise of many, Molex discontinued an unprofitable smartphone component, even though it was a high-profile product made for a valued customer. It also exited the mobile antenna business and closed a legacy plant that was a sentimental favorite of several executives, despite losing money for years.

Each of Molex's divisions used the five dimensions to identify and close the gap between their current results and what could be accomplished. One division found that to get the right people in the right roles based on Comparative Advantage, a dozen managers had to be replaced. Because managers now earned roles based on their contribution mindset, aptitude, sense of urgency, and passion rather than credentials or tenure, opportunities opened for many others. Another division began investing in high-value, high-growth opportunities where it had the capabilities to create superior value for the customers.

Based on the widespread application of key principles and the five dimensions, Molex discontinued nine thousand unprofitable products, closed eleven unprofitable plants, prioritized which plants and products to invest in, and reassigned or replaced two-thirds of its leaders based on Comparative Advantage. Then, leveraging what it learned from all this work, Molex developed a new framework for managing product life cycles and prioritizing innovation and growth.

After changing its paradigm, Molex started generating significantly improved returns, quadrupling its 2013 earnings. It is now on a path to industry-leading profitability. This transformation has created exciting, synergistic opportunities for its employees while funding profitable growth and acquisitions in new areas, such as medical devices and aerospace.

Molex Earnings Variation 2014–2024 (2014=1)

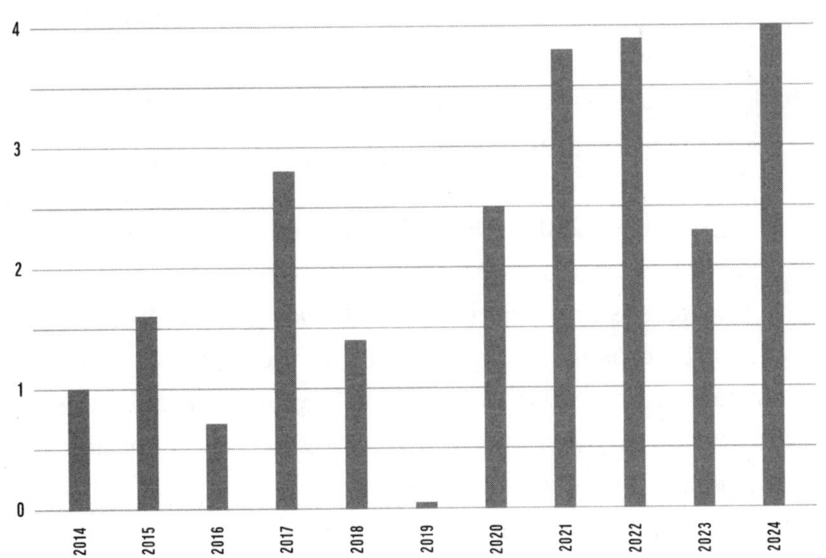

Just as important, Molex has learned not to rest on its laurels or be content with current successes, recognizing that there will always be much more to do. It makes a point of continually evaluating the underperforming portions of its portfolio and adjusting its offerings based on competitive advantage and Mutual Benefit.

TRANSFORMING INVESTING

Since the 1960s, our company has had a policy of paying a dividend of 10 percent, enabling us to reinvest 90 percent of earnings. This isn't just a point of difference; it's a game changer for creating value. Our continual reinvestment has funded Koch's remarkable growth and made possible a broad range of improvements, innovations, and acquisitions.

We could have grown even faster were it not for a self-limiting paradigm. For years, we tended to limit ourselves to investments in companies in which we could acquire 100 percent ownership or majority control. We failed to see that we would have an even wider range of opportunities by also making minority structured investments (such as preferred stock and loans with warrants) and avoiding the premium you need to pay to acquire a controlling interest.

We still had this paradigm when we created Koch Equity Development in 2003. KED was created to help other Koch companies find and evaluate acquisition opportunities.

Despite the limitation in our thinking, KED got off to a great start, advising on the acquisition of INVISTA in 2004 and Georgia-Pacific in 2005. By 2011, we'd paid off the debt associated with those purchases and were generating more liquidity than we could invest at good returns.

With so much capital earning low returns, we started looking for new and better ways to invest, which caused us to recognize our flawed vision. While it may seem strange to consider KED's initial contributions in this light, be mindful that failure often results from the complacency that can come from success. That is one reason why it's critical to continually challenge what you are doing—exploring a wide range of alternatives with an eye toward beneficial **Options**.

This is especially important when the environment for your investments is altered radically, as it was after 2007. As you see in the following chart, rates for two-year Treasury notes fell from 5 percent that year to less than 1 percent in 2011 and stayed there for most of that decade. These extremely low rates resulted in poor liquid returns and made acquisitions expensive, especially those that carried a control premium. When we offered to acquire Georgia-Pacific in 2005, a time of "normal" interest rates, no one bid against us. Had we tried to acquire GP in the interest rate environment following 2011, we probably wouldn't have been successful.

In 2012, KED began to embrace a much different paradigm. Instead of limiting itself to 100 percent ownership or majority control, KED began seeking partnerships and minority

30

PRINCIPLE:
OPTIONS

The future is uncertain, yet the decisions you make today can greatly affect your ability to succeed in the future. This is why Options and optionality play a crucial role in decision-making. Possessing an option provides the ability or right, but not the obligation, to take an alternative course of action.

There are three types of options: exchange, contractual, and operational.

Everyone involved needs to be encouraged to understand what options are available and the benefits, costs, and risks of each. To determine whether acquiring, granting, or building an option would be profitable, you need to apply Marginal Analysis in estimating whether its future risk-adjusted value would be greater than its cost.

investments. KED also let it be known that Koch was willing to consider almost any type of investment—not just the "usual suspects," like those involved in manufacturing and industrial processes.

Market Yield on 2-year Treasuries[35]

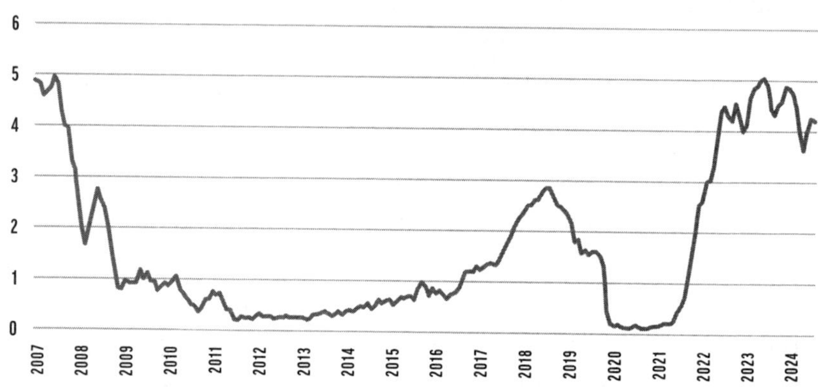

Just as important, KED decided it needed to create unique and flexible capital structures—solutions tailored to satisfy specific customer needs instead of the traditional funding solutions offered by big banks and investment funds. This was based on applying our Risk and Mutual Benefit principles. As long as KED believed we would be compensated for the risk we were absorbing, we were open to an investment.

KED's new way of thinking reflected the principle of Mutual Benefit. It required carefully listening to counterparties and creatively providing win-win solutions. This differentiation was quickly validated. The family that owned American Greetings, the second-largest greeting card company in the world, selected KED over other suitors for the financing needed to take their company private. That transaction was so beneficial that the family began recommending KED to other potential customers.

At Koch, we strive to apply a win-win philosophy in all we do. We seek to understand what our core constituencies value and then cooperate with them to achieve mutually beneficial outcomes. Trust is the foundation for such relationships.

Although it was relatively small by Koch's standards, the American Greetings deal had an outsized effect on our brand. The market, initially caught off guard, now realized that KED was a differentiated capital source interested in more than just 100 percent ownership and industrial assets.

Using this momentum, KED quickly completed a long list of mutually beneficial transactions. It structured equity for GE Aviation, helped ADT Security and Solera go private, assisted Meredith's buyout of the *TIME* magazine group, partnered with the Getty family to regain control of Getty Images, helped the DeSoto family grow MITER Brands tenfold in five years, completed the purchase of Transaction Network Services and Infor, and aided in the acquisition of Molex. KED's earnings from 2012 to 2024 increased more than twentyfold.

Thanks to our principle-based framework, KED avoided another common failure. The investment industry is often criticized for cultivating short-sighted, win-at-all-cost opportunists. These individuals don't seek the long-term, mutually beneficial relationships that are key to lasting success. Koch learned this lesson the hard way in the 1990s after hiring unprincipled investment bankers. They corroded our culture by forcing out good employees who challenged their violation of our principles. These violations included manipulating financial scorecards to show profitability where they had losses and seeking bonuses based on inflated profit projections versus actual results over time. In contrast, KED used a principled approach in building

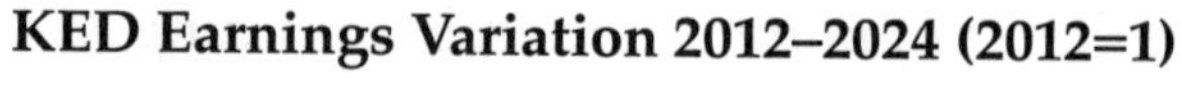

KED Earnings Variation 2012–2024 (2012=1)

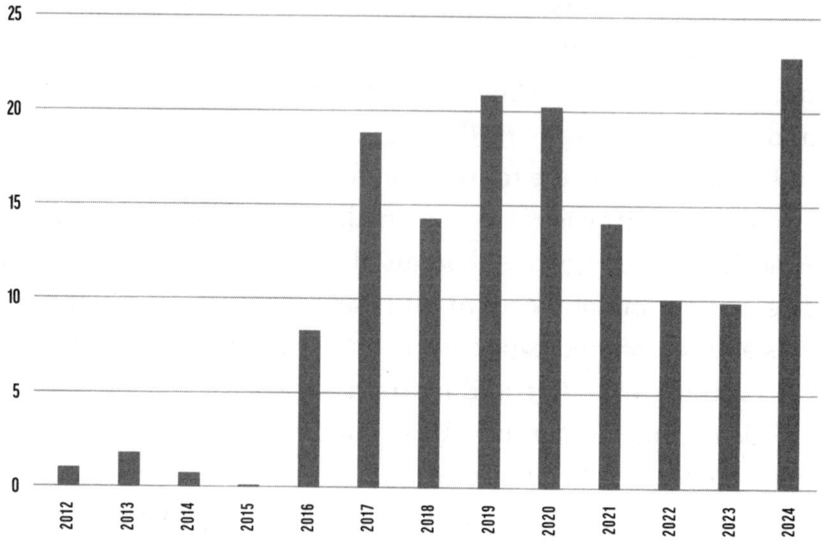

its small team, recruiting talented and contribution-motivated Koch employees and similar candidates from outside Koch.

Of course, not every investment initiative has been successful. When KED decided to expand its field of opportunity exploration to Europe, where there are many closely held companies, it struggled to navigate that region's varied cultures and failed to find partners who shared Koch's vision and values. But, because we opened an office in the region, the local leader felt the need to make investments, which we did. To get approval, unrealistic financial assumptions were made and the investments performed poorly.

KED closed its London office in 2022, having achieved little to show for its efforts, except for lessons learned. Our strategy violated the principle of Virtuous Cycles of Mutual Benefit because we didn't have the capabilities to be successful, given the cultural and economic environment there.

KED also undermined its long-term focus on Mutual Benefit by sometimes negotiating deals with counterparties that were too one-sided. While this created short-term profits for KED, it did not build lasting partnerships or create virtuous cycles of mutual benefit. In fact, a private equity sponsor, notorious for driving hard deals, accused KED of becoming the loan sharks of Wichita.

————

These and other failures have been important reminders of the need to consistently understand and apply principles, including **Overcoming Entropy and Bureaucracy**. For KED to succeed long term, it needs to be the preferred partner in the market and promote positive outcomes for all its core constituencies. Failures have been an effective teacher in this regard, even more so than KED's successes.

> **31**
>
> PRINCIPLE:
> ## OVERCOMING ENTROPY AND BUREAUCRACY
>
> Entropy, the tendency for disorder to increase, afflicts human affairs just as it does the physical world. For individuals, organizations, and society, there are always many more ways for things to go wrong than for them to go right.
>
> In organizations, the most common manifestation of entropy is bureaucracy, which results from detailed rules and procedures, rigid hierarchies, and perverse incentives that bring about loss of the knowledge, ideas, and motivation of employees.

These four case studies are representative of what is required to build a successful business long term—and the inevitability of failures when we aren't guided by principles.

To avoid this tendency, we strive to continually transform our ability to apply Principles of Human Progress.

HOW YOU CAN APPLY THESE PRINCIPLES

- What do your customers value most? What capability should you build to deliver it better than anyone else?
- Which of your products and activities are profitable and which are not?
- Where are you relying on averages or sunk costs? Are you applying Marginal Analysis?
- What product, service, or process should you grow, maintain, or exit? What's your plan to test that decision?
- Are you identifying your customers' unmet needs? How can your team satisfy them?

CHAPTER 7

HOW TO TRANSFORM YOUR CAREER—AND LIFE

When we are no longer able to change a situation,
we are challenged to change ourselves.
—VIKTOR FRANKL[36]

BIG IDEAS TO WATCH FOR

- Strive to be in the role that fits you, rather than climbing the ladder. Find ways to contribute that align with your strengths and passions.
- Success requires taking appropriate risks and being a lifelong learner. Progress comes from stepping outside your comfort zone and experimenting with new paths.

One of our greatest joys is seeing people transform their careers and lives by applying Principles of Human Progress. Everyone we've worked with has experienced failures. Yet those who've turned to principles have ultimately achieved success, often surpassing their highest hopes.

You saw this reality in chapters 2 and 3, when we told our stories of personal transformation. Yes, we've both had plenty of failures, and we can safely predict that we'll have plenty more.

But time and time again, principles have enabled us to learn from our mistakes and exceed our own expectations.

In this chapter, we'll showcase just a few of the many people at Koch who've done the same by applying principles.

Of the many principles at play here, the one that stands out is Empowerment. Your success depends on breaking the barriers that stand in your way, whether internal or external, that prevent you from becoming all that you're capable of being. At Koch, a primary role of every supervisor is to help remove these barriers by ensuring employees have roles that fit their gifts and empowering them to contribute.

At its most fundamental level, Empowerment involves learning and developing your gifts and pursuing your passions. When you do, you're more likely to find roles that fit those gifts, enabling you to make a bigger contribution, achieve greater success, and self-actualize.

When someone is struggling or stagnating in their career, the most likely culprit is that they aren't in the right role. A good example is when Chase fired himself from Koch Fertilizer and took a seemingly lower position. It proved to be a smart decision—for him and the company.

Other common barriers include being deficiency moti- vated—that is, fixating on what you lack instead of discovering and developing the gifts you have. Arrogance, a lack of integrity, or a sense of entitlement are other common characteristics that hold people back. These internal barriers make you less likely to maximize your contribution and be successful.

There are plenty of external barriers too. You may have had a supervisor who micromanaged everyone or was narrow- minded. Maybe you worked at a company that stifled you with top-down rules. Perhaps you didn't have the proper "pedigree" (work experience, college degree, or cultural background).

We've worked hard to break down many such barriers at Koch, but even after decades of effort, we still have work to do.

That's why the stories you're about to read inspire us, and we hope they inspire you. They remind us of what's possible when we empower everyone to achieve their potential. Just imagine what could happen if all our 120,000-plus employees were motivated to contribute, create, face reality, take on new challenges, cooperate, and help others succeed. Abraham Maslow defined this as realizing one's potential—what he described as being "everything that one is capable of becoming."[37]

Helping each employee along this path is a critical responsibility of supervisors at every level. They must respect employees as unique individuals, continually evaluate and adjust their roles and responsibilities so they can best contribute, and provide meaningful work that fits their talents and passions as well as receive feedback that helps them grow.

You're about to meet four employees who were empowered to self-actualize. Each one overcame internal barriers, external barriers, or both. We hope you're able to see yourself in some of these stories. And we hope that, like these Koch employees, you're able to move past failure and achieve more than you thought possible, both in your career and your life.

Before we dive in, though, we want you to keep two important things in mind.

First, transforming your career is a journey, not a destination. These employee stories don't end when they break a barrier. In fact, that's where the real story starts. Self-actualizing is a never-ending process. For every obstacle in the rearview mirror, there's another ahead of you. The principle of Virtuous Cycles of Mutual Benefit is at work here too. The more progress you make, the more progress you *can* make by continually applying principles.

Second, the people you're about to meet broke barriers in large part because they work at a company that values Empowerment. We realize not every business does, perhaps including your own. If that's the case, changing your company's culture or where you work is essential for finding fulfillment.

If you're a supervisor or aspire to be one, please read this chapter with an eye toward learning how to create an environment of Empowerment. If you're not a supervisor, this chapter may help you see things at your company that need to change or that you can do differently.

Advocating for a culture that empowers people can require courage, but it's worth it. After all, your long-term success is at stake.

And if you're stagnating in your current job, don't forget you have another option: Come work for Koch! We're always looking for people who want to contribute and achieve their potential.

FINDING A FULFILLING ROLE

"I have to become a manager to advance."

Chances are you've heard this sentiment. Maybe you believe it. This is easily one of the most common paradigms in business, pushing people to "climb the corporate ladder," which includes becoming a supervisor. Even then, there's pressure to keep climbing until you manage the managers. Surely *then* you'll be happiest and make the most money, right?

This is the wrong way to think about what role is best for you. Deep down, you already know it's wrong-headed, even if you've never publicly challenged the conventional wisdom about ladder-climbing.

Groundbreaking research by the think tank Populace shows why it's easy for people to end up in supervisory roles, even though they'd prefer to be individual contributors. It's the fallacy of status.

According to this research, 92 percent of people say they believe others define success based on achieving social status.[38] They associate supervising with status, so they think they need to become a supervisor to succeed in the eyes of other people.

But it turns out most people don't really value status; they just assume others do. Populace also found that 97 percent of people say they personally define success as being able to use their talents to pursue their own interests, regardless of whether that improves their social status.[39]

The problem is that many don't act on their own views. They feel like they're the only ones who think this way, so they chase status even though they don't personally value it. Almost everyone agrees that we don't *want* to climb the ladder unless that's where our talents and interests lead us.

What would happen if more people actually acted on their *true beliefs*, pursuing their passions regardless of social status? There's someone at Koch who demonstrates the answer.

Shakkthi Balasubramanian grew up in Chennai, India. As a student, he discovered his aptitude for solving math problems, then applied it by taking courses in databases, networking, and server management. After he finished his education, he took a job in his city's booming information technology industry. He knew he had a passion for IT.

Shakkthi's first role wasn't what he wanted. He was stuck taking calls and giving scripted responses, with little opportunity for creative thinking or problem solving. He moved to different companies over the next few years, pursuing more fulfilling jobs that dealt directly with IT.

Seven years in, Shakkthi fell into the supervisor trap. His expertise had expanded to the point that one of his employers thought he'd be a good manager. Shakkthi took the job because it seemed to be the natural next step in his career. Besides, everyone else said supervising was the way to go. For eight years, he worked in various management roles. When he moved to Koch Global Services in 2019, he was given his biggest management job yet.

But Shakkthi wasn't happy, either before or after he joined Koch. As a supervisor, he felt his creative fire was burning out because he wasn't addressing technology challenges. When he told his friends about his frustration, they told him it was too late to go back. He genuinely believed that if he stopped being a supervisor, he would go down the corporate ladder, not up. He feared that pursuing his passion meant taking a demotion and felt that status was better than accomplishment, no matter how miserable it made him.

Thankfully, Shakkthi felt empowered in his work at Koch. He also benefited from another principle: Changing Paradigms. He began to shift his thinking about the necessity of being a supervisor, driven by his desire to find fulfillment.

Shakkthi had the courage to approach his supervisor, saying he'd like to focus his skills on IT—not managing. His supervisor was supportive, recognizing that everyone should seek roles where they are most passionate and can make the greatest contribution. He urged Shakkthi to come up with ideas for a better role.

Shakkthi soon found a non-supervisory role as a solutions architect. Despite his initial nervousness, he embraced the opportunity to fully explore his creativity and curiosity.

One of his first projects was to rethink how to equip an office building with new technologies. He proposed moving from on-site servers to cloud-based ones. It was a smart move, helping reduce infrastructure costs and creating an environment for employees to operate securely and conveniently anywhere in the facility. Solving problems like that made Shakkthi happier than he'd been in years. He was finally contributing in ways that fit his passions.

Shakkthi has been thriving in his individual contributor role ever since. He has found innovative ways to help Koch facilities improve access to data for real-time decisions, enhance productivity, and speed up the delivery of products to market. All of this brings him a real sense of accomplishment. That's why he got into IT in the first place.

Shakkthi's success even inspired one of his friends to leave his own supervisory role. Remarkably, that friend was one of the people who had previously told Shakkthi that he should remain a supervisor. By shifting his focus from climbing the ladder to pursuing his passion, he is creating much more value—and also making more money.

In Shakkthi's words: "My wife tells me that I'm happier and more energetic. I can feel the difference too—I'm thinking of big ideas again!"

CONFRONTING A TOP-DOWN CULTURE

Few mistakes are more common in business than imposing a top-down culture on employees. Leaders justify it with any number of excuses: This is the way we've always done it. The people at the top know best. How would employees know what to do without so many rules?

Whatever the excuse, the inevitable result is that employees suffer. They're forced into roles that don't fit their aptitudes. They're prevented from innovating, contributing, and achieving their potential. And these external barriers can create internal barriers. When you're told what to do—or what you can't do—you often give up or doubt your own strengths. Maybe the leaders really do know best.

Chieko Yamamoto encountered this kind of corporate culture. She grew up in Japan, and like her father before her, she wanted to work in manufacturing there. She applied for a job at Molex (long before it was acquired by Koch), where she encountered major barriers, right from the get-go.

After receiving her application, Molex told Chieko that she should seek a job in sales, not manufacturing. The reason? Sales had a higher percentage of female employees, so she'd be a better fit. This was barrier number one: the corporate assumption that women should work in a sales job.

Instead, Chieko pressed for the role she really wanted. She succeeded, only to find barrier number two: a bureaucratic culture with inappropriate gender expectations.

Chieko was told by colleagues that, as a woman, it was her job not only to memorize the favorite tea of each of her male colleagues but also to make it for them. She was also told never to question her male leaders; she just had to accept whatever they said. This environment prevented Chieko from exploring her aptitudes and making a bigger contribution. She even began experiencing self-doubt—an example of external barriers creating internal ones.

Frustrated, Chieko left the full-time workforce for two years after having children. When she returned in 2005, she put aside self-doubt and began to push against the barriers that held her and countless others back—especially those involving gender.

Chieko's example was not only one of Empowerment but also Challenge. She had the courage and willingness to respectfully question her leaders' decisions, actions, and proposals. She challenged the idea, not the person, in a spirit of constructive improvement and solutions.

Chieko's refusal to sit back and stay quiet paid off. In 2008, she became the first woman at Molex to serve on the consumer and commercial solutions leadership team. Her supervisor told her not to be afraid. Given the culture at the time, that was a tall order for a woman in her thirties whose peers were all men in their fifties.

Nonetheless, she challenged Molex's approach to customer service, which involved answering every customer question with a customized response. This had created an enormous backlog, which Chieko suggested could be fixed by using a web-based solution. Once implemented, the new system provided immediate and accurate answers—a better outcome for both Molex and its customers.

Koch's acquisition of Molex in 2013 only strengthened Chieko's willingness to challenge the company's culture and advocate for roles where she could better contribute. She quickly took to Koch's principle-based approach, looking for ways to apply the concepts she was learning to further strengthen Molex. Yet even then, colleagues told her that it was better not to rock the boat.

Once again, Chieko refused. The leader of Koch's Principle Based Management capability encouraged her to challenge him and other leaders. Impressed by her enthusiasm and desire to contribute, he offered Chieko a job, telling her that she could help transform Molex. Her own husband, a former Molex employee, doubted that real change was possible, but Chieko had long since broken that internal barrier. She accepted the position.

Like Shakkthi's, Chieko's new role struck many as a demotion, since she went from being a supervisor to an individual contributor. But her salary didn't decrease, because Koch's compensation philosophy is based on contribution, not hierarchy. She actually had more earning potential, since her new role gave her a chance to make a bigger contribution.

Chieko contributed to transforming Molex's culture from within. In 2014, she started supporting the same division where she had previously worked, helping them see how using principles is more effective than following rules. She also helped identify many gaps in Molex's application of principles, working with company leaders to enact necessary changes. These included terminating leaders who fostered a culture of control rather than Empowerment.

Chieko now works in the United States. Her role supports all of Molex—not only in Japan, but across the world. She's thriving because she's empowered to challenge failed practices and help chart a path to success for a major business. Molex has made substantial progress but still has room for improvement. We're confident it can continue transforming, thanks in large part to the work of principled people like Chieko.

If you work in a company that's defined by top-down rules, make sure you haven't internalized them. You have to break mental barriers about your own abilities before you can break barriers in the rest of the business. Whatever your role, have the courage to question conventional wisdom, which sometimes is more foolish than wise.

The good news, as Chieko proved, is that most company cultures can be changed. It takes time, but more than that, it takes principled employees—people who challenge themselves and everyone around them to continually do better. If you find yourself in a stagnating company culture, find a new company.

In Chieko's words: "It hasn't always been easy, but if I can help others understand how the power of these principles can help them realize their potential, that's a dream come true."

STARTING AT THE BOTTOM

Have you ever felt like you're stuck in a dead-end job?

Virtually everyone does at one point or another. Our respective experiences working fields and shoveling cow manure spurred each of us to apply ourselves and find a path that better suited our gifts. But what about people who start with far fewer resources and opportunities than we did? What's the secret when starting with very little?

We'll begin our answer with the Contribution Motivated principle. No matter who you are, how much you have, or what job you hold, you have the ability to succeed by using your gifts to improve other people's lives. You need to act on this insight, feeding your desire to make a difference. Once you do, you can continually enhance your effectiveness and success.

We prioritize this principle in our culture. It involves hiring and retaining those who are, first and foremost, contribution-motivated people—like Juan Perez.

> **32**
>
> PRINCIPLE:
> ## CONTRIBUTION MOTIVATED
>
> Personal success and fulfillment—in any field or endeavor—come from helping others in ways that are mutually beneficial. Alexis de Tocqueville called this acting out of an "enlightened regard for themselves," which "constantly prompts them to assist each other."[40] This principle of Contribution Motivated can be vital to an organization or society's success.
>
> Being contribution motivated enables people to discover, develop, and utilize their abilities to succeed by helping others. They are energized by continuously trying to improve, innovate, transform, and creatively get results—which enables them to live lives of meaning. The more people contribute, the better they feel about themselves and the more they tend to be rewarded, so the more they want to contribute.

Juan's early life was defined by struggle. Born and raised in Mexico, he was fourteen years old when his father died. After seven difficult years, he immigrated to the United States and ended up in Wichita, Kansas, where he married and started a family.

Juan needed money to make ends meet. He took orders at a deli for a while, then moved to janitorial work. By that point, he had two young children, with a third on the way. Unable to support his wife and children on his limited wages, Juan knew something had to change, for his family's sake.

It would have been easy for Juan to fall into the trap of being deficiency motivated, a classic internal barrier. Thankfully, Juan was contribution motivated, so he looked for ways to do more and devoted all his energy to the search. He got his chance when he saw a newspaper job fair advertisement for Koch-Glitsch, which makes products and solutions for the refining and chemical industries. Juan slept in his car in the parking lot of the Koch campus where the job fair was held, just so he could be first in line for an interview the next morning. He was hired as a forklift driver.

Once he was on the job, Juan's desire to contribute expressed itself in his consistent willingness to learn new things. If something needed to be done on the shop floor, Juan was the first to volunteer and was quick to help others. He often asked if the team needed extra help during the weekends. If they didn't, he took it upon himself to study blueprints and other materials to better understand the work his team was doing. Juan's supervisors recognized his drive and expanded his responsibilities, giving him more opportunities to learn and contribute.

Juan's learning and experimentation quickly made it clear that he had a real aptitude for machines. In short order, Juan became a machine programmer.

That was thirty-six years ago. Juan continued to distinguish himself by his relentless desire to learn, apply himself, and increase his contribution. Until the day he retired in 2021,

Juan always worked hard to understand new technology and stay on the cutting edge. By applying principles, Juan overcame obstacles to lead a life he had only dreamed about.

Principles have also transformed Juan's family. His experience at Koch led him to encourage his children to learn new skills and seek new opportunities. When he saw that both of his daughters had an aptitude for math, he suggested they try accounting. They did, and before long, both were hired at Koch. Juan's oldest daughter has been here for eighteen years and leads the Americas region of the Koch global treasury team. His younger daughter is flourishing in Koch's Human Resources data and analytics department.

Juan and his family demonstrate the transformational power of principles. Principles can change your life's trajectory, even when you have nothing or feel unable to do anything meaningful. Not everyone is like Juan, but everyone has aptitudes that they can discover and develop with an eye toward helping others.

Have you found yours? If not, be willing to experiment to unearth them. If you have, be ready to work hard to develop them into a valued skill. Once you start, you'll find that you never have to stop—and the further you go, the more success you'll achieve.

In Juan's words, "By applying these principles, I learned to believe in myself and my abilities. I learned how to create value for the company, and for myself and my family. My family and I have had more opportunities than I ever imagined, and for that, I am forever grateful."

SUCCEEDING ON A SECOND CHANCE

Everyone makes mistakes. But some mistakes can make it much harder to find productive work and a fulfilling life. Case in point: About one in three American adults has a criminal record, which often limits job opportunities.[41] How do you succeed if you're in that situation?

Richard McMichael asked himself this very question not long ago. As a college student, he got caught selling drugs, resulting in a five-year sentence at a Kansas correctional facility. Overnight, Richard went from having a promising future in petroleum engineering to living in a prison cell with seemingly no future at all.

A criminal conviction is one of life's toughest external barriers. It's standard practice in the corporate world to discriminate against people with criminal records. Business leaders often think: Why take a chance on someone who broke the law? How can you really know if they've reformed?

Making matters worse, the very existence of that external barrier can easily create an internal barrier. If companies are just going to turn you away, why apply for a job at all? Once you're out of prison, it may seem easier to turn back to crime. Indeed, it may seem like the only path.

Richard refused to fall into that vicious cycle. While behind bars, he started reading books by successful entrepreneurs in hopes of charting a similar course. He also enrolled in an online college program to earn an accounting degree. He didn't *have* to do these things, but he refused to let barriers destroy his future.

As his sentence ticked by, Richard set his sights on a particular company. He spent many days on a prison work crew that picked up trash along Kansas highways. He could see Koch's headquarters in the distance and decided to try and get a job here. After earning his online degree, Richard applied for an entry-level accounting role at Koch, while still serving time.

One of the biggest reasons that Richard wanted to work here was that he knew we had "banned the box." That means we don't automatically disqualify candidates who have felony convictions. Our focus on principles has caused us to realize that people who've made mistakes still have skills and the capacity to contribute.

The hiring manager who interviewed Richard was impressed by his eagerness to contribute. Since he met all the qualifications, she offered him a job. Richard accepted, determined to make the most of his second chance. Since he couldn't drive due to restrictions on his license, he rode a bike from his work-release facility to Koch. It was a sixteen-mile round trip every day, rain or shine.

Richard's manager wanted him to succeed. Instead of limiting his responsibilities to what was in his job description, she challenged him to use his coding skills, which he'd taught himself in his spare time, to automate tasks. She believed he'd find higher-value opportunities to contribute.

One of his first automations resulted in what could have been a costly mistake: a significant overpayment to a financial institution (which was quickly resolved). Instead of being punished, Richard's manager told him that mistakes are inevitable in innovation. She then introduced him to an automation leader who helped hone his coding skills.

Since then, Richard has automated more than 150 tasks in just two years, freeing up countless hours for company accountants to devote to more productive work. He also developed a model that generates $2 million in value annually. Richard is now a marketing analyst for Molex.

Richard is truly fulfilled. He recently said, "Three and a half years ago, if you told me I was going to be here, I would have been the happiest guy in prison."

———

All the principles you've encountered in this chapter are evident in Richard's story. He embodied Empowerment by breaking barriers. He was changing paradigms while in prison. He embraced Challenge to learn new skills and disrupt the status quo. And he is definitely contribution motivated.

Richard is also a great example of applying the principle of Transformation. He has radically altered his life's trajectory, going from a prison cell to becoming a highly productive member of society. In 2024, Richard's accomplishments were acknowledged by the governor of Kansas, who pardoned him and cleared his record.

Richard's story reminds us that incredible things are possible when we commit to transforming ourselves. Long-term success entails continually seeking help to acquire new knowledge and skills. Being a lifelong learner is essential.

Transformation is only possible in an entrepreneurial culture where employees are eager and willing to drive change from the bottom up rather than waiting for a top-down grand plan. While some transformations are big steps forward, many are the cumulative result of employees continually challenging and pushing themselves and their teams to find new ways to create value.

In Richard's words: "For the first time in years, I actually got to contribute. I've also developed better relationships in my personal life."

———

What does transformation look like for you? Your backstory may not be as dramatic as these examples, but chances are, you're capable of transformation. Whatever your role or wherever you are in your career, you have opportunities to go from working at the margins to moving forward farther and faster than you ever imagined.

EMPOWER YOURSELF

These stories don't come close to covering all the barriers you may encounter. And we can't stress enough that for every barrier you break, there's another ahead of you. That's why Empowerment is a never-ending process.

HOW YOU CAN APPLY THESE PRINCIPLES

- What are your aptitudes? What are you passionate about? How are you using these attributes in your current role and in your life?
- Does your work enable you to apply your greatest gifts every day?
- Do you feel like a supervisory role is essential for your success? If your gifts and passions lie elsewhere, do you have the courage to find a role that better fits your strengths?
- Are you growing or coasting? What's one way to lean more toward growth this week?

CHAPTER 8

HOW TO DO THE RIGHT THING

*How selfish soever man may be supposed, there are evidently
some principles in his nature, which interest him in the fortune
of others, and render their happiness necessary to him, though
he derives nothing from it, except the pleasure of seeing it.*
—ADAM SMITH[42]

BIG IDEAS TO WATCH FOR

- Stewardship over signaling. Doing the right thing means respecting others' rights and acting with integrity—not chasing trends or appearances.
- A principle-based approach gets results; one where employees just follow rules does not.
- Mutual Benefit creates real value. Long-term success comes from helping others succeed, not from trying to benefit at the expense of others.

Social pressure on business is nothing new. But the 2020s have seen a wide swing in what people expect from business leaders on hot-button issues.

In 2020 and 2021, many companies faced unprecedented demands to do more to address racial discrimination and inequality. Around the same time, the business community faced increased pressure to commit to a carbon-neutral future. Koch has always believed in equal rights and environmental stewardship, but most others had a different approach. This has changed. By 2025, polls indicated that an overwhelming majority of Americans wanted businesses to stay out of political issues and current events.[43]

Given these conflicting opinions, what's the right thing for a business to do?

Principle-driven leadership starts by recognizing that the most basic role of business is to help people improve their lives by providing products and services they value more than their alternatives, and to do so responsibly while consuming fewer resources. This means business has an essential role in contributing to a society of equal rights and mutual benefit by respecting the rights of employees, customers, community members, and other constituencies.

When a business fulfills this role, more people have the opportunity to contribute and live a life of meaning, while employees are empowered to realize their potential regardless of race, gender, or other characteristics. In such an organization, safety is the highest priority, and the environment is proactively protected.

Unfortunately, many businesses don't satisfy these requirements, despite their best efforts or public claims. They're failing to fulfill these roles because, rather than applying proven principles, they've adopted flawed approaches such as Diversity, Equity, and Inclusion (DEI) and Environmental, Social, and Governance (ESG).

These approaches don't work because they ignore key principles that foster progress. This brings to mind Nobel laureate Milton Friedman's warning that "one of the great mistakes is to judge policies and programs by their intentions rather than their results."[44]

We don't say this in a judgmental way. To the contrary: We're sympathetic because we've had plenty of our own failures despite our good intentions. Our experience has deepened our appreciation for many principles, such as Stewardship.

Stewardship requires compliance with all laws and regulations and always acting in a manner that reinforces a bottom-up system of equal rights. It guides our approach to beneficial diversity and inclusion, and it has transformed our effectiveness in safety and the environment. We're applying it throughout Koch, led by our Stewardship capability, which we created in 2020. The group is now comprised of twelve leaders and more than two hundred subject matter experts.

We don't just want to avoid repeating past mistakes, as important as that is. We want to ensure that Koch fulfills its role in helping people improve their lives. To understand why we're so serious about this, let's consider what our company has been through.

33

PRINCIPLE:
STEWARDSHIP AND COMPLIANCE

The essence of Stewardship is recognizing our obligation to always act in a manner that respects the rights of others. Everyone should have the right to live as they choose, so long as they don't violate the rights of others. This empowers employees to realize their potential regardless of race, gender, or other characteristics.

Businesses respect others' rights by providing goods and services that help people improve their lives and doing so responsibly. It is also essential that businesses give safety the highest priority, be environmentally responsible, and comply with legal requirements.

Nothing is more important than human life. Thus, the safety of all those with whom a business interacts is the top priority. Similarly, proper regard for the environment starts by giving priority to the highest-consequence risks. This means implementing the best environmental practices—even if not required by law.

RISK AND COMPLIANCE

We know from painful experience that good intentions don't necessarily lead to good results. In the 1990s, our best intentions didn't stop many failures, some of which were disastrous.

By far, the worst was the death of two teenagers from a leak in one of our gas liquids pipelines. Upon discovering the leak, they started their car to go inform authorities, which ignited the fumes, killing them.

That tragedy shook us to our core.

Our policy has always been to only operate a pipeline when we are convinced it is safe. We had previously shut down that pipeline due to corrosion concerns, restarting it only after repairs and tests. A subsequent investigation found that, while we had regularly inspected it, the pipeline contained a strain of bacteria that accelerated corrosion much more rapidly than had ever been known in the US. The resulting legal judgment against us was extremely high, but it paled in comparison to the two deaths.

Clearly, we needed to do things differently. So we turned to principles such as Risk and Knowledge.

We realized our tragic failure was a knowledge problem. We identified the source and cause of the accelerated corrosion, shared the findings inside and outside Koch, and developed new corrosion-detection measures that are now used by us and others in the industry.

Additionally, we created an environmental excellence initiative to enlist every employee in establishing Koch as an international leader. It resulted in an enormous improvement in our environmental compliance, including reductions in leaks of all kinds. These and our other efforts have greatly improved our performance. For example, the US Environmental Protection Agency (EPA), in its 2015 Toxic Release report, ranked Koch the best for pollution prevention initiatives.[45] To this day, our employees are continually exploring new ways to apply technology and analytics to help detect corrosion in our systems before even the smallest failure occurs.

This progress led us to more urgently improve all applications of our Stewardship principle for safety and the environment, especially after acquiring Farmland's fertilizer business, INVISTA, and Georgia-Pacific in the early 2000s.

These acquisitions increased our number of employees more than fourfold and added hundreds of operating sites. We also had to correct serious environmental, health, and safety problems that existed at those companies prior to our ownership. The worst issues were at INVISTA, which we addressed through a formal agreement with the EPA.

Given the stakes, in 2004 we put a heavy emphasis on compliance: "Strive for 10,000% compliance, with 100% of us fully complying 100% of the time. Ensure excellence in environmental, safety, and all other compliances. Stop, Think, and Ask."

We hammered away at the message that compliance was everyone's job and rolled out detailed rules and

34

PRINCIPLE:

RISK

Risk and reward are inseparable and a basic fact of business, as well as life. But not all risks are equal. Risks involving human safety and compliance need to be approached differently than those associated with the profitability of an investment. Risk decisions also need to be made in a manner consistent with our principles. This encompasses eliminating catastrophic risks—like those that could lead to injury, loss of life, or a major environmental issue—and optimizing other risks.

Before pursuing opportunities, risk and potential rewards need to be understood. We must then determine whether to absorb, mitigate, or avoid those risks. We align the interests of all employees and agents so they make decisions based on a risk philosophy that maximizes the long-term success of the company.

procedures across Koch. We also created a risk management capability and established annual awards to recognize outstanding environmental, health, and safety performance. And we ramped up our efforts to communicate our principles to as many people as possible as quickly as possible.

This sounded good, but it was another case of judging a program by intentions. Requiring employees to fully comply 100 percent of the time put the emphasis on perfection rather than reducing harm. Put another way, by focusing on eliminating minor violations, we distracted employees from preventing major disasters.

We have had a number of cases where a disaster was avoided only because employees deviated from this rigid requirement. One such case was at a petrochemical plant where the operators interpreted 10,000 percent compliance to mean they should never use a flare because doing so would result in a minor compliance violation. (Flares are a safety valve for reducing unstable pressure in processing units.) A serious incident during an operational upset was only prevented because a supervisor immediately waived the requirement. He knew that flaring was the right decision to avoid much greater harm.

Our approach was also a barrier that kept our employees from transforming their ability to contribute. We thought it was bottom-up empowerment, but by setting a faulty vision, we made it top-down compliance. Employees were required to spend their time complying with highly prescriptive procedures, such as checking boxes on countless lists. What we should have done was empower them to apply principles to improve results.

This is the essence of a principle that is required for Stewardship: Principle-Based vs. Rule-Based. Consistently doing the right thing requires applying principles, not being bound by rigid rules.

We should clarify that a principle-based approach is not an absence of rules. But when policies, processes, or procedures are necessary, they must be continually challenged and improved in light of principles. When rules undermine progress, they should be modified or eliminated.

To be clear, our compliance programs did provide performance improvements. We earned high-profile awards from OSHA and the EPA. But our rigid approach was rule-based rather than principle-based. As such, it held employees back from making even greater improvements. To cure this problem, we took out the 10,000 percent requirement in 2018 and changed our Compliance principle to Stewardship and Compliance, which now reads: "Act with proper regard for the rights of others, especially regarding safety and the environment. Comply with all laws and regulations. Stop, Think, and Ask."

This new language reflects the need for every employee to respect the rights of others, including their life and property. Instead of binding them by rigid rules, this language encourages employees to be principled problem solvers.

A BETTER SOLUTION THAN DEI

Our focus on Stewardship couldn't have come at a better time. It has enabled us to better handle the global pressure to adopt Diversity, Equity, and Inclusion (DEI) initiatives, which, because of how they were structured and implemented, contradicted our principle-based framework.

At Koch, we value the benefits of a diverse workforce and seek to foster a workplace where employees are respected and included. Such an environment is essential for a successful business and a successful society. But the only way we've found to realize this vision is by applying principles. For decades, treating individuals with dignity and respect has been ingrained in our culture. Respect is itself a principle necessary for good Stewardship.

People are more likely to share their opinions and ideas and engage in effective challenge when a culture of respect and trust exists. It requires being truthful, especially when having difficult conversations. By providing feedback that helps people deal with reality and improve, we are showing respect. Anything less lacks integrity and usually leads to bad outcomes.

That's a stark contrast to DEI's rule-based approach, which holds that a unilateral, top-down emphasis on checklists, quotas, and rules is the way to achieve a more diverse workforce. This typically devolves into superficial changes at best and policies in the name of *equity* (in place of *equality*) that are worse.

The most destructive element in DEI is equity. It is the opposite of equal rights, which recognizes that everyone has the right to live as they choose, so long as they don't violate the rights of others. *Equal rights* requires removing barriers that unjustly hold certain people back so all people have the opportunity to realize their potential. *Equity*, on the other hand, assumes social justice should be judged based on whether different groups of people achieve equal outcomes—and action is required to ensure they do. But given the enormous diversity in gifts and life

---

35

PRINCIPLE:
RESPECT

Treating everyone with dignity and respect doesn't just lead to better outcomes. It's the right thing to do. It is disrespectful to believe you can know everything about a person and to judge an individual—positively or negatively—based on group identity or other characteristics.

Respect enables you to build relationships with people outside your normal circles or comfort zones. This expands your knowledge and perspective, enriches your experience, and enhances your ability to learn and contribute.

circumstances, achieving equal outcomes requires holding some back in order that others may get ahead. This requires coercion and the continual violation of equal rights, inevitably leading to tragic consequences. Rather than leading to a system of mutual benefit, it creates conflict and a perpetual "us versus them" mentality that stifles progress.

Once again, we were reminded of Friedman's warning about the difference between stated intentions and actual results.

DEI advocates generally push for a greater percentage of underrepresented groups in management and new hires, while publicly shaming corporations that fail to meet their demands. Many businesses have responded by sponsoring affinity groups that categorize people with common outward characteristics such as heritage (ethnicity, race, nationality, language), gender, sexual orientation, and religion. Although these factors obviously inform an individual's experiences and perspectives, no single characteristic should be used to define another person. It's disrespectful to judge a person—positively or negatively—based on group identity.

Instead of imposing the top-down approach of DEI, we adopted a bottom-up framework of equal rights, Mutual Benefit, and Comparative Advantage. We have found that this leads to an inclusive environment and genuine progress.

We don't categorize people based on one of their observable characteristics. Rather, we use principles to guide us toward diversity and inclusion that is mutually beneficial for employees and the company. We celebrate the uniqueness of each individual. We educate our employees about the benefits that come from seeking out contributions from team members with a diversity of backgrounds, experiences, perspectives, and talents. And we encourage building relationships with people outside our normal circles or comfort zones.

This is the essence of our Stewardship principle: Acting with proper regard for the rights of others means we promote equal treatment for everyone rather than favoring one group over another. We recognize that certain groups have been unfairly discriminated against, and that today some people still face much greater barriers to success than others. Our approach is to take a person's unique experience into account when shaping their role. We are committed to helping them succeed as an individual.

Our principled approach was put to the test during the summer of 2020, following the murder of George Floyd by a Minneapolis police officer. In the nationwide upheaval that followed, many Koch employees and constituents called for us to "do something." They saw other companies launching DEI initiatives and wanted us to do the same.

But we weren't interested in merely sending a signal that we were concerned about injustice and discrimination. Instead of giving in to these social pressures, we turned to principles—especially Stewardship, Respect, and Bottom-Up vs. Top-Down to guide our way forward. We wanted to ensure that these principles more fully informed our actions with employees, customers, community organizations, and everyone else.

Most notably, company leaders initiated conversations with employees who wanted Koch to adopt DEI. The goal was to listen and learn from the personal experiences of employees and better understand their concerns about Koch's gaps and opportunities for improvement.

These interactions, many of which were led by Dave Robertson (Koch's president at the time), were often difficult and emotional, but they were absolutely worthwhile. They resulted in all of us gaining an enhanced understanding of how principles lead to better outcomes rather than racial quotas, affinity groups, and other forms of identity discrimination.

We also encouraged our employees to get involved in the many initiatives we support to remove the barriers in communities that hold people back. These include a significant focus on areas such as the criminal justice system and education, where racial discrimination has been particularly harmful.

Koch's approach worked then and still does today. Our focus on principles has contributed to a renewed culture, where all employees are valued and empowered, instead of a culture of box-checking, race-based exclusion, and pitting people against one another. Because of our adherence to principles, Koch has avoided the internal tumult that divided many other companies and hurt their ability to fulfill their role in society.

Others began to realize the inherent problems with a rule-based approach to DEI. As *Harvard Business Review* reported, the typical DEI initiative "purports to end inequity but instead sustains it at great cost to marginalized populations."[46] Such failures have led many major companies, including big banks and tech firms, to make big cuts to their DEI programs. Similarly, many universities no longer require faculty or student applicants to write a statement about how they would enhance DEI.

There is plenty of evidence that a rules-based approach leads to failure. As *The Washington Post* reported:

A comprehensive review of 31 years of data from 830 mid-size to large U.S. workplaces found that the kind of diversity training exercises offered at most firms were followed by a 7.5 percent drop in the number of women in management. The number of black, female managers fell by 10 percent, and the number of black men in top positions fell by 12 percent. Similar effects were seen for Latinos and Asians.[47]

The article also reported that mandatory, top-down programs led to the worst results.

Remember Friedman's warning about the difference between stated intentions and actual results. Despite its promises, DEI has proven counterproductive both to diversity and inclusion. Thankfully, principles provide an effective path to making a difference in these vital areas.

A BETTER APPROACH THAN ESG

The same insights hold true for Environmental, Social, and Governance (ESG).

Like DEI, ESG is inherently top-down, with a focus on imposing rules and checking boxes. Many businesses have embraced and proudly publicized specific ESG commitments, especially regarding the environment. One of the most popular is achieving net-zero greenhouse gas emissions by a set date, regardless of a company's ability to meet that goal. Many of the companies that made such commitments without the capabilities to achieve them now face lawsuits accusing them of fraudulent business practices. Here is yet another powerful warning about the distinction between stated intentions and real results, not to mention the liabilities that come from empty virtue signaling.

Our own failures on safety and environmental issues in the 1990s enabled us to see ESG's problems much earlier. We're committed to achieving better environmental results—that's one reason we place such a high emphasis on creating more value while consuming fewer resources. To make that vision a reality, we turn to Stewardship, not ESG.

The incompatibility between our principle-based approach and ESG became clear when banks and rating agencies started evaluating customers according to ESG's top-down, one-size-fits-all criteria. We began facing customer inquiries into how we were performing relative to these standards. Community organizations asked similar questions.

These inquiries turned into threats that came to a head in 2021, when several Koch companies were given ultimatums by customers to commit to ESG quotas or cease doing business with them. These demands put sizeable segments of several of our businesses at risk. We realized we had to effectively communicate why our principle-based approach provides much better results than rule-based initiatives such as ESG.

Perhaps the best example of our responses was at Molex. In 2021, Molex was informed by an important potential customer that it had to sign on to the customer's ESG commitments to do business with them. Instead of going along with this rule-based demand, Molex spoke with that company's leaders to understand exactly what they valued. They made clear they wanted their suppliers to increase their percentage use of renewable energy. Knowing that's what the customer valued, Molex found new energy sources that satisfied that need. As a result, Molex was approved as a vendor without making an ESG commitment that would cause it to sacrifice principles.

Our approach catches many of our customers by surprise because it's profoundly different from what they are used to. This shows how ingrained top-down is in most corporate cultures. But when they see that our approach produces real results, fostering experimentation and innovation, expanding opportunities for individuals, and responsibly creating more value with fewer resources—their perceptions change. Most no longer worry whether we check their boxes, because they see that even when we don't, we do what matters to them. That's the principle of Mutual Benefit.

Voluntary exchanges tend to be mutually beneficial because both parties believe they will be getting more of what they value than they are giving up. Involuntary transactions, however, are win-lose. Whether legal, through tariffs or subsidies, or illegal, through fraud or theft, win-lose transactions are harmful to society. In contrast, succeeding by benefiting others makes everyone better off.

In retrospect, these challenges to our principle-based framework were enormously helpful for Koch. They drew attention to the many perils of a rigid, rules-based approach, reminding us of our earlier failures with compliance and helping us avoid similar mistakes. They also made clear that we needed to fully apply Creative Destruction to a greater extent on environmental issues. We couldn't simply wait for customers to pressure us to "do the right thing."

In keeping with our Stewardship principle, Koch employees have embraced the challenge to be entrepreneurial in finding new and better ways to achieve transformative environmental solutions. The resulting progress has far exceeded what we would have accomplished had we only been focused on checking a box.

One of the most remarkable innovations is mRegz™ AirCompliance, a breakthrough monitoring network developed by Molex and FHR under a formal cooperative research and development agreement with the EPA.

This network is a solution to leaks at industrial sites, which are both a significant safety risk and source of greenhouse gases, accounting for approximately 25 percent of emissions. We designed this system for industrial facilities like FHR's that have millions of valves, flanges, and connectors that can leak.

Before mRegz, the only way to detect leaks was by manual inspection, a process that required ongoing labor-intensive emissions monitoring. Even under EPA standards, it wasn't possible to inspect every connection all the time.

The mRegz system uses sensors to detect leaks, so it's always on, and as approved by the EPA, it eliminates the need for manual inspection. It's also able to detect emissions at much more sensitive levels—as much as a thousandth of current methods. And it gives operators the ability to respond and share information immediately.

We can now quickly identify and respond to emissions from leaks that have the potential to affect our employees or people in surrounding communities. Because the mRegz system is sensitive enough to pick up minute variations in air quality, we've even been able to alert neighboring worksites of their emissions before their own manual monitoring detects them. This is an unexpected, but significant, benefit for us, our neighbors, and our communities.

This experiment led to another cutting-edge product from Molex: an application that can quantify corrosion in pipes before failures occur. Innovations like these have greatly improved our sites' capability to operate safely and responsibly. Koch Engineered Solutions has also developed a superior pipe corrosion detection system that we make available to other companies.

We have made numerous other safety improvements over the years, many of which have been recognized by the US Occupational Health and Safety Administration (OSHA). One such example is INVISTA's Victoria, Texas, plant. OSHA has awarded Victoria its highest safety classification four times since our acquisition.

Koch has also made many other significant environmental improvements. For example, our two refineries have reduced greenhouse gas emission intensity by 19 percent since 2010. In addition, they both have built large-scale solar plants that will further reduce that intensity. The EPA has recognized our energy accomplishments by awarding Koch its highest honor: ENERGY STAR Partner of the Year four years in a row.

WHEN RULES ARE WRONG

Our commitment to a principle-based approach rather than one-size-fits-all rules still requires that we fully comply with all government laws and regulations. We do so regardless of whether we think they are beneficial, and even if they are counterproductive. When we believe rules are harmful, we work to persuade authorities to modify or eliminate them and replace them with more effective standards.

When laws and regulations undermine the ability of businesses to create good profit—which comes from making a contribution in society—everyone is harmed. Laws and regulations are particularly harmful if they are overly intrusive or numerous. Today there are more than a million federal regulations and several times that many state regulations. At such staggering levels, regulations become destructive, holding back innovation and progress, including on environmental and social issues. Time and time again, we have found that our Stewardship principle is essential for helping people improve their lives.

Don't get us wrong: Business should be held to very high standards. But principles do that more effectively than rules. That includes the demands made by those pushing DEI and ESG. Many business leaders are tempted to cave in to those demands and adopt whatever rules are in fashion because they believe it shows they have good intentions. But when businesses empower their employees to realize their potential by creating value for others, life gets better for everyone.

The path that gets results is paved with principles. It's the proven way to move forward.

HOW YOU CAN APPLY THESE PRINCIPLES

- What social pressures are you facing today? Is your response making things better, or are you just doing what you think others expect you to do?
- Review a process in your organization. Does it empower employees to solve problems or reinforce rule-following? What could be improved?
- Can you identify a company policy or decision that seems well-intentioned but does not produce real results?

PART II: SUPPLEMENTARY CONTENT

Scan to see how these principles work in practice. Access case studies, leader stories, short videos, and practical frameworks showing how these principles have been applied inside real organizations—what worked, what didn't, and why.

HOW YOU CAN TRANSFORM SOCIETY

HOW BUSINESS CAN CONTRIBUTE TO SOCIAL PROGRESS

*[The] rapid spread in this country of the philosophy
of enlightened management . . . will surely change
the whole society toward improvement, and therefore
must be considered to be revolutionary.*

—ABRAHAM MASLOW[48]

BIG IDEAS TO WATCH FOR

- Businesses contribute to society when they apply their capabilities to create value and solve problems in people's lives.
- When businesses hire for values and aptitudes, not credentials, they realize better results and empower more people to contribute.

The US is gripped by some very big problems. The economy is booming for many people but is a bust for many others. Unprecedented numbers of Americans think their children will be worse off than they are. "Deaths of despair" are soaring, driven by substance abuse and suicide. Tribalism and other forms of division have turned much of the country into warring camps. There are too many challenges to list here.

What role does business play in solving these problems and contributing to progress in society? Unfortunately, for many people, the answer is some version of "none."

For some on the Left, business is antithetical to social progress. It may even be responsible for the crises in the US. Those who hold this view see business as a necessary evil, at best. They want the government to be responsible for directing the economy, taxing and regulating companies as part of a top-down attempt to drive progress. According to this argument, business can't be left to its own devices, or the problems will get worse.

Some on the Right hold a different yet equally limiting view of business. They think that the sole role of business is to generate profit and returns. Under this view, greed is good, and every moment business spends caring about society is wasted.

We reject both views.

We believe in good profit. Business *must* care about solving problems in people's lives. By creating value for customers, businesses contribute to progress and succeed long term. Far from being a necessary evil, business is a positive good when it operates according to Principles of Human Progress. And when it does, history shows that business is the most effective institution in the world at fostering progress.

If that seems far-fetched, consider some of the vitally important things that business does, which most people now take for granted.

Before today is over, you'll likely eat three square meals, as will more than 300 million Americans. So will the vast majority of the world's more than eight billion people. This is nothing short of a miracle.

For nearly all human history, putting food on the table was a daily struggle for most. Hunger and malnutrition weren't just rampant; they were the norm, and starvation was a constant reality. But over the past two hundred years, people have pioneered incredible innovations in crop productivity, harvesting practices, transportation, storage, and more. We've disproven Thomas Malthus' infamous prediction that a growing world couldn't possibly feed everyone. Business is a big reason why. From the large farm to the neighborhood diner, businesses continually increase food supply to meet growing demand.

Or consider the transformation in human lifespan. Two centuries ago, you were statistically unlikely to live until age forty. Now, you'll likely live until you're nearly eighty. People are living longer, healthier, and happier lives because of incredible breakthroughs in medicine, nutrition, and other fields.

Even more incredible innovations are in the works. Artificial intelligence is enabling faster drug discovery. Gene-editing technologies are making personalized medicine more precise and widely accessible. Robotics are delivering cancer-cell therapies at a fraction of the cost. While advances are the result of many different factors, business plays the most critical role in the discovery and distribution of these modern miracles.

Overall, our quality of life would have been unimaginable to previous generations—the cars we drive, the size of our houses, the sheer number of retail options we have available. And we wouldn't have any of this without energy. Where does this access to affordable, reliable, and abundant energy resources come from? Business plays the leading role. In the last two decades alone, natural gas extraction techniques have significantly improved the standard of living in America while benefiting the environment.

In chapter 1, you read about the "Great Enrichment"—the sudden improvement in human existence since the 1700s. It was the result of more and more individuals discovering and applying their unique gifts. They have mainly done so by

36

PRINCIPLE:
CAPABILITIES

Long-term success comes from a focus on building capabilities that enable you to create superior value and to apply them where you can create the most value, both for others and for yourself. Being capability bounded, not industry bounded, allows you to create virtuous cycles of mutual benefit in multiple businesses and industries.

Creating superior value requires many capabilities—especially ones that are complementary and mutually reinforcing. Building superior capabilities requires employees who create their own virtuous cycles—who self-actualize. You may have advantaged facilities and technologies, but they don't last without contribution-motivated employees who continually transform themselves and the business. Employees who create knowledge and contribute to a principle-based culture are your ultimate capability.

working in businesses. And huge numbers of people have had a go at starting their own business.

As a society, we need to continue this upward trajectory, tackling the challenges of today. Government and philanthropy have an important role to play. The next two chapters will examine how businesses can interact with those institutions in a principled and effective way.

This chapter, however, will look at how business can continually contribute to progress in society by applying principles to improve its performance. This is the primary way that companies move the needle on pressing problems. Instead of defaulting to advocating for public policy or funding charity, business leaders should first ask: How can my company create value for society by doing what we do best—and continually doing it even better?

We have found the principle of Capabilities very helpful in answering this question. Capabilities are to a business what abilities are to an individual—the things you do that help you succeed. Practically, you first have to understand what your capabilities are. Then, you have to figure out where you can apply them to create the most value for others and society.

Another key principle here is Mutual Benefit. A business should only apply its capabilities in ways that are win-win for itself and society. This isn't self-sacrifice or charity, and it's certainly not winner-take-all. Long term, no one benefits if a business neglects its core function of creating value or tries to play a zero-sum game, succeeding by making others worse off. Businesses stagnate and ultimately fail if they don't generate good profit. When Koch has succeeded as a business, we've contributed to social progress. When we've fallen short as a business, we've missed an opportunity to do so.

Thankfully, our missteps have helped us find better ways to achieve success. Let's look at two examples of how principles have enabled us to help tackle some truly big societal problems.

THE ECONOMY: PROGRESS VS. PARTICIPATION

One of the biggest challenges in America is that more and more people are being excluded from progress. They see the advances in the economy—the cheaper goods, the new technologies. But they also see that much of their lives is being disrupted. What good is a cheaper television if you lost your job at the factory?

This reality has caused many people to believe that America can either embrace the fast pace of economic progress and leave people behind, or it can limit the pace of progress and keep people employed and society stable.

This is a false choice. The best economic progress happens when more people are empowered to participate in that progress. When fewer people do, the result is the kind of social crisis we have today—a combination of economic stagnation and rising resentment. This is a recipe for disaster, as many countries throughout history have experienced. Without a dramatic change, this crisis could quickly spiral out of control.

Addressing this crisis requires action at every level of society. Public policy must change, insofar as it tries to protect people from progress and pushes them to believe that innovations will actually hurt them. That includes protectionist policies such as tariffs that try to protect industries—and even countries—from change while raising costs on everyone and disrupting the supply chain. Education plays a big role too. Our current system fails to prepare people for our dynamic economy and a lifetime of learning.

But how can business help?

One answer can be found in hiring practices. At their best, businesses draw workers from a broad pool, recognizing that a diversity of talents and experiences contributes to creating good profit. That includes hiring from communities that have been—or are being—left behind. People who have been laid off from a factory shouldn't be stuck on the sidelines for the rest of their lives. Everyone benefits if they can find a new and better job.

Unfortunately, companies frequently have hiring barriers that prevent people from contributing, like calling for candidates to have a four-year degree or some other credential. This can exclude otherwise qualified job candidates—especially those from struggling communities.

Nearly 44 percent of jobs in 2021 were limited to those with a college degree.[49] That excludes the 62 percent of Americans over age twenty-five who don't have a degree[50]—more than 150 million people.[51] And estimates say that nearly three-quarters of jobs will require at least some college education by 2031.[52] That often seems wise—don't you want someone with a resume that proves they're qualified? But life isn't that simple, and unless these requirements are specifically tailored, they can hurt the business while worsening the lives of people being left behind.

Thankfully, Koch has learned how to mostly avoid this trap. In hiring and promoting, we've sought to apply the principle of Contribution Motivated, recognizing that a candidate's desire to make a difference, coupled with their talent, matters more than any degree or prerequisite.

Think back to chapter 2, where you met Sterling Varner, who had no college degree. He rose to become president and COO at a time when other companies wouldn't have considered him for those roles.

That said, our application of principles has been far from perfect. We had credential requirements for many hires, most notably in information technology and accounting. Our mistake became clear in the mid-2010s as we struggled to fill jobs because of competitive pressures from technology companies and financial services firms, hurting our performance and threatening to derail our competitiveness long term. We also routinely hired people with the right professional credentials who didn't last because they lacked what we really needed—namely, the desire to succeed by creating value for others.

In 2018, our senior management came to realize the extent to which the company was using college degrees as a requirement for technical roles. It prevented many talented, intelligent, and motivated people from being hired. We had long known that people are more than their level of education, but we still needed to fully implement our principles.

This required transforming our HR capability. Rather than "checking boxes" based on a resume, the new HR leadership began looking at each candidate's unique blend of values, aptitudes, and experience, as well as their motivations.

Mackenzie Postma shows the benefit of this principle-based approach. She grew up in rural Michigan and took an online IT course at a local community college. She was very talented, yet because she lacked a four-year degree, our recruiters historically would have ignored her. But in 2021, we hired Mackenzie. A new individualized assessment program—which we built as part of our HR rethink—revealed that she had a high aptitude for the work we needed. She's now a software engineer at Koch Global Services.

Or consider the story of Jarrod Benson. As a teenager working a summer job at a local company, he painted lines at one of the parking lots at Koch headquarters. At age eighteen, he became an aircraft parts machinist in Wichita, and he learned through that job that he was good at troubleshooting and solving problems. He also realized this skill set applies in technology, so he began working on computers in his spare time. At twenty, he moved into IT roles at local companies.

Jarrod applied for IT roles at Koch over a five-year period, but he was repeatedly rejected because he was self-taught and lacked the required credentials. Fortunately, a current employee referred him to our HR team, saying that Jarrod had the values and abilities we wanted. We hired Jarrod in 2005.

Jarrod quickly proved himself, moving into a leadership position in 2009. In 2013, his supervisor challenged him to take a role transforming the cybersecurity capability. As he built his team, he realized his own department still had a degree requirement. He knew that didn't make sense since he—the department's head—didn't meet its own standards. So in 2014, he worked with HR to remove those requirements and hire people based on aptitudes and interests. Today, Jarrod is Koch's chief information officer.

In other areas, we've developed new systems that are tailored to finding people who are contribution motivated and have the right talents. After years of struggling to find good people, accounting began to rethink credential requirements. This led to a partnership with Wichita State University. The school wanted to recruit students who otherwise couldn't afford college, and Koch wanted candidates with the ability and desire to contribute. So in 2021, we designed an apprenticeship program that lets students earn money while learning accounting on the job. Most participants go on to work for Koch, helping them build a better life and giving the company better talent.

Across the company, we've launched experiments, programs, and partnerships to improve our ability to identify and develop people who are contribution motivated. One of the most exciting initiatives is our IT Skill Development Program in partnership with Catalyte. The program uses artificial intelligence to identify people who have the aptitudes for IT, regardless of educational backgrounds and professional experience. All these efforts are helping people who may have otherwise been left behind.

When companies look only or mainly at credentials, they can effectively discriminate against people because of their family's income, their place of birth, their previous career choices, and other factors that have no bearing on their individual aptitudes and mindset. Welcoming a broader array of applicants is essential to ensuring a future in which more people can participate in societal progress.

That's especially true when it comes to people with criminal records. One of the most perverse forms of the credentialing problem is refusing to hire people who've run afoul of the law—even after they've paid their debt to society. Criminal records are usually a kind of "anti-credential," an indelible mark that prevents people from finding meaningful work. This hurts their opportunity to have fulfilling careers and hurts society by increasing criminal recidivism.

It also hurts businesses. A staggering 77 million Americans, or about one out of every three adults, have a criminal record of some kind.[53] A company that won't consider even those who've reformed has written off a huge number of people who could contribute.

But that's exactly what many companies do, as did Koch for decades. Fortunately, we ditched this practice in 2015. We "banned the box," removing the section on our job applications that asked candidates if they had a criminal record. Wherever allowed by law, background checks are run only after they have been evaluated like any other candidate.

In the ten years since we "banned the box," we have extended job offers to more than seventeen thousand people with a criminal record. Our experience has been that when these individuals are in the right roles and given the chance to contribute, they make a meaningful difference for themselves, their families, and Koch.

Nationwide research confirms that when companies de-emphasize credentials overall, they're more likely to find successful hires, saving money and time in the hiring process.[54] This makes sense: Someone's values and aptitudes—not a degree—are the best indicators of their future contributions.

By acknowledging this truth, businesses have an enormous opportunity to make a societal difference. If more of them rethought or rejected credentials, people who've been displaced by the rapid changes in the economy could be welcomed into exciting new job opportunities without having to earn a four-year degree—a task that's often impractical.

Businesses could help find new ways to get them up to speed in this fast-paced economy. So instead of being left behind, they would help move society forward, applying their unique talents to create value.

This vision of economic inclusion and shared progress is achievable. If just a fraction of companies took this road, many more contribution-motivated people could fill millions of job openings. Some of the biggest benefits would flow to overlooked people and undervalued communities, who would be empowered to participate in society's progress. And in many cases, this will enable more companies to achieve better long-term success.

This approach illustrates what it means for business to succeed while enabling social change.

COMMUNITY-BASED SOLUTIONS: LAWYERS TO THE RESCUE

Our approach to hiring reflects a deliberate effort to better apply principles, with the goal of sparking progress for the business and society. Other times, however, the opportunity for social change arises unexpectedly. That was the case with our legal capability, which found a powerful way to make a difference only after we addressed its failure to fully apply our principles in business dealings.

For a long time, our legal capability had a reputation for being too tough. While it was led by principled people who were aligned with our vision, they emphasized one-sided winning rather than win-win relationships. In litigation, they were as aggressive as possible, and in contract negotiations, they'd quibble over things that were much more valuable to our counterparties than they were to us. Other businesses had a saying: "In a 50-50 deal, Koch gets the hyphen." While some in the legal community would view this as a badge of honor, we did not. This approach didn't align with the principles of Mutual Benefit, Partnership, and Respect, among others.

As we got feedback, we realized that our legal capability was hurting the company. In more than a few instances, we lost out on deals because counterparties didn't want to work with us after their initial interactions. In other cases, we weren't even given the opportunity to consider an acquisition because of our legal reputation.

We initiated a leadership change in 2016 so that the legal capability would better apply Economic Thinking, focus on Division of Labor by Comparative Advantage, and forge mutually beneficial partnerships. These changes quickly paid off, which happens when principles are faithfully applied. The legal department began doing a much better job of fulfilling its core business functions. But the changes also helped us discover an opportunity we didn't expect—a chance to further contribute to social progress.

Our new general counsel and his team saw opportunities for our lawyers to help with an issue that Koch has long cared about: fixing our broken criminal justice system. Inspired by Koch's support of criminal justice reform policies, they realized that our lawyers could help people who'd been harmed by the system. The lawyers could find greater fulfillment in their jobs at Koch, while positioning the company as a preferred partner with communities and other businesses.

Since the 1970s, Koch has worked to end the two-tiered nature of the system, in which well-connected people and less fortunate people often get treated very differently. We've also sought to reform one-size-fits-all punishments that do more harm than good, while helping people reintegrate into communities once they've paid their debt, with the goal of breaking the cycle of crime.

While our government affairs team had long played an effective role on the policy front—contributing to historic victories such as the federal First Step Act in 2018—our legal team discovered they could also be effective on a pro-bono basis. Specifically, our lawyers could provide free legal services to remove barriers for people who've run afoul of the system.

These pro-bono services cover a wide range of important issues: helping get a nonviolent criminal record expunged or pardoned; helping a person with a criminal record get a driver's license so they can drive to work; helping veterans who'd been dishonorably discharged for drug-related offenses regain their benefits; or even helping free people who'd been wrongly incarcerated. This is the definition of Mutual Benefit. Our communities gain the contributions of those leaving the criminal justice system; our lawyers pursue uniquely fitting and fulfilling work; and people who are struggling to disentangle themselves from the criminal justice system get their lives on track. Win-win-win.

Our pro-bono initiative got off to a bumpy start. We quickly discovered that Kansas Supreme Court rules prevented lawyers licensed in other states (as many of ours were) from doing pro-bono work. After successfully pushing for a change to that rule in 2018, the initiative began in earnest in Wichita. That first year, our lawyers worked to expunge dozens of criminal convictions, helping people access jobs, education, and housing.

About 60 percent of our lawyers participate in this work. They report greater fulfillment and want more pro-bono opportunities. The initiative has also been helpful for recruitment and retention. The nonprofits we partner with love it, too, as do the people receiving the free legal services. Many of these groups have shoestring budgets, and the people they serve often had no access to legal expertise. Now they have world-class legal help, making them much more effective at improving lives.

After their initial success, the team saw an even bigger opportunity to scale the pro-bono initiative. They asked themselves: "If this initiative worked with Koch's attorneys, why not bring it to Koch's preferred law firms?" They issued a "force multiplier" challenge to fourteen firms in 2020: Would they direct their own pro-bono hours to Koch's initiative? Some of these firms have thousands of lawyers, so if they got involved, the pro-bono initiative could grow dramatically.

All the firms got involved. Like us, they saw an opportunity to help their lawyers become more engaged, strengthening their own business effectiveness. This also expanded the benefits of the program to the communities where these firms operated. Once again, win-win-win.

The pro-bono initiative went national. Lawyers from Koch and the various law firms were suddenly supercharging criminal justice work. The National Association of Criminal Defense Lawyers got help protecting innocent people. The Innocence Project got help exonerating people who had been wrongly convicted. And hundreds of people got the legal counsel they couldn't otherwise afford.

This work is transformative. Our nonprofit partners tend to have enormous demand for their services. But they're limited by the lack of resources—resources that the pro-bono initiative frees up. As one nonprofit leader told our legal team, his organization has saved "millions if not tens of millions of dollars" that it would have spent on outside legal help. It's now devoting that money to helping more people.

The pro-bono initiative has expanded to provide free legal services to more than 350 nonprofits addressing everything from poverty to foster care to substance abuse and beyond. When a local group needs help with buying a second property, the initiative provides it. When an organization in a single state wants to go national, the initiative helps write a fifty-state human resources manual. Lawyers are applying their passions to drive societal progress, helping hundreds of nonprofits transform their effectiveness.

To date, the pro-bono initiative has provided more than twelve thousand hours of free legal service. One of Koch's partner firms has pledged ten thousand hours of its own. In recognition of its efforts, Koch was one of two winners of the Pro-Bono Institute's 2025 Corporate Pro-Bono Partner Award. And there's plenty of room for further progress.

There are thousands of lawyers at hundreds of businesses and law firms whom we hope to get involved, virtually all of whom are required to do some pro-bono work. Some of them do effective work, but many don't. We're now developing partnerships with corporate legal departments, as well as law schools such as Villanova. If more lawyers get involved in a transformative effort like the pro-bono initiative, they'll make a remarkable difference—in their lives, in the lives of others, and across our society.

For our part, we're glad our principles led us to this opportunity. It never would have happened if we hadn't challenged our legal capability to more fully apply them, in a spirit of Mutual Benefit. Once you get on a principled path, doors can open that you never expected, including ones that lead to social change.

WHERE YOU CAN START

These examples may not resonate with your business or organization. You may have different capabilities. You may be in different industries. But you can still apply this principle-based approach.

There are a great many challenges in America today, far beyond the economic exclusion and criminal justice system that we've discussed. Whatever problem you seek to solve, the place to start is by identifying your capabilities. What does your business do that makes it successful?

From there, think expansively about how those capabilities can be applied. At Koch, we realized that improving how we hired could help tackle the crisis of people being left behind. But we didn't realize that by improving our legal team, we could help scale criminal justice efforts nationwide. We had to change our paradigms and experiment. You should expect to do the same.

If you succeed, you will join the long list of businesses that have helped solve some of the biggest problems in human history. Businesses are eliminating world hunger. Businesses are transforming the environment for the better. Businesses have done—and are doing—extraordinary good for billions of people. Where can you make the biggest difference?

HOW YOU CAN APPLY THESE PRINCIPLES

- How can your company's capabilities be applied to address big problems in your community or society while improving performance?
- Review the hiring and advancement criteria at your organization. Are they unintentionally excluding high-potential candidates? What changes might draw out contribution-motivated candidates?

CHAPTER 10

HOW BUSINESS CAN SHAPE BETTER PUBLIC POLICY

*. . . a wise and frugal Government, which shall restrain
men from injuring one another, which shall leave them
otherwise free to regulate their own pursuits of industry and
improvement. . . . This is the sum of good government. . . .*
—THOMAS JEFFERSON[55]

BIG IDEAS TO WATCH FOR

- The way businesses interact with government has big implications for society.
- Companies should work against corporate welfare, even when it appears to be in their short-term interest. Long-term success comes from creating value for others, not from special treatment or government handouts.
- Policy over party. Support principled policies regardless of which political party initiates them.

For centuries, business has helped solve many of society's biggest problems. But business can't solve every problem. Other institutions play important roles, especially government and philanthropy, and business necessarily interacts with them.

First, let's acknowledge an overlooked fact: Neither government nor philanthropy can succeed without business. Government depends upon the resources that companies generate, including the taxes that they and their employees pay. The same is true for philanthropy, which is ultimately funded directly and indirectly by business profits.

Business should also enable government and philanthropy to embrace their most productive roles. Think of this as another application of the principle of Division of Labor by Comparative Advantage. Let's start with what government does best.

We understand the government's role in the same way that scholars have described it for generations. According to sociologist Max Weber, government is the entity that has a legal monopoly on the use of force in a geographical area.[56] Not the most eloquent definition, but it's accurate. And for the record, "force" isn't inherently bad. We should all be glad that someone is authorized to protect our family from assailants. We should all be glad that people pay taxes for things such as roads, social safety nets, and other public goods that aren't otherwise provided by business or civil society. Government force is necessary where competition and cooperation don't work as well.

That leaves a lot for government to do. But it also defines the limits of appropriate government action. Every company should help government stay on the straight and narrow by supporting its proper actions and holding it accountable when it oversteps.

For example, business should advocate for equal rights while opposing government's infringement of those rights. The loss of liberty is harmful to everyone and ultimately holds back human potential and all of society. And there's a reason we say *equal* rights: Good government provides a level playing field, which is one of its most important responsibilities. At its best, public policy gives individuals and businesses the space to find new ways to create value and help people improve their lives.

Unfortunately, government frequently exceeds these boundaries, often at the urging of business. When it does, it generally violates the principle of Bottom-Up vs. Top-Down, among others.

In a top-down society, government decides how people should live their lives. This prevents the knowledge dispersed throughout society from being put to productive use, which is required for increased prosperity. Such control also undermines progress by stifling people from discovering, developing, and applying their talents.

A bottom-up society empowers people. It unleashes their creativity, initiative, and Talents, resulting in beneficial outcomes beyond what anyone could have planned or predicted. Everyone benefits when behavior is mostly governed by general principles rather than detailed rules, freeing individuals to use their gifts and knowledge to tackle problems and pursue opportunities.

Here's some of what we've learned (including through failure) about how business can move public policy in a more principled direction.

CORPORATE WELFARE: AN ENEMY OF PROGRESS

Koch has always opposed corporate welfare as a matter of principle. By this, we mean any government policy that gives a business or organization an unfair advantage. Corporate welfare is an egregious example of a top-down approach.

Corporate welfare takes many forms, from tariffs and direct subsidies that benefit one company over another to regulations that help established businesses hold off new competitors. Then there are occupational licenses, loans and loan guarantees, eminent domain abuse, bailouts, and many others.

Whatever its form, corporate welfare is the opposite of Principled Entrepreneurship, which holds that companies should pursue good profit, that which is earned by creating value for others. Your business or organization needs to recognize that long-term success is incompatible with corporate welfare, no matter how much it seems to benefit you in the short term.

Corporate welfare is a form of political entrepreneurship, not Principled Entrepreneurship. Rather than profiting by creating value for others, it involves profiting by taking from others, which corrupts the political system. It also corrupts the country's culture by leading people to believe that success comes from harming rather than benefiting others.

The problem with corporate welfare is that it always—*always*—impedes progress. It pushes businesses to focus on securing handouts instead of creating value, solving problems, and improving lives. Society loses when a business abandons its core mission of creating value for others. Corporate welfare also pits companies against one another, not through natural and beneficial competition, but by preventing others from making a contribution and succeeding.

Corporate welfare blocks smaller businesses from growing and start-ups from getting off the ground. When a company is propped up by government, what chance does a would-be competitor have? The damage is worst for those with the least, such as entrepreneurs from disadvantaged communities who are prevented from getting started by established players with the power of government on their side.

Established businesses struggle in the long run too. They're so focused on getting corporate welfare that they stop innovating and creating value for customers.

The decline of American auto manufacturing is a cautionary tale. Automakers spent so many years lobbying for self-serving protectionist policies that they didn't keep up with advances in manufacturing or focus on game-changing innovation. To see where corporate welfare leads, look at Detroit, which used to be one of America's great cities but became a shell of its former self. Yet instead of changing their ways, automakers want even more protectionism. Who suffers the most? It's not the executives, who inevitably benefit from bailouts. It's the workers, their families, the community, and society as a whole, all of which suffer as the companies fail.

This failure to envision and deliver the future—to apply the principle of Creative Destruction—is the inevitable result of corporate welfare. Given that there are tens of thousands of these ruinous policies at every level of government, it's undeniable that Americans are worse off. The best evidence shows that since 1980, regulations—many of which are blatant examples of corporate welfare—have lowered the income of the average American by $13,000.[57]

If anything, these numbers undersell the real damage. Corporate welfare has prevented businesses from creating untold innovations. With a level playing field, our society could be decades ahead of where we are now, with technologies that improve lives in ways we can't imagine.

Corporate welfare corrupts business, causing it to undermine long-term value creation in favor of short-term financial gain. The allure of short-term gain is why so many businesses support corporate welfare. Koch has encountered this reality many times in our attempts to improve public policy. Our inability to stop more corporate welfare has been one of our biggest failures.

One example was when Charles founded Business Leaders Against Subsidies and Tariffs—BLAST—in 1977. He persuaded Nobel Prize winner Milton Friedman to chair its academic advisory board after agreeing to tone down the name to Council for a Competitive Economy. Whatever the name, it failed because most of the business leaders we approached said that while they agreed with us in theory, they wouldn't join. They were dedicated protectionists of their own businesses.

One business leader who refused to join said, "I love what you and Milton are doing, but it won't work in my industry. My company makes jeans, and if we go out of business, who will make our boys' uniforms in time of war?"

This is the typical refrain from the corporate welfare recipient: "I know corporate welfare is bad in general, but I'm different, I'm special." They aren't different or special. Their approach is unprincipled and shortsighted, not recognizing the need to contribute to succeed long term. This is how we get the boundless examples of corporate welfare that exist today, from sugar subsidies that enrich a few companies but make all products that use sugar more expensive, to government loans for manufacturers, to requirements that intra-US shipping only happen on US-built ships. All this corporate welfare raises costs, reduces choices, distorts markets, and stifles opportunities for everyone else.

This failure forced us to recognize that most businesses would never voluntarily give up their goodies. They were too convinced that corporate welfare was necessary for their success. Instead, we needed to focus on individual Americans— the ones being hurt.

To do that, Charles created Citizens for a Sound Economy in 1984, which was much more successful. It rallied Americans to fight policies that hold people back, including top-down mandates that prop up businesses, worsen poverty, and otherwise make people's lives worse. In 2004, the group changed its name to Americans for Prosperity, which continues to fight corporate welfare to this day.

Focusing on the American people has worked, perhaps most notably in eliminating occupational licensing requirements for many jobs. Established companies push for these licenses—which often cost thousands of dollars and require thousands of hours in a classroom—to block competitors, including individuals who start with nothing. Around one in four jobs requires a license, up from one in twenty in the 1950s.[58] As a result, people who want to pursue their passions can't, from those who want to open a hair-braiding business to would-be interior designers, among hundreds of licensed careers. Elevating these victims' voices has resulted in all fifty states taking principled steps to lower licensing burdens, eliminate some licenses, or prevent the creation of new licenses.

We've also made a point of opposing corporate welfare that seems to benefit Koch.

In the 2010s, we could have hopped on the corporate welfare bandwagon by opposing the Keystone XL Pipeline. That pipeline would have brought cheaper Canadian crude oil to refineries in the South, reducing the competitive advantage of our Minnesota refinery. But we supported that pipeline on principle, even though it would have reduced our short-term profits.

Similarly, Koch opposed all mandates and subsidies for ethanol plants, even though we owned several. While the Keystone pipeline project was killed and ethanol mandates survive, we continue to advocate for what we know is right—namely, a level playing field with no preferential treatment, for us or anyone else.

We fared better with the Border Adjustment Tax. In 2017, the Republican-controlled House of Representatives proposed increasing taxes on imported goods while subsidizing exports. This was a clear-cut case of corporate welfare for domestic manufacturers, including Koch.

We would have profited handsomely from the tax. For example, our sizeable exports of chemical intermediates from INVISTA would have become tax-free. It also would have benefited Georgia-Pacific, which primarily buys domestic southern pine trees to produce paper products, while its main competitors rely on imports, which would have been more expensive because of this new tax.

All told, the Border Adjustment Tax could have given us at least $1 billion of extra profit per year, but we opposed it anyway. Across the economy, the Border Adjustment Tax could have cost consumers more than $1 trillion, with the least fortunate being hit the hardest. That's not progress; it's picking Americans' pockets.

We fought hard to kill this tax, funding efforts to help Americans see that if it passed, they'd pay through the nose. They, in turn, pressured Congress to ditch this terrible idea. Despite enjoying early support from some influential members of Congress, the Border Adjustment Tax was quickly abandoned.

Corporate welfare is just as prevalent at the state and local levels. We fight it there too—even when it takes unexpected forms.

In the early 2010s, we drew up plans to construct a new building at our Wichita, Kansas, campus. It required moving a city street that ran straight through the land we wanted to use. When we discussed our proposal with the city, officials offered to pay for moving the street. We refused on the grounds that since Koch wanted to move it, Koch should cover the cost, more than $6 million. It would have been easy to stick taxpayers with the bill, but that would have been wrong, because it's corporate welfare.

The system is so distorted by corporate welfare that it would be nearly impossible to completely avoid it. Koch only participates in incentive programs where they already exist or have become embedded in the law. But even when we do, we actively oppose rather than lobby for them. If we could somehow end all subsidies tomorrow, including those that benefit Koch, we would be thrilled. The challenge is to get other businesses to focus on creating value rather than seeking handouts.

This is where you come in.

We recognize that it's hard to say no to other people's money and special treatment for yourself. But whatever your business or industry, you need to realize that corporate welfare only hurts you in the end. (Remember Detroit!) You may think your story will turn out differently, but it won't. Even if you're benefiting from special treatment, you're missing out on the much greater benefits that come from good profit.

Corporate welfare is a classic example of short-term interests clouding much better long-term benefits. This is the principle of **Time Preference**.

> **37**
>
> PRINCIPLE:
> # TIME PREFERENCE
>
> Other things being equal, people prefer the satisfaction of a given value now, rather than later. This time preference varies from person to person and for the same person at different periods. The higher your time preference, the more willing you are to sacrifice a benefit in the future to get what you want now. The lower your time preference, the more you are willing to forgo a benefit now to bring about a better future.

Our long-term focus has been essential to Koch's success. It is why our owners reinvest 90 percent of earnings and seek employees who are contribution motivated and have a talent that will help us create long-term value. Invariably, these are employees who have lower Time Preferences.

When you advocate corporate welfare, you're also turning others against you—and not just other companies that don't have your handouts. People don't like businesses that get ahead by holding others back. If that describes you, you're sowing the seeds of your own destruction while undermining the economy as a whole.

Instead of going down that road, practice Principled Entrepreneurship. Lobby against the policies that unfairly benefit you. Help your customers and communities understand why corporate welfare is harmful, both to you and them. And as you rally others to achieve a level playing field in your industry, you'll be able to lead your own business to even greater success.

That's where business should always be—succeeding by helping others succeed, not through special-interest handouts that cause others to fail. If you truly want to shape better policy, the best place to start is opposing corporate welfare.

WHEN—AND HOW—TO SUPPORT POLITICIANS

At Koch, we want policies that empower people to contribute to society and lead fulfilling, meaningful lives. Hence, our long-running opposition to corporate welfare and our support for criminal justice reform and other beneficial policies. We want policies that enable businesses to contribute by pursuing good profit, such as lower taxes, eliminating unnecessary and harmful regulations, limiting government spending to those essential things that only government can do, and other policies that lead to human progress.

In our representative form of government, good policies are only possible when they have the support of politicians. Given this reality, business needs to find a productive way to encourage politicians to do the right thing—that is, to pass prin-cipled policies.

Unfortunately, politicians have a long history of pursuing unprincipled, counterproductive ideas. Our struggles to defeat corporate welfare in the 1970s and 1980s are proof. While we recognized that politicians were partly to blame, we avoided getting involved in efforts to elect candidates for decades. (We did make modest contributions through our corporate political action committee simply to ensure we had a seat at the table on policy discussions.)

By the early 2000s, however, we were concerned that policy was moving in an even worse direction than normal. Government had gone beyond its proper role in many ways, rejecting the voluntary cooperation and competition that drive better results for everyone in society.

The Clinton administration tried to pass an unprecedented government intrusion into health care. The Bush administration launched counterproductive wars in the Middle East while convincing Congress to expand entitlements, extend federal control over education, and pass massive bailouts for big banks—policies that did tremendous damage while adding trillions of dollars to the national debt.

The Obama administration made deals with Congress to enact trillions more in wasteful spending. They also passed harmful health care and banking bills. The latter gutted the community banking that small businesses rely on. What's more, President Obama burdened the economy with unprecedented numbers of top-down mandates.

So in the lead up to the 2010 elections, we started supporting groups tied to one political party as they directly engaged in electoral politics. Little did we know how big a failure this focus on partisan politics would be!

The groups we supported were guided by political consultants who told them that to see better policy, they should go all in to help Republicans win control of Congress. The opportunity seemed ripe, since John Boehner, the soon-to-be Speaker of the

House, was promising $100 billion in cuts to wasteful spending. We supported that vision, hoping to see even more substantive reforms.

Up until that point, we had gone to great lengths not to identify with either political party. We had long criticized both Republicans and Democrats when they passed lousy policies (as they both frequently did). But we hoped that our support for efforts to elect Republicans would encourage them to choose a more principled direction, especially on spending and debt.

Like many of our experiments, this decision to only support candidates from one party failed. When John Boehner left office, instead of cutting spending as promised, he capitulated and helped *add* $100 billion to the federal budget. On issue after issue, not only did Republicans not solve big problems, they actively made those problems even worse.

Another story crystallizes why partisan-focused efforts don't work. A US senator who received funding from groups we supported in the 2014 midterm election told his colleagues that they should vote for a bill we opposed. He said they didn't have to worry about how we'd react. His reasoning: We were in the bag for Republicans. "Who else are the Kochs going to support?"

Not long after, we ended our support for that experiment. By focusing our support on party instead of policy, we had clearly failed.

Instead, we took a step back and asked ourselves: How could we make a difference in public policy that is consistent with our principles?

It dawned on us that we had failed to apply many of our principles. We violated Experimental Discovery by not challenging groups making bigger bets than they should have. We also violated **Alignment of Incentives**. While we've learned how to apply that principle at Koch, we hadn't in other areas, such as the relationship between business and government.

Aligning incentives starts with eliminating perverse incentives, which cause employees to suboptimize their ability to create value or even to destroy value. It is also important to align incentives for the company's other core constituencies, such as customers, suppliers, shareholders, co-investors, communities, and governments.

In short, we had given both political parties a strong incentive to continue acting badly—and no incentive to act better. Practically, aligning with one party gave us the worst of both worlds: Allies took us for granted while opponents demonized us.

We started supporting new and smaller experiments in the late 2010s and early 2020s. Instead of a *party-first* approach, we took a *policy-first* approach. We advocated for principled policies, then went to people across the political spectrum to build support. This strategy reduced the alienation of politicians from one side of the aisle while also avoiding the mistake of giving a free pass to the party on the other side. We supported efforts that welcomed politicians from both parties into a growing coalition. The famous abolitionist Frederick Douglass summed up

> **38**
>
> PRINCIPLE:
> ## ALIGNMENT OF INCENTIVES
>
> A company's future depends on providing incentives that motivate its core constituencies to help maximize the company's long-term success.
>
> This starts with employees. You need to seek to align employees' interests with what will be beneficial for them and the company. This alignment provides roles, work, authorities, and rewards that motivate employees to make the maximum contributions to their organization and ultimately to the business' long-term success.

this approach best: "I would unite with anybody to do right and with nobody to do wrong."[59]

Far from stepping away from electoral politics, this approach helped us find new and better ways to do even more. For instance, we're now supporting groups that participate in the primary elections where political parties select candidates. This way, they can help ensure that voters have at least one candidate in the general election who is likely to move policy in a principled direction.

Naturally, there are many critics who reject this approach. The political parties don't like it for obvious reasons. Neither do most political consultants, since they tend to make their careers by catering to one party or the other. True, we don't get invited to as many fancy fundraisers or photo ops as we used to, but that's a plus in our book.

You may hear complaints that this is all about "leverage" and getting politicians to "do our bidding." We've even been called "political kingmakers." But that criticism isn't factual. Many people undoubtedly support politicians in the hope of getting handouts for themselves. But the candidates we support know that picking business winners and losers or otherwise hurting Americans risks losing our support in future elections. Our goal is to only support those politicians who, on balance, act consistently with Principles of Human Progress and back policies that help people, not hurt them.

This approach has led to much more success than our earlier efforts.

In the late 2010s, we began supporting efforts that contributed to historic and bipartisan federal policy victories, including health care legislation that gave veterans more choices, a law that gave terminally ill patients the right to try potentially life-saving treatments, and the biggest criminal justice reform in decades. Our efforts also helped pass tax reform without many of the special interest giveaways that lawmakers would have included.

These policies resulted from bottom-up efforts to unite Americans and to show politicians that when they pass principled policies, they can count on us to let voters know they did the right thing. For instance, we supported groups that advocated for President Biden's decision to end America's longest war, the twenty-year war in Afghanistan, notwithstanding the way it was done. Before that, the groups we support praised the Obama administration for its work on criminal justice reform and occupational licensing. Praising Democratic presidents would have been much harder to do under a partisanship-first approach.

The progress has been even more exciting in the states, the true laboratories of democracy. In the early 2020s, our support for groups with the courage to do the right thing helped them overcome Republican corporate welfare programs, including fifty-two innovation-stifling health care laws in twenty-six states. They also successfully blocked large subsidies, most notably in Florida, where Americans for Prosperity helped eliminate the Republican governor's business slush fund. They never could have done that under the old approach, because Republicans wouldn't have listened. But once AFP made clear that they'd lose support if they continued the destructive program, those politicians voted to stop bribing companies to come to Florida on the taxpayer's dime.

We're heartened by these developments, but we believe even bigger victories are yet to come. We're still experimenting and improving our approach, building broad coalitions to tackle the biggest policy challenges of the day.

Can you or your business do the same? Absolutely. Whether it's at city hall, the state capitol, or the United States Congress, you can help deliver better policies—the kind that uphold equal rights and empower more people to succeed.

You're unlikely to succeed by blindly backing politicians from a single party. We learned that the hard way. But you can succeed if you back politicians from either party who, on balance, support beneficial policies.

THE ROAD TO REAL POLICY CHANGE

Every business is affected by public policy. It plays an outsized role in determining whether business is a force for good and whether companies succeed or fail. Your business can help guide the government in a more productive direction. Obviously, this isn't easy, so here are some tips that will help you.

1. View every policy through the lens of principles.
You'll quickly find that many policies are profoundly unprincipled. They're top-down, not bottom-up. They show little respect for the least fortunate, including equal rights. They disempower people instead of empowering them. And so on.

If a policy is built on an unprincipled foundation, you should not only avoid it, but you should actively oppose it. That could be as simple as writing an op-ed in your local paper, running ads on social media, or maybe even lobbying against it. Whether your business is big or small, you have many ways to speak out.

Remember also that principles require taking a long-term view over a short-term one. Corporate welfare often looks good in the here and now, but it shortchanges the country and ultimately cripples your ability to create the most value. Special-interest handouts always do more harm than good in the end.

2. Focus on policy, not political parties.

The former allows you to build coalitions from the bottom up, while the latter winnows the number of people who will work with you. Your business will suffer if you alienate people by focusing on partisan politics. You stand a far greater chance of success if you try to ally with people from all different perspectives who have shared values and goals.

3. Only support policies based on good Economic Thinking.

4. Not every problem needs a policy solution.

Government's role is limited. Sometimes, as you read in the previous chapter, your business can help drive solutions through its day-to-day operations and innovations. At other times, the solutions can be found in corporate philanthropy. That is the subject of our next chapter.

39

PRINCIPLE:

ECONOMIC THINKING

Economics is the study of choice in using scarce resources that have alternate uses. Good economic thinking seeks to understand these trade-offs so the greatest value can be created for people throughout society. For a society to be prosperous and progress, it must generate measures of what people value and the availability of resources to satisfy those values. Such measures can only arise when policies enable voluntary exchanges that reveal these trade-offs.

HOW YOU CAN APPLY THESE PRINCIPLES

- What corporate welfare does your company get? How can you publicly oppose it?
- Find opportunities to participate in non-partisan coalitions to advance beneficial policy goals. Who are the partners (business, nonprofit, or civic) that could help?

CHAPTER 11

HOW TO TRANSFORM CORPORATE PHILANTHROPY

*Community is a consequence. It results when
people come together to accomplish things that
are important to them and succeed.*
—RICHARD CORNUELLE[60]

BIG IDEAS TO WATCH FOR

- Corporate philanthropy needs to be grounded in principles just like the rest of your business.
- Solving big problems demands many partners working across institutions over time. Think shared vision, values, and complementary capabilities.
- Collaborating across differences leads to broader, more innovative solutions.

For business to succeed and endure, it doesn't just need principled government policy; it needs a healthy society overall. While the pursuit of good profit is the primary way that companies help strengthen society, corporate philanthropy is also a valuable tool for contributing to well-being and progress.

There are two kinds of corporate philanthropy. The first is donating to local charities and worthy causes, such as supporting youth mentoring programs and college scholarships, or funding civic and cultural institutions. At Koch, we place great value on contributing time and resources in this way to make our communities better. But this chapter is about the second kind of corporate philanthropy. It's about donating with the goal of sparking and supporting social change—transforming society's institutions for the better, so they consistently empower all people to have better lives.

In 2022, US corporations donated more than $36 billion to charitable causes. Foundations, which rely on corporate profits, gave another $103 billion.[61] But when it comes to achieving social change, not all corporate giving gets beneficial results. Many businesses implement giving programs based on activist demands or political pressure, which can make things worse, not better. It's also common for companies to want to be seen "doing something." They pledge to write big checks and bask in media fanfare. All too often, those checks never get written, and those that do often have little to show for it.

Koch's philanthropy doesn't make those mistakes, but it still has often fallen short.

Here's what we've learned through trial and error: Corporate philanthropy needs to be grounded in principles, just like the rest of your business. One of the most important is **Partnerships**.

Good partnerships are essential to the long-term success of any kind, and giving is no exception. Rather than trying to do it all ourselves, we fund groups with shared vision and values, and the complementary capabilities to make an expansive vision a reality. This is yet another example of the wisdom of Frederick Douglass we mentioned in the previous chapter: "unite with anybody to do right and with nobody to do wrong."[62]

The largest recipient of Koch's corporate giving by far is Stand Together, a philanthropic community that Charles founded in 2003. It unites hundreds of business leaders and philanthropists to support and scale thousands of promising projects nationwide. Stand Together helps catalyze bottom-up solutions to America's biggest problems, such as a failing education system, substance abuse, generational poverty, challenges in the economy and health care system, the criminal justice system, antisemitism, foreign policy, the ability of people to exercise their free speech rights, and more.

Across all its efforts, Stand Together pursues a broad strategy—addressing the root causes of problems instead of just chipping away at the edges. This approach has sparked social movements that are driving lasting change.

Stand Together is a fairly recent development in our history of giving. Let's explore some of the lessons we learned before its creation and ongoing evolution.

COMMON MISTAKES

Well-intentioned corporate giving often fails because it starts from a narrow personal or philosophical perspective, often that of the CEO.

40

PRINCIPLE:
PARTNERSHIPS

Partners are those who join with us in any form, manner, or endeavor. Beneficial, lasting partnerships have three requirements:

- **Shared vision:** For every type of endeavor and relationship, there must be an understanding and agreement on the vision—what they are jointly trying to accomplish and the best way to accomplish it.

- **Shared values:** Partners share the values necessary for making the joint undertaking successful long term. At a minimum, these include honesty, mutual respect, humility, knowledge sharing, and a commitment to continual transformation.

- **Complementary capabilities:** Each partner brings something different and important to the success of the endeavor. When both parties are intellectually honest and open about their strengths and weaknesses, they can apply Comparative Advantage to determine the division of labor that will generate the greatest results.

Of course, business leaders have their own values and world-views, and it's natural for their companies to focus on efforts that align with those beliefs. But expecting or demanding complete agreement with the CEO's—or anyone else's—ideas limits effectiveness.

Charles learned this the hard way. In the 1960s and '70s, he looked for philanthropic partners who aligned 100 percent with his understanding of Principles of Human Progress. He focused on libertarians, supporting dogmatic abstract thinkers such as Murray Rothbard, Robert LeFevre, and others. His laudable goal was to help them inspire the rest of the country to understand and apply principles, leading to the creation of a better society for everyone.

PRINCIPLE:
OPENNESS

41

An open society encourages honest exchanges of knowledge, opinions, and ideas, based on a system of equal rights that respects the dignity of each person.

Unfortunately, today's trend is against Openness. Differences have become dividing lines. Those who disagree are demonized or canceled. Closed-minded people retreat into insular and protectionist groups, reinforcing their own biases and preventing the exploration of different perspectives through civil discourse.

But this dogmatic, theoretical approach didn't work. Sure, it led to some interesting dinner conversations—and some knock-down, drag-out fights—but it sparked almost no social change. When you aim for 100 percent alignment, you spend more time arguing over intellectual purity than pursuing practical results. That's not a recipe for inspiring others, much less broad societal transformation.

Rigidity also runs counter to the lessons of American history. Our country has generally solved problems more effectively than others because we've empowered people with a diversity of perspectives to pursue change together. Far from limiting progress, different perspectives have been crucial to finding a path forward. When people with different views but similar goals unite, there's a greater chance for innovative, creative solutions.

No one has described the quintessential American approach better than the philosopher-historian Alexis de Tocqueville. Writing in the 1830s, he noted that when Americans determine a goal, they look for "mutual assistance; and as soon as they have found each other," they unite.[63] This spirit helps explain the strength of American communities and the progress of our society.

This insight bears on corporate philanthropy because it shows the importance of **Openness**.

At Koch, we recognize the vital role of Openness in bringing about progress, both in the business and through corporate philanthropy. Innovation flourishes when we encourage the free flow of ideas, well-designed experiments, and Challenge. Openness helps us overcome entropy in society, our organizations, and our lives.

Without Openness, you're closed to new knowledge, especially the knowledge that other partners bring to bear. In other words, you assume that you have all the answers. But when you embrace Openness, you find new and better ways to tackle challenges because you welcome new and innovative ideas. Openness and the principle of Humility go hand in hand.

The 100 percent alignment that Charles sought in his early giving wasn't open, so it limited his partnerships and thus his effectiveness. He gradually changed his approach to philanthropic partnerships to one that only requires a shared vision on the issue being addressed.

Chase experienced a similar paradigm shift in the mid-2010s when his sister, Elizabeth, launched an organization called

Unlikely Collaborators. She brought together a diverse group of people with a broad set of beliefs, and by sharing her problems and personal story, she helped the group become more open and willing to work together. She guided participants through an exercise to help them discover their North Star—the goals and values that guide their lives. Seeing so many people look beyond their differences and come together to help one another make progress profoundly influenced Chase.

Koch's philanthropy is now guided by Openness, enabling us to greatly increase our partnerships and effectiveness. Consider the story of Stand Together and Van Jones.

Van was a political appointee under President Obama. In 2011, he organized a protest outside a Stand Together conference. To put it mildly, Van is nowhere near 100 percent aligned with how we think about solving societal problems. Had it been the 1970s, we never would have worked with him, and Van likely wouldn't have worked with us. Yet because of our shared desire to fix the broken criminal justice system, we learned the importance of collaborating with others, even if we disagree on other issues.

Long story short, such unlikely alliances (and there were many others) paved the way for dozens of meaningful reforms that improve justice and public safety. The list includes the passage of the federal First Step Act—the most significant criminal justice reform in decades. As Van said after that bill became law, "We started working together to get some other people free, but the reality is, those of us who worked on this, we got some freedom." By working together instead of going it alone, we got "to see the country differently and do more good."[64]

As this story shows, an open approach to partnerships lets you more fully tap into the power of the Division of Labor by

Comparative Advantage. You'll be more effective if you work with those who complement your strengths and make up for your weaknesses. Put simply, you can accomplish more together than you can separately.

This brings up another common mistake in corporate philanthropy—the tendency to support a single solution to a problem rather than seek out many partners with complementary capabilities. While most businesses understand the need to work with other companies—including suppliers, distributors, investors, and so on—they often take a narrower view regarding philanthropy. If they care about poverty, they have their anti-poverty group. If they care about helping students, they have their education group. It's also rare for businesses to work together with other corporate or family foundations.

This path is doomed to failure because of the scale of the problems that need to be solved. A challenge like generational poverty can't possibly be addressed by a single organization or even a handful of groups, no matter how large and well-financed they are. You need a diversity of partnerships that tackle societal issues from as many angles as possible.

Stand Together is grounded in this insight. (The name is actually a reference to Partnerships.) When tackling societal challenges, there is no silver bullet. Instead, you need an ecosystem of solutions. Far from being a one-stop shop, Stand Together fosters that ecosystem by working with hundreds of community-based groups, universities, and companies; thousands of educational innovators; and millions of grassroots activists.

Stand Together's partners work across the major institutions in society that affect a person's life, including communities, education, business, and government. All of them are necessary to solve the biggest problems and empower people to succeed.

This comprehensive approach has enabled our philanthropy to make a bigger difference just in the past few years than we did in the previous fifty years combined.

We believe that applying a comprehensive approach can do the same for you. Regardless of the resources your business may have, make sure the groups you support have the necessary vision and values—and that together, you have the capabilities needed to really make progress on the problems you hope to solve. Help them focus on doing what they do best, taking into consideration what other groups are doing on the same issue. And take a broad view regarding potential partners instead of going it alone. All of this will improve your effectiveness.

This approach has enabled Stand Together to make real progress on a host of pressing issues. One of the best examples is in education.

AN EDUCATIONAL AWAKENING

Transforming education has long been one of our philanthropic priorities. We want every person to be motivated to discover, develop, and apply their gifts, empowering them to live a life of meaning and fulfillment. Education is key to this vision.

Given our North Star, we reject the one-size-fits-all model that has dominated public and private education alike for centuries. It puts students on a *de facto* assembly line, treating them the same while ignoring their gifts. Rather than stimulate students to discover and develop their gifts, this approach tends to drain their energy and motivation. Only 31 percent of eighth graders are proficient in reading, and 26 percent are proficient in math—numbers that have fallen despite record investments in public education.[65] By the time kids reach twelfth grade, less than a third report being at all engaged in their studies.[66]

Students shouldn't be treated like cars on an assembly line. They should be empowered to take the road that's best for them—because that's the road to a better life and a better society. This is "individualized education." And it works.

But until recently, philanthropic efforts to transform the education system in the United States did not work. In fact, they failed miserably.

For the better part of three decades, state and national efforts to help students find better schools became mired in the us-versus-them quagmire. The divides came down along familiar lines—public schools versus private schools, teachers' unions versus parents, and so on. It was a dogmatic purity test rather than a focus on results. And people who should have been allies fought each other. Some said charter schools were best, while others said private schools were better. Major philanthropists promoted their preferred models, refusing to partner with others. Amid the division, the failing education *status quo* prevailed, hurting more students with every passing year.

By 2020, many of us who'd worked on education knew something had to change.

The COVID-19 pandemic created unprecedented demand among families for better options, but the same old approach was only capable of achieving the same lack of results. Instead of pitting people against one another and insisting on ideological purity, we needed to unite behind a commitment to better education, no matter where it took place—in private schools, public schools, parochial schools, homeschools, microschools, you name it. We needed everyone who cared about individualized education to do their part to achieve broad and flexible reforms that let families pick what's best for them. Just as important, we needed to show that everyone could benefit from these reforms, including public schools and teachers.

Stand Together worked with many philanthropic partners to increase support for groups that could foster this new approach. It quickly paid off. Within five years, twenty-seven states passed more than seventy education reforms that have benefitted tens of millions of students. The list includes Education Savings Accounts and tax credits, which give students thousands of dollars to spend on the public or private school that best fits their needs. Other reforms ended the longstanding practice of "ZIP Code assignment," which forces kids to go to bad public schools in their neighborhood instead of better public schools nearby.

These reforms passed in large part because they united people across various divides. They encourage public schools to up their game because money now follows students who switch schools. If a public school starts providing the education students need, parents don't have to choose between public school and private school. Teachers benefit, too, especially when they're freed from one-size-fits-all "seat time" mandates that force them to teach different studenwts the same way. Instead, teachers can find new and better ways to help students learn in the way that's best for them. That's why they became teachers in the first place.

But changing policy is just one piece of the puzzle. What good is the ability to choose the school that's right for your child if there aren't better options from which to choose? And what good are better options if families don't know about them in the first place? To truly create an ecosystem of solutions in education, we needed a more expansive vision of Partnership, based on Openness.

This insight led Stand Together to work with thousands of educational innovators who are finding game-changing ways to help students learn.

In some cases, they helped longstanding partners transform. Charles and his wife, Liz, founded Youth Entrepreneurs in 1991 to help students learn core economic concepts and how to start a real business. By 2020, however, it was clear that the program's true power came from empowering teachers to motivate students to discover their gifts. The group was renamed Empowered, and today, it helps fifty-five thousand educators in all fifty states (and ninety countries!) put their students on a path to lifelong learning and fulfillment.

Another big effort is VELA, which Stand Together helped cofound in 2019 with the Walton Family Foundation. This community of entrepreneurs provides alternatives to conventional education and has supported more than four thousand education startups and learning models in all fifty states.

These educational startups take many forms. Summit Christian Academy in Colorado is a homeschool collaborative that offers a classical academic program with specialized pathways, including an aviation program where students receive flight training.[67] Path of Life Learning is a microschool designed for military families, offering flexible two- or four-day learning options and customizable curricula so families can build the academic program that works best for them.[68] Barefoot University Forest School, created by two moms in Texas, connects families with organized forest-school experiences to supplement their education.[69] VELA founders serve low- and middle-income families, and over half of these founders are from communities of color. They've already served more than five million students.

Another innovative Stand Together partner is Sal Khan, an education entrepreneur who built a tech-driven platform that's helped more than a hundred million students globally. His latest project is called Khanmigo. It uses artificial intelligence to help teachers tailor education to students' individual needs, essentially giving students a digital tutor that helps them gain mastery of a subject. Khanmigo can be used in any educational setting, including public schools. As more teachers implement it, millions of students could benefit.

And then there's Joe Liemandt. Joe is a successful software company executive who cofounded Alpha School, a model that enables students to experience more academic growth than traditional school students.[70]

How? By using machine-adaptable learning and other forms of artificial intelligence to teach kids in ways that best suit their learning aptitude, and by hiring coaches to keep kids motivated to learn. Students learn at twice the rate of the best private schools in just two hours per day, leaving the rest of their time at school free for project-based learning. Joe is now looking for ways to supercharge his model by applying gamification to fuel students' passion for learning.

These partners—and there are many more—show a comprehensive strategy in action. Changing laws isn't enough. You also need to change the education landscape itself, while empowering families to discover their options and demand better. Is there still work to do? Absolutely. More than 50 percent of students in the US now have access to better education because of reforms, compared to just 20 percent before these efforts began. But tens of millions of kids still need help.

Whether or not education is the philanthropic issue that motivates you, we urge you to apply comprehensive strategies, involving many partners across multiple institutions to maximize effectiveness.

THE IMPORTANCE OF MOVEMENTS

At its best, a comprehensive and principled approach to corporate philanthropy can make a bigger difference than you may realize. It can spark movements that transform how other people approach solving society's problems. That's how you achieve an altogether different scale of effectiveness.

We think of movements in light of "tipping points"—the point at which an approach to solving a problem takes on a life of its own and gains momentum well beyond your direct involvement. That's when the principle of Changing Paradigms is fully realized. People can't even imagine doing things the old way because the new way is obviously superior. It becomes what people expect. In education, for instance, we'll reach a tipping point when the typical American family expects that no matter where they send their children to school, they'll receive an individualized education that helps transform their lives.

If changing paradigms at the societal level seems like a tall order for corporate philanthropy, we assure you it's not. Such a shift may be underway as we write this, thanks to a movement that's changing how Americans deal with substance abuse.

Nearly fifty million Americans struggle with a substance use disorder.[71] Maybe it's drugs. Maybe it's alcohol. Maybe it's both. Regardless, the human cost is heart-wrenching. People with incredible potential are being cut off from a life of contribution and meaning. In so many cases, they're losing their lives. Shortly before we wrote this book, life expectancy in the United States declined for three years in a row. Deaths from drug and alcohol abuse were a major reason why.[72]

Sadly, substance abuse has largely been viewed through an unhelpful paradigm, one that sees those who struggle with addiction as problems to be solved rather than the source of the solution. Popular treatment programs say that substance abuse defines people. In this view, you can't escape addiction; you can only manage it. Medical treatments often reflect the same assumption. We see this in the widespread use of methadone, which can save lives yet is addictive itself and has debilitating side effects. Replacing one drug with another is not a long-term solution.

A better approach, based on Principles of Human Progress, is to focus on people's intrinsic dignity. This approach empowers them to leave substance abuse behind and move forward by developing their gifts, believing in themselves, and contributing to the lives of others.

People like Scott Strode show what's possible. He struggled with substance abuse—both drugs and alcohol—for many years. Thankfully, he discovered that he could beat it by exercising with others. In 2006, he founded The Phoenix, a peer-to-peer physical fitness program that's free for anyone who's been sober for just forty-eight hours. The Phoenix surrounds you with a supportive community full of people who've also struggled with addiction. They show up for one another and help one another overcome their shared barrier.

The result? The Phoenix is more than twice as effective as most traditional recovery efforts. That's the magic of the Empowerment principle.

Scaling The Phoenix proved difficult. After a decade of hard work, Scott had helped about fourteen thousand people—an impressive number, but a drop in the bucket given the nation-wide substance abuse crisis. Through experimenting with different models, Stand Together enabled The Phoenix to expand to more states and shift its focus from building new gyms to building an online platform that empowers volunteers. Soon, The Phoenix was being used by tens of thousands of people in more than twenty-five hundred communities. Scott attributes this rapid growth to a consistent application of Principle Based Management, which helped him see that his approach is grounded in the dignity of every person and enables them to believe in themselves.

But that was just a stepping stone. As The Phoenix began expanding rapidly, its team started thinking really big. Scott and his team challenged themselves to find ways to bring their Empowerment paradigm into the broader culture. Culture, after all, is where movements are made and where society is shaped at a fundamental level.

In 2022, Stand Together and The Phoenix launched an effort called One Million Strong. The goal was to change how people think about addiction, which we believed could happen when The Phoenix helps more than a million people in recovery. One Millon Strong highlights The Phoenix's empowerment-based approach, showing how it's fundamentally different—and better than deficiency-based approaches. It partners with musicians and the broader music industry to spread the word using their platforms. Many musicians have gotten involved because they're personally passionate about this issue.

One Million Strong started in a remarkable place—a music festival in Kentucky called Bourbon and Beyond. Alcohol is central to the event's identity, but the organizers wanted to be clear that the concert was for everyone, including those who choose not to drink. They invited One Million Strong to host a premier "sober space" right in the heart of the concert grounds. From there, One Million Strong took off.

In 2023, One Million Strong got the entire music industry's attention with an open letter in *Billboard* magazine. It was signed by fifty-one music executives and artists, with musicians from Aloe Blacc to Melissa Etheridge pledging their support. Marcus King then took One Million Strong on tour, wrapping his bus in its iconic logo. Entertainment giant Live Nation embraced it as the company's premier addiction recovery program for its forty thousand employees, proclaiming it "Sober Nation." iHeartMedia spread the word during "Sober September." AEG—which runs Stagecoach and Coachella—now hosts One Million Strong sober spaces at its festivals. Many venues now include high-end mocktail programs with the One Million Strong brand.

This is a game changer for people trying to beat substance abuse. Rather than hiding in basements and feeling ashamed or excluded, they're now able to wear their sobriety on their sleeve. (Scott Strode sports a "Sober" T-shirt most of the time.) Instead of being defined by their addiction, these men and women are free to do the things they love.

By the time you read this, The Phoenix will have achieved its goal of supporting more than a million people in recovery, and that's just the beginning. One Million Strong is rapidly becoming something that concertgoers expect. While Stand Together and The Phoenix anchored the early efforts, artists and industry leaders are now taking action organically. Given the outsized voice that musicians have in our culture, the message of empowerment may soon spill over into other areas of life, including the way people raise their kids or lead their businesses.

That's what a movement looks like. And this paradigm change—from deficiency to strengths, from addiction to empowerment, from shame to self-actualization—could very well transform millions more lives for the better. It's happening because One Million Strong taps into a powerful principle: Requirements for Human Action. To succeed long term—in business or philanthropy—you must enable people to understand what you're trying to achieve and empower them. When people become dissatisfied with their lives, are exposed to a better life, and find a path to achieve it, they will act.

This movement strategy is being applied to many key issues, not just education and addiction. Your corporate philanthropy can contribute to such movements too. There's nothing wrong with contributing where your business is located. We do that also. But if you aim to spark broader progress and tackle society-wide challenges, principles can help you achieve those greater results.

Business leaders naturally think as big in their business as their capabilities allow. Why not think the same way regarding your philanthropy?

WHERE TO BEGIN

Corporate philanthropy can be one of the most fraught and frustrating parts of a business. But it can also be among the most rewarding things you do.

In addition to the principles we've mentioned, we recommend a heavy focus on Experimental Discovery. Start with small bets to see what works and what doesn't. Pursue plenty of partnerships to find the ones that can help you achieve your goals. And look for partners who have the capabilities to tackle big problems at scale.

On that note, if this approach interests you, reach out to Stand Together. They work on hundreds of issues with thousands of partners. You can find more information at StandTogether.org.

Whatever cause you care about, don't make the mistake of thinking you know best, like we did early on. And don't put all your eggs in one basket, assuming that you can build the best poverty-fighting, education-fixing, or other problem-solving institution the world has ever seen. You'll achieve far more if you unite with others. Take it from our sixty-plus years of failure, learning, and ongoing transformation.

HOW YOU CAN APPLY THESE PRINCIPLES

- Are your company's philanthropic efforts designed to make a lasting difference?
- Identify one cause you or your business teams care about. How could you support it with time or resources? What other partners would be helpful?
- How can you make your philanthropic strategy more comprehensive to get better results?
- Think of a movement, such as the one underway to transform education, that you believe is needed. What principle helped it grow, and how could you apply that insight?

PART III: SUPPLEMENTARY CONTENT

Scan to explore what principled leadership makes possible. Discover stories, essays, videos, and practical resources that examine how these principles shape culture, enable continual transformation, and contribute to long-term progress—inside organizations and beyond them.

HOW TO LIVE A LIFE OF MEANING

*Ever more people today have the means to
live, but no meaning to live for.*
—VIKTOR FRANKL[73]

We've spent the last eleven chapters talking about how Principles of Human Progress can help you become a principle-driven leader, find success and overcome failure in business. But we want to close on an even more important note. These principles can help you find meaning in your life. If this is something that you're looking for, you're not alone.

Today, our country faces a crisis of meaning. A staggering 57 percent of Americans are trying to find more purpose in their lives.[74] An even higher percentage of millennials—75 percent—say they lack purpose altogether.[75] We're talking about more than one hundred million people who have yet to find meaning and fulfillment. How can they discover what they're looking for?

Our friend, the social scientist Todd Rose, points to the answer. In his book *Dark Horse*, he wrote that most people believe that to live a fulfilling life, you must pursue a successful career at all costs, regardless of whether that success aligns with your own North Star. But Todd, drawing on the best research, says the opposite is true. Real personal and professional success comes from building a life around what you find fulfilling. In other words, those who chase success by putting aside the things that are meaningful to them are likely to miss out on both.

It's fashionable to assume that success in business comes at the expense of pursuing a life of meaning and purpose. This assumption is in the phrase *work-life balance*, which implies a direct trade-off between living a meaningful life and having a successful career—something that must be "balanced," so the trade-off doesn't become too severe.

But in our experience, nothing could be further from the truth. There shouldn't be a trade-off; they should be mutually reinforcing. We've found that the best way to succeed in your work is to apply the principles we've described in this book in every aspect of your life. As you do, your success in business will reinforce your personal fulfillment. This is why we call them Principles of Human Progress.

Both of us have come to this conclusion in our own way. And to share more about that, we'll each speak to our personal experience.

———

Charles

As a young man in my early- to mid-twenties, I was utterly lost. I had a good job as a consultant in Boston and all the trappings of early career success. But I knew I wasn't living up to my potential. I felt empty. That changed once I returned to Wichita and immersed myself in the discovery and study of Principles of Human Progress. The more I learned about them, the more I looked for opportunities to apply them in all aspects of my life. As I did, the more meaning and purpose I found.

When I married Liz, these principles helped shape the most important and meaningful relationship of my life—one that has been going strong for fifty-three years. I could talk about how we've applied Partnership, Division of Labor by Comparative Advantage, and Virtuous Cycles of Mutual Benefit to make it work so well, but the reality is much simpler and more beautiful. Liz is good at everything I'm not, and we've dedicated ourselves to making each other better. If I didn't have Liz, I wouldn't have experienced the greatest joy in my life, which comes from my family. Nor would I have been able to achieve nearly as much in business, philanthropy, or anything else. She is living proof that a shared commitment to living by these principles helps you find meaning and fulfillment in every part of your life.

I turned ninety while we were writing this book. Virtually all my living friends have retired. But not me. People often wonder why I work every day or why I'm writing yet another book. Wouldn't it be better, they ask, if I gave it a rest and sat on a beach? My response is always the same: "Why, do you want me to die?" I'm still going strong because I've found meaning—because I'm striving to realize my potential, even now. For me, a good day is when I've found a way to contribute. I couldn't imagine living any other way. That's the power of principles, and thanks to them, I still wake up every day excited to make a difference.

Chase

In my early forties, I went through a painful divorce. It made me take a step back and ask if my life was on the right track—whether I was truly living up to my potential. From the outside, things seemed great—a good job, a loving family, and great friends. But after a lot of reflection, I realized there was so much more I could be doing.

I made some big changes. I focused on the principles that could best help me align my life to my purpose and passion—principles like Openness, Comparative Advantage, and Partnership. I asked myself, "What would you do if you weren't afraid?" I rekindled my passion for music. I founded Stand Together Music to tap in to the power of music and help artists leverage their platform for good. I put a band together and we named it 2ŁØT after the second law of thermodynamics and a recognition that the concept of entropy is real for all of us. Or as Bob Dylan wrote, "He not busy being born is busy dying."[76]

I also got more involved in my local community in Wichita—something I'm passionate about. And I redoubled my commitment to raising my kids according to these principles. But instead of Sunday lectures like I endured, I created games and prizes to make it fun and engaging. Sometimes I think I'm learning more from them than they are from me!

Far from distracting me from my work responsibilities, my newfound sense of purpose made me even more passionate and effective in my job. I have achieved more in the past five years than I did in the previous twenty, finding new ways to contribute to Koch as we adapt and transform to meet the opportunities and challenges of the twenty-first century. Principles haven't just transformed my life in the past tense; they're transforming my life more and faster every day. If I continue to follow this course, I'm confident my life will continue to get better.

———

Our experiences aren't unique. We've seen these principles transform the lives of countless colleagues over the years. From Shanghai to Chicago, from Bergamo to Bangalore, we've seen people apply them in their families, their community groups, their churches, and every part of life. Their determination to lead principled lives has invariably helped them make a bigger difference at work.

But why? It comes down to synergy—when your selfish desire for personal success fuses with your selfless desire to contribute to the lives of others. At that point, your success becomes inextricably tied to helping others succeed. You're realizing your potential—and achieving far more than you otherwise could by helping others do the same. This is the essence of human progress and an important reason for looking to these principles as your guide.

This is the insight we want to leave you with. Take the principles that you've read about in this book and practice them in every aspect of your life. Pursue success by first pursuing a life of meaning—not the other way around.

May these principles help you find the meaning and purpose that make life worth living. And may you experience the glorious feeling of accomplishment—not only in your work, but in all you do.

PRINCIPLES IN BRIEF COLLECTION (IN ALPHABETICAL ORDER)

ACCOUNTABILITY

Abraham Maslow believed the role of management is to create the "social conditions in any organization so that the goals of the individual merge with the goals of the organization."[77] Accountability is one of the essential factors contributing to this merger.

Accountability occurs when a person bears the consequences (good or bad) of a decision or action. It starts by establishing clear decision rights and building a culture of Principled Entrepreneurship. This helps avoid inaction, abdication, plunging, or finger-pointing.

Personal accountability is an unpopular concept these days. As economist Thomas Sowell observed: "We seem to be getting closer and closer to a situation where nobody is responsible for what they did but we are all responsible for what somebody else did."[78] Accountability, properly understood, is to take account of what happened and appropriately recognize those who contributed positively or negatively to the results. We always want to understand the full context of the outcome and whether behavior was consistent with Our Values when determining the appropriate response.

In a business, Accountability for positive outcomes could lead to building greater capabilities resulting in additional opportunities. For an individual, it could lead to expanded and new opportunities to contribute and increased rewards. We recognize and reward contributions that build capabilities and generate results—including past contributions that haven't been fully rewarded. And we don't penalize well-designed experiments that fail, as they create knowledge leading to better decisions.

Accountability for negative outcomes could lead to a change in direction, structure, or personnel, or even exiting the business. For an individual, it could lead to additional coaching and feedback, adjusting responsibilities, or, when the person isn't a fit, leaving Koch. In such cases, it gives individuals the opportunity to start with a clean slate where they can better contribute.

For Koch to succeed, every initiative needs an owner with clear responsibility who is held accountable for its results in harmony with our principle-based framework. Ongoing coaching and feedback help employees understand what is and what is not working. The goal is to help individuals learn and improve. Providing feedback, especially when related to performance gaps, is not enough. Accountability includes the necessary follow-up to ensure sufficient progress is being made and to determine the appropriate action when it is not.

As Charles Koch wrote in *Good Profit*, "Holding ourselves and others accountable also requires courage and intellectual honesty, especially when we are faced with the unpleasant task of dealing with the performance or behavior issues of a coworker. A culture that lacks accountability lacks integrity and cannot survive, let alone thrive."[79]

ALIGNMENT OF INCENTIVES

Koch's future depends on providing incentives that motivate our core constituencies to help maximize the company's long-term success.

This starts with our employees. We seek to align their interests with what will be beneficial for them and Koch in harmony with our principle-based framework. This alignment provides roles, work, authorities, and rewards that motivate them to make the maximum contributions to their organization and ultimately to Koch's long-term success. This includes contributions in building capabilities that have generated or we believe will generate results—including past contributions that haven't been fully rewarded. And we don't penalize well-designed experiments that fail, because they create knowledge leading to better decisions.

We structure incentives to align the interests of employees with the interests of the company, our customers, and society. As psychologist Abraham Maslow taught, "This includes the need for meaningful work, for responsibility, for creativeness, for being fair and just, for doing what is worthwhile, and for preferring to do it well."[80]

Employees also need to feel they are working for a good company and are benefiting others as well as themselves.

Additional key aspects include:

- Using incentives to guide employees toward activities and areas where their abilities and interests will enable them to create the most value.
- Structuring incentives to attract, motivate, and retain principled entrepreneurs, without putting a limit on compensation.
- Basing compensation on overall contribution to Koch's long-term success, not just on a specific set of accomplishments.
- Rewarding contributions, such as knowledge sharing, that benefit other employees and parts of Koch.
- Aligning incentives starts with eliminating perverse incentives—those that cause employees to sub-optimize their ability to create value or even to destroy value.

Examples of perverse incentives are:

- One-size-fits-all point systems or pay grades, detailed formulas, profit sharing, and cost-of-living adjustments, regardless of an individual's contribution.
- Automatic raises and pay based on title, credentials, seniority, experience, or number of reports.
- Rewarding short-term earnings or the performance of the employee's unit, regardless of the effect on Koch's long-term success. Financial compensation

for hitting targets that aren't tied to value creation, such as meeting budgets or exceeding sales goals.

It is also important to align incentives for the company's other core constituencies, such as customers, suppliers, shareholders, co-investors, communities, and governments. Doing so by understanding their subjective values greatly enhances Koch's long-term success.

Some examples:

- By consistently practicing Stewardship and Compliance—especially regarding safety and the environment—providing good jobs, and supporting effective nonprofits, we make our communities better, and they will want us to succeed.

- Persuading retailers to increase our premium shelf space by demonstrating that our products will improve store traffic.

- Motivating our suppliers to create the most value for us by empowering and rewarding them appropriately.

- Designing the compensation for advisors, agents, or consultants to share in our gain so they are motivated to achieve better outcomes.

- By understanding what governments value, acting with integrity, and keeping commitments, we improve the chance they will allow us to earn good profit by creating value in society.

BOTTOM-UP VS. TOP-DOWN

For all the millennia of human existence, life was miserable. Nearly everyone was born into poverty, lived in poverty, and died young. As recently as two hundred years ago, 90 percent of the world's population lived in extreme poverty. But then, something remarkable began to happen: Life started to get better and better for more and more people. The flat line representing average well-being became a hockey stick, suddenly and sharply improving—and it has not stopped. Today, less than 10 percent of people live in extreme poverty, even though the world's population is now almost eight times what it was two hundred years ago.

What happened? In short, certain societies haltingly but increasingly began to move from top-down—where a few people controlled the many—to bottom-up, where more and more people enjoyed greater opportunity to live as they saw fit, although it has been an uneven process that remains incomplete. They were more fully able to apply their abilities and knowledge to better their lives and the lives of others.

A top-down approach presumes those in control know what's best for everyone else. Those at the top typically seek power, rely on one-size-fits-all approaches, and use detailed rules and coercion that stifle others. No matter how well-intentioned, a top-down approach only benefits those at the top.

A bottom-up approach respects the inherent worth of each person and unleashes creativity, initiative, and talent. When behavior is governed by this principle, the outcome exceeds what anyone could have planned or predicted. Everyone benefits when behavior is mostly governed by general principles rather than detailed rules, freeing individuals to use their gifts and knowledge to tackle problems and pursue opportunities.

This approach does not mean decentralizing all decisions or equally distributing authorities. Leaders should only make decisions for which they have the demonstrated capability, while seeking and using the input and challenge of others who can improve those decisions. For example, a facility manager is most likely in the best position to make decisions that affect the whole facility. With a bottom-up approach, the manager seeks and uses the input and challenge of those who have relevant knowledge. However, with a top-down approach, managers simply impose their decisions, which undermines the culture and leads to worse results. They are guilty of "the fatal conceit."[81]

Bottom-up does not mean employees are free to do whatever they feel like. We strive to create the conditions where employees are motivated to do what is beneficial for Koch and themselves. The responsibility of every supervisor is to enable their employees to understand how and be motivated to maximize value in harmony with our principle-based framework. This bottom-up approach benefits everyone—employees, Koch, and society.

CAPABILITIES

Koch's long-term success has come from a focus on building Capabilities that enable us to create superior value and to apply them where we can create the most value both for others and for ourselves. Being capability-bound, not industry-bound, allows us to create virtuous cycles of mutual benefit in multiple businesses and industries.

Creating superior value requires many capabilities—especially ones that are complementary and mutually reinforcing. This starts with our overarching capability, Principle Based Management, that guides all the others through its five dimensions: Vision, Virtue and Talents, Knowledge, Comparative Advantage, and Motivation.

Principle Based Management has led our businesses to transform their ability to succeed in a variety of environments by modifying their visions and strategies to fit the conditions they face. Just as important is exiting when a business doesn't have and can't add the necessary capabilities.

Building superior capabilities requires employees who create their own virtuous cycles—who self-actualize. We have numerous advantaged facilities and technologies, but these don't last without contribution-motivated employees who continually transform themselves and Koch. Employees who create knowledge and contribute to our principle-based culture are our ultimate capability.

To succeed in the future, we prioritize improving our capabilities and building and acquiring new ones. This necessitates strengthening our internal capabilities, collaborating with others who have complementary capabilities, and acquiring organizations with superior ones.

CHANGING PARADIGMS

A paradigm is the shared set of assumptions, theories, and methods that guide the work of individuals and groups. All of us have them. Paradigms help us make sense of the world. They shape our approach to problem-solving, innovation, and the pursuit of knowledge. They become our "truth"—even when flawed or untrue. A flat earth, witch-burning, and lobotomies used to be generally accepted paradigms. Thankfully, our understanding has improved, and most of our paradigms are better.

Thomas Kuhn, philosopher of science, noted that when most people are faced with a new paradigm, they tend to ignore, deny, or even attack the new way of thinking rather than giving it a chance.[82] This is especially true for those who don't know how to change or have a vested interest—such as a career or reputation built on the current paradigm.

Attacks on those advocating a new paradigm by those wedded to the existing paradigm have always been common. The seventeenth-century church imprisoned Galileo for suggesting Earth orbited the sun. For decades, nineteenth-century doctors rejected the new paradigm of germ theory because it implicated their dirty hands as a source of disease transmission and high mortality rates. When Einstein introduced the theory of relativity, it was attacked by the scientific community. Einstein welcomed the criticism and even insisted that his theory pass three tests to be considered valid.

A longstanding paradigm in business is the belief that a top-down approach is best, with leaders dictating how everything should be done. In the early 1990s, when we introduced MBM® to our metal fabrication plant in Italy, the response of the union leaders was: "This might work in the US, but it won't work in Italy. Here, managers think. Workers work. You're asking us to do the manager's job." Applying MBM there required a paradigm shift.

Following are additional examples of business-related paradigms that are inconsistent with Principle Based Management:

- Forcing employees into roles they aren't good at or don't care about, rather than fitting the role to the comparative advantage of each.
- Defending rather than challenging the status quo.
- Using averages to make decisions rather than applying Marginal Analysis.
- Hiring based on credentials rather than virtue and talents.
- Increasing revenue that is unprofitable.

Changing paradigms begins by recognizing that something is amiss, such as not getting the results we expected. Our initial reaction tends to be only giving lip service to the needed paradigm shift, to changing the form but not the substance. Thus, it often takes outside intervention to bring about real change, which can mean removing those, including leaders, who are holding back progress.

CLOSING GAPS

Successful entrepreneurs are never satisfied with the status quo. Those who become satisfied are soon no longer successful. Even if they are the best in the world, the innovations and improvements by others—Creative Destruction—will inevitably make them obsolete. To continue to succeed, entrepreneurs need to envision the gap between the value of what they are creating today and what is possible. They are always driving Creative Destruction.

A principled entrepreneur envisions what could be accomplished when proven principles are fully applied. At Koch, we seek to close the gap between what we are doing, however good, and what we could be doing if we were fully applying our principle-based framework. The application of these principles enables us to continually see additional opportunities for improvement and growth for ourselves and Koch.

Closing Gaps is more than benchmarking. Benchmarking is the process of measuring our performance against those known to have superior practices and performance. It is useful to learn from others and identify performance gaps, but we also must compare our actual performance to what we believe is possible. It is relatively easy to spot gaps when we are not performing well. But success can be particularly difficult to overcome because it makes us overconfident and complacent. Instead, we should be humble, open to the fact that no matter how well we are doing, we can always do better, learn what is possible, and discover how we can improve.

Supervisors must foster a culture that encourages experimentation and discovery, building knowledge networks and pursuing hunches about where we have gaps. This helps us avoid the natural tendency toward stagnation and decline. This can be done by using the five dimensions of Principle Based Management to regularly discover gaps in our methods and results. Effective use of technology and data can also greatly enhance our ability to gain new knowledge and insights that stimulate opportunities for improvement and growth.

A restless discontent, fueled by a vision of a better state and a belief that such a state can be realized, spurs never-ending cycles of improvement and transformation for employees and the company.

CONTRIBUTION MOTIVATED

Personal success and fulfillment—in any field or endeavor—come from helping others in ways that are mutually beneficial. Alexis de Tocqueville called this acting out of an "enlightened regard for themselves," which "constantly prompts them to assist each other."[83] This principle of Contribution Motivated has been vital to Koch's success.

From Abraham Maslow it has become generally accepted that most individuals must first satisfy their basic physical needs and then their communal needs, as well as achieve a sense of self-worth. Individuals for whom any of these needs are seriously unfulfilled tend to be driven by them, which he called being deficiency motivated. In this state, people often act in unhelpful or even counterproductive ways, such as being defensive, resisting feedback, hoarding knowledge, undermining colleagues, and complaining without offering solutions.

Being contribution motivated enables people to discover, develop, and utilize their abilities to succeed by helping others. They are energized by continuously trying to improve, innovate, transform, and creatively get results—which enables them to live lives of meaning. The more people contribute, the better they feel about themselves and the more they tend to be rewarded, so the more they want to contribute.

As difficult as it is for individuals to contribute when deficiency motivated, it is almost impossible when negatively or destructively motivated. They can be driven by tribalism; narcissism; the will to power; jealousy; a lack of integrity, humility, or respect for others; or the desire for vengeance for real or imaginary injustices. Organizations with a culture of negative motivation typically have no purpose other than advancing their own power or profiting by any means.

We prioritize this principle in our culture. It involves hiring and retaining people who are first and foremost contribution motivated, and reinforcing that motivation through individualized roles and responsibilities, coaching, development, and rewards.

CREATIVE DESTRUCTION

Successful businesspeople stand on ground that is "crumbling beneath their feet," wrote economist Joseph Schumpeter in 1942. He described Creative Destruction as "the process of industrial mutation" which "incessantly revolutionizes the economic structure from within, incessantly destroying the old one, incessantly creating a new one."[84]

As entrepreneurs create new businesses, products, services, processes, methods, or types of organizations, less-effective ones become obsolete. It is apparent that consumers benefit as new alternatives that better serve them are brought to market. What is not obvious is that, over the long term, Creative Destruction benefits virtually everyone. It makes people throughout society better off, not only by continually creating better products and services, but also by creating better, safer jobs available to more people.

Those whose businesses or jobs are threatened or lost due to Creative Destruction often don't take this long-term view and try to stop it. When they succeed, progress is stifled, disproportionately harming those who are worst off. Progress is maintained by ensuring those who are hurt in the short term learn new skills and have the opportunity to benefit long term from innovation and higher productivity.

At Koch, we recognize that the future is unknown and unknowable. This is why our Vision is open-ended and embraces Creative Destruction. It focuses us on building the capabilities that enable us to continually create new opportunities and transform. This requires seeking disruptive innovations through internal development and acquisitions, and shedding products, assets, and businesses that are unprofitable or worth more to others. When we drive Creative Destruction faster than our best competitors, we are successful.

Creative Destruction originates with employees who are principled entrepreneurs, who recognize that however well they are doing today will soon not be good enough and are willing to change the paradigms, methods, and tools that helped them succeed in the past. This happens when employees find a role where they have the opportunity, ability, and passion to innovate and create value, thereby experiencing the glorious feeling of accomplishment.

DIVISION OF LABOR BY COMPARATIVE ADVANTAGE

A fundamental Principle of Human Progress is the Division of Labor by Comparative Advantage and the resulting increase in cooperation. Specialization by Comparative Advantage with voluntary exchange and teamwork is much more effective at satisfying people's needs than any other form of organization. This occurs when every employee is in the role where they can make the greatest contribution relative to what else they could be doing and what other employees could do.

Employees have a comparative advantage in a group when they can perform an activity at a lower opportunity cost than others. For example, selling is typically a comparative advantage of successful salespeople, even though they may also be very good at sales analysis. This gives sales analysts a comparative advantage at doing analysis, even when they are not as proficient at it as outstanding salespeople. Employees and groups who take account of their comparative advantages (not just competitive advantages) contribute more and thus are more successful.

In staffing, this principle calls for each of our organizations to begin with a clear vision of what capabilities are needed for making the greatest contribution. Contribution-motivated individuals with the optimal diversity of talents and interests can then be selected to build the needed capabilities.

Roles and responsibilities are designed not only to fit each employee's talents and interests but in relation to the roles and capabilities of other employees in a way that optimizes the group's overall performance. This is accomplished through an ongoing dialogue between employees and supervisors with assistance from others. It includes supervisors giving employees frequent, honest feedback to help them understand their performance and how to increase their contribution. It is also essential that supervisors solicit feedback from employees regarding what would enable the employee, the supervisor, and the group to improve.

Because conditions and people are always changing, roles and responsibilities need to be continually reassessed to maximize each individual's contribution and the organization's overall performance. When an employee leaves, is added, or changes roles, responsibilities throughout must be reevaluated.

One way everyone can contribute is by identifying potential employees who would strengthen their team and other parts of Koch. A beneficial division of labor by comparative advantage requires a diversity of employees who are contribution motivated and have a variety of aptitudes or skills that will increase our ability to profitably expand our current businesses, solve existing or anticipated problems, or capture new opportunities.

ECONOMIC THINKING

Economics is the study of choice in using scarce resources that have alternative uses. As economist Thomas Sowell observed, there are no solutions to economic problems, only trade-offs.[85] Good economic thinking seeks to understand these trade-offs so we can create the greatest value for ourselves and others.

In economics, scarcity means that using a resource in one way prevents you from using it in another. For example, the choice to use gold to make jewelry means that same gold cannot be used to make electronic components, coins, or dental crowns. The highest-valued alternative not chosen is the opportunity cost of that gold.

All economic decisions involve costs and benefits, but not all involve money. Choosing a financial investment involves money. Choosing what to listen to during your commute does not. Both have an opportunity cost. Because we want to employ resources—including people and their time—in the most valued way, opportunity cost must always be considered.

Marginal Analysis is an important element in good economic thinking that can greatly improve business decisions. Marginal Analysis considers the benefits and costs associated with a specific change. Mistakes to be avoided include inappropriately considering unrecoverable costs (sunk costs) or using totals and averages that hide or subsidize unprofitable assets or activities.

In keeping with our Vision, we strive to create mutual benefit by delivering products and services that customers prefer over alternatives, as well as profitability for Koch. The magnitude and risks of a decision should determine how much to invest in analysis, including the range of outcomes to consider.

Good economic thinking and, thereby, good decision-making require accurate measures of scarcity and relative value. Thus, for a society to be prosperous and progress, it must generate measures of what people value and the availability of resources to satisfy those values. Such measures can only arise from voluntary exchanges in the form of relative prices.

The same is true for an organization, which is why we base our decisions on measures derived from economically sound prices set by these conditions.

All decisions, large and small, benefit from Challenge and good economic and critical thinking. Thousands of employees making better decisions every day provide a major competitive advantage and can be the difference between success and failure.

EMPOWERMENT

As Abraham Maslow taught: "Every person is, in part, his own project and makes himself."[86] When individuals believe they have a gift that can be developed and are free to determine and control their own lives, they are empowered to contribute, make a difference, and realize their potential. Empowerment is facilitated by a contribution mindset and a supportive, inclusive environment. It is hindered by barriers—both internal and external to the individual.

Internal barriers include doubts and limiting beliefs. If someone feels incapable of contributing or afraid of making mistakes, they will fail to become all that they can be. Internal barriers can cause someone to give up before they start. While few begin with everything in their favor, everyone has a gift that, if cultivated, can improve their circumstances. Individuals who believe in themselves—who realize they have something to offer— have discovered their unique gift and are more motivated to develop valued skills and contribute. They are more likely to develop an accurate sense of self-worth, realize what they are capable of becoming (self-actualize), and live a life of meaning.

External barriers exist when the key institutions of society—education, business, communities, and government—hinder or impede an individual's journey of realizing their potential. Removing all such barriers is essential. People become empowered when they are enabled to discover, develop, and apply their gifts; communities provide the support they need; businesses empower employees to succeed by contributing to the betterment of others; and governments protect the rights of every individual and ensure equal treatment.

Koch's success depends on empowered employees who apply Principles of Human Progress. Effective supervisors empower employees to be the best they can be, providing the conditions necessary for contributions (Requirements for Human Action). They help them understand and internalize Koch's (and their group's) Vision, ensure they have roles that fit their gifts, and provide the necessary resources and opportunities to learn and try new things. Empowered individuals are capable of extraordinary things.

EXPERIMENTAL DISCOVERY

As commentator George Will reminded us: "The future has a way of arriving unannounced."[87] In our rapidly changing world, competitors are constantly improving, and what customers value is constantly changing. No matter how superior a company's knowledge, products, and services, it cannot stay in business unless it makes improvements and innovations at least as fast as its most effective competitors. Doing this successfully requires that a business apply Experimental Discovery and Creative Destruction to its vision, strategies, products, services, and methods. All businesses must continually innovate, which usually involves numerous changes in direction, leading to the discovery of new paths.

Progress—whether in business, an economy, or science—comes through experimentation and failure. Those who favor a "grand plan" over experimentation don't understand the role that failed experiments play in creating progress in society. As Einstein supposedly said, "Someone who has never made a mistake has never tried anything new."[88]

Such failures can effectively signal what doesn't work. When dealt with quickly and efficiently, they minimize waste and redirect scarce resources to what does work. A market economy is an experimental discovery process in which business failures are inevitable. Attempts to eliminate any risk of failure only ensure greater failure.

For Experimental Discovery to work, we have to design experiments properly and recognize when we are experimenting, so we can learn and limit the bet accordingly. Koch companies have suffered whenever we didn't recognize we were experimenting and made bets as if the risks were small when they were not.

Since the future is unknown, we can never predict with certainty which investments will be profitable. To drive Creative Destruction, we encourage numerous well-designed experiments to determine which new businesses, products, services, processes, methods, or type of organization will be successful. We also limit the size of experiments by considering the risk and magnitude of gain or loss.

A well-designed experiment starts with a hypothesis and the goal of learning whether it is valid. If done properly, it leads to new knowledge that brings about change, even if our assumptions or hypotheses are disproven. We learn even more when we explore a range of possibilities that includes the areas of greatest uncertainty and potential.

Confusing as it might seem, failure and getting results are not mutually exclusive. As Einstein is believed to have observed, "Failure is success in progress."[89] A failed but well-designed experiment is valuable if it generates lessons that lead to positive results. A true failure is a failure to learn because of poorly planned or impulsive action.

To encourage Experimental Discovery, we don't penalize well-planned experiments that fail since they fuel the necessary flow of small and frequent bets that generate discovery and learning. This is vital to innovation, growth, and long-term profitability. It is also motivating, as experimenting to discover new ways to create value makes work more interesting and exciting.

HEADWINDS AND TAILWINDS

We have long emphasized the importance of continually improving to drive rather than be a victim of the increasing rate of Creative Destruction. But in recent years, as the speed and magnitude of these changes accelerated, a heightened sense of urgency was required to not only improve but transform our performance.

This led our businesses and capability groups to apply the principle of Headwinds and Tailwinds to transform their ability to succeed in a variety of environments by modifying their visions and strategies and building the required capabilities.

Headwinds exist for a product where its long-term opportunities and profitability are being seriously eroded by declining demand or a reduction in the barriers to entry. These winds can be generated by, among other things, competition from new technologies or products, unfavorable changes in consumer preferences, or government interventions.

Tailwinds exist for a product where its long-term profitability has the potential to greatly increase. These winds can be generated by, among other things, new technologies, products or strategies, favorable changes in customer preferences, or distortive government subsidies and mandates.

Wherever a headwind or tailwind exists it creates competitive forces in the opposite direction. The effects of headwinds are lessened by negative factors, such as those listed above, which deter new entrants, investments, and innovations. The effects of tailwinds are lessened by stimulating a flood of new competitors, investments, and innovations.

The Headwinds and Tailwinds principle has been a major factor in our recent successes. It helps us decide whether to enter or remain in a business, based on whether we have or can build the right capabilities for whatever conditions exist.

HUMILITY

Arrogance—an exaggerated sense of your own importance or belief that you are better than others—is the enemy of humility. It is a highly destructive trait for individuals and organizations. It blinds people to their limitations and biases them against the contributions of others. Lack of humility is so destructive that Pope Gregory listed pride as one of the Seven Deadly Sins more than fourteen hundred years ago.[90] Arrogance has led to the downfall of many once-successful societies, organizations, and individuals.

To be humble is to understand and accept yourself as you really are and accept others as they really are. Having an accurate sense of self-worth begins by believing you have inherent value as a person—which has nothing to do with title, status, or money—and then discovering your talents and developing them into valued skills. Admitting when you need help, can't do something well, or need to improve is liberating. It frees you to focus on how you can best contribute and allows others to do the same.

Intellectual honesty is closely related to humility. It is dedication to truth and constructively dealing with reality, even when it is painful. Instead of our only looking for evidence to support our ideas and views, intellectual honesty leads us to sincerely seek constructive feedback and strive to see things as they really are, rather than how we wish them to be. This is difficult because even when we ask for criticism, we often want praise. We constructively deal with reality by stopping unprofitable endeavors, being realistic about threats that could harm our business, and experimenting to create better results. People who are intellectually honest change their paradigms when those paradigms are holding them back.

Maintaining humility when we've been successful is especially challenging. The minute we believe our success is inevitable or feel we are entitled to our success, we're in serious trouble. True humility is reflected in our willingness to hold ourselves and others accountable for results and behavior consistent with Our Values. We should have high expectations of ourselves and others, willingly admit our mistakes, make corrections when we fall short of these standards, and give credit where credit is due.

INTEGRITY

Integrity is such an important principle that we list it first in Our Values. Integrity means being committed to and living by a beneficial moral code. Imagine how much better the world would be if everyone acted with complete integrity, with their word as their bond, and never did anything they wouldn't want others to know about. There would be much less need for all the time and money spent on controls, litigation, and security.

Acting with integrity requires courage because doing the right thing is sometimes difficult or uncomfortable—especially when it involves challenging your supervisor or others who can affect your future. We are always expected to do what is right rather than what is easy, even if it makes us subject to criticism or ridicule. When things aren't going well or there is pressure to improve results, we must resist the temptation to cut corners. It is never acceptable to compromise safety, compliance standards, or our principles for a short-term gain. What good are principles if we abandon them under pressure?

Integrity is the foundation for trust and mutually beneficial relationships with all our constituencies. Trust is earned by helping others succeed, keeping commitments, being honest, sharing credit for success, making tough decisions in a timely manner, admitting mistakes, and proactively taking corrective action when you fall short. You build trust and a reputation for integrity over time by demonstrating that you are a good steward and will always strive to do what is right.

Integrity is important in everyday interactions and decisions. This requires providing timely and honest feedback that will help your coworkers, including proactively pointing out when someone is making a mistake or headed for failure and providing praise when it is genuine and earned. It also requires speaking up when you have been asked to do something you're not good at. Integrity spurs a sense of obligation and willingness to take such actions even when difficult.

KNOWLEDGE

Knowledge is more than data, facts, or information; it's about applying understanding and know-how profitably to improve results. Societies are most prosperous when knowledge is plentiful, easily accessible, relevant, and inexpensive. Such knowledge results from openness, free speech, challenge, free association, mutually beneficial trade, and market signals, including prices and profit/loss. Anything that restricts the creation and use of knowledge distorts reality and hinders progress.

One of society's greatest sources of knowledge is what each individual knows about their specific needs, preferences, and circumstances; what they are and are not good at; and how they can best contribute. Because this knowledge is widely dispersed, it is impossible for one person or a small group to make optimal decisions for everyone else. That is why prosperity and progress require a bottom-up approach in which individuals are empowered to develop and apply their abilities.

No matter how capable our employees may be, our company cannot possess all the knowledge necessary to succeed long term. To overcome entropy and at least match the creative destruction of our best competitors, we need a culture that values lifelong learning and innovation. This includes:

- Building broad knowledge networks to enable us to acquire the most valuable knowledge from any and all sources (Republic of Science).
- Employees developing the personal knowledge that enables them to solve problems, identify opportunities, and discover better ways of doing things.
- Internally sharing our ideas and knowledge, soliciting and providing challenge (Scientific Method and Challenge), and identifying and closing gaps.

- Developing reality-based measures and doing marginal analysis to help us learn what works, improve results, and increase our rate of transformation.
- Conducting well-designed experiments (Experimental Discovery).

Hayek recognized that human progress is not the result of human design but of experimentation and centuries of accumulated knowledge. The institutions, customs, and traditions we take for granted reflect far more wisdom than any one person can possess. As Sir Isaac Newton said, "If I have seen further, it is by standing on the shoulders of giants."[91] Likewise, the organizational knowledge embodied in our principles and processes has developed over time. Today's employees benefit from the culture, know-how, and practices developed over the years by employees they never met.

Principles such as Integrity, Humility, and Openness are vital to, and promote respect for, this organizational knowledge. At the same time, our principle-based framework encourages us to continually challenge our paradigms and update our vision of what is possible so we can innovate, transform, and succeed long term.

LIFE OF MEANING AND SYNERGY

Viktor Frankl, a psychiatrist and Holocaust survivor, believed that we all need "the striving and struggling for a worthwhile goal ... the call of a potential meaning waiting to be fulfilled ... The more one forgets himself—by giving himself to a cause to serve, or another person to love—the more human he is and the more he actualizes himself."[92]

While imprisoned, Frankl learned that even when experiencing great difficulty, we have the power to choose our response. He gave the example of "men who walked through [the concentration camp] comforting others, giving away their last piece of bread."[93] Those who did so had a better chance of surviving because it gave them a reason to live. Frankl also taught that when people have no meaning in their lives, they default to the destructive paths of power or pleasure.

Psychologist Abraham Maslow believed that this pursuit of meaning is a deeply personal journey because everyone differs in their aptitudes, interests, goals, experiences, and circumstances. We increasingly self-actualize as we learn about ourselves—what we care about, as well as what we are and are not good at. This better enables us to contribute and succeed and to help others do the same.

In Maslow's view, we most fully self-actualize when we can achieve what he called *synergy* by resolving the "dichotomy between selfishness and unselfishness ... when by pursuing [our] own self-interest, [we] automatically benefit everyone else, whether [we] mean to or not."[94] He believed it was possible for societies and organizations to create these conditions. (See Alignment of Incentives.)

Maslow and Frankl found that people prefer meaningful work to meaningless work. Studies have found some janitors to be among the most self-actualized hospital employees. Those in hospitals that enable them to understand how they contribute to the well-being of patients and to the smooth functioning of the hospital can experience deep satisfaction and meaning in their work. Similarly, Maslow explained that "washing the dishes can be the most meaningless chore or it can be a symbolic act of love for one's family."[95] Thus, what's important is not the nature of the work itself but our understanding of its purpose and who it is helping.

As employees, we find greater meaning in our work when we understand how it contributes to improving other people's lives and the overall success of the company. Feedback, recognition, and rewards help us understand what is valued by others, thereby enabling ourselves and others to experience greater synergy, and our organization and society to experience greater success. (See Motivation.)

MARGINAL ANALYSIS

Marginal Analysis involves evaluating the benefits and costs associated with a specific change—it's what occurs "at the margin." It helps us improve business decisions, eliminate waste, and discover profitable opportunities.

Marginal Analysis asks, "What is the profitability of additional units of production, of one more or less plant, or of a larger versus a more modest investment?" It looks at the benefits and costs associated with a specific change. We call it *marginal* not because it is unimportant, but because it is incremental, occurring at the margin. This makes it a much more powerful tool than working with averages or totals.

We make most decisions using Marginal Analysis, which requires understanding the difference between costs and benefits that are incremental and those that are not, such as sunk costs. Only by making decisions on the appropriate margin will a business consistently enhance its profitability and eliminate waste.

When used properly, Marginal Analysis is an indispensable management tool. For example:

- If we wanted to add a team member, we would determine what more could be accomplished for the incremental cost. If a team member were to leave, we would determine whether the savings of not replacing the employee would exceed the value foregone.

- In a plant with excess capacity, the marginal cost up to full utilization would simply be the incremental cost incurred (which may vary significantly from the average cost), plus any effect on the market. The marginal cost of producing an amount exceeding the capacity would also include the necessary investment.

- In deciding what to do with a poorly performing plant, we use Marginal Analysis to compare the net present value of continuing to operate with that of shutting it down or selling.

- In considering an innovative new feature or technology, we estimate the remaining resources, risks, time, and opportunity cost involved in realizing the benefits. We then determine whether the risk-adjusted potential is high enough to sufficiently overcome these cost factors.

Marginal Analysis requires establishing an optimized base case (OBC) that can be compared to alternatives. An OBC includes known, incremental, low-cost improvements. It is essential that the base case be realistic.

Effective marginal analysis requires good knowledge systems. Traditional accounting practices tend to rely on historical transactions, totals, and averages, causing unprofitable assets or activities to be hidden or subsidized by those that are profitable, leading to poor decisions. In contrast, when we apply Marginal Analysis with the appropriate data focused on the profitability of individual customers, products, services, plants, offices, staffing, and other assets, we greatly improve decision-making.

MEASURES

As Einstein observed, "Not everything that counts can be counted, and not everything that can be counted counts."[96] That is why we strive to measure things that matter—things that lead to profitable action—even when it is difficult to do so. And it is why we avoid relying on measures that do not provide insights leading to improvements and innovations.

It is essential for us to have measures that help us understand reality and properly focus our efforts. Such measures include profit/loss and return on capital consumed. Rather than relying on averages or total profitability, we need to know the profitability of business strategies, customers, products, services, plants, production units, suppliers, and activities. Our measures need to provide the information required for Marginal Analysis. The goal is not precision but knowledge regarding future changes and opportunities to improve.

Many of these measures are largely subjective and qualitative rather than quantitative. Important areas to measure include:

- **Culture:** Progress in applying Principle Based Management, including the effectiveness of supervisors.
- **Opportunity Cost:** An activity is truly profitable only when it is more profitable than the most profitable opportunity foregone.
- **Stewardship and Compliance:** Performance in eliminating the conditions and events that have harmed or could harm people or the environment and in complying with all applicable laws and regulations—all classified by seriousness.
- **What Each Customer Values:** Not only what the customer values as a company but also what its relevant decision-makers value.
- **Price-Setting Mechanisms:** Based on various supply-and-demand scenarios that cause marginal competitors to increase or decrease production or prices.
- **Our Competitive Position:** Where we stand in the value we create for our customers and the costs of providing it versus present and future competitors.

- **The Value and Cost of Activities:** Benchmark versus the best in the world regardless of industry.
- **Allocation and Profitability of Overhead Costs:** Whether costs are allocated according to the businesses that drive them and are profitable to each business.

Knowing what drives profitability is important. If we are doing well, is it because of favorable market conditions or our competitive advantage? Given that we tend to work on what gets measured, it is essential that we measure the right things—especially if rewards and recognition are involved. Measuring and rewarding revenue will drive more revenue. Focusing on costs will drive cost reduction. Using either as the primary measure of success will destroy rather than create value.

It is imperative for every business, facility, unit, and team to continually evaluate its measures. This requires critical thinking to determine whether each measure is driving mutually beneficial outcomes. All employees need to know which parts of their work are profitable, based on measures that help them understand what to start, stop, change, or improve.

MOTIVATION

Motivation (from the Latin word meaning "to move") is what prompts us to act. It is not a feeling, emotion, or what makes a person happy. A person's motivation comes from a combination of what is within them (intrinsic) and their environment (extrinsic). Thus, to have an organization of contribution-motivated people, we address both factors.

We start by selecting contribution-motivated employees who define success as making a positive difference for others and have a strong desire to do so (intrinsic). We then strive to select supervisors who will create an environment (extrinsic) that motivates employees to maximize their contributions to Koch's long-term success. (See Alignment of Incentives.) We reward results rather than activity; otherwise, we unintentionally motivate employees to do work that is wasteful.

We also recognize that for individuals to act, they not only need to be dissatisfied with the status quo, but they also need to have a vision of a better state and a belief that it can be achieved. (See Requirements for Human Action.) Just as profit and loss can help satisfy these three conditions for entrepreneurs, roles, feedback, and rewards can help satisfy these conditions for employees.

Rather than using rigid, formulaic pay structures that fail to consider what an individual has contributed (whether positive or negative), we attempt to reward employees according to the long-term value they create. This includes contributions to culture, current results, and building capabilities that we believe will generate results. When employees understand how they earn and can increase their compensation, they become more fully motivated to increase their contributions.

Effective supervisors are motivated to help their employees self-actualize, rather than control and stifle them. They prioritize building trusted relationships and learning how to motivate each employee based on what is important to them, given their subjective value—such as pay, doing meaningful work they are good at and care about, having some control over their activities, and the opportunity to be creative and develop. (See Life of Meaning and Synergy.)

MUTUAL BENEFIT

In 1776, Scottish economist and philosopher Adam Smith observed that people in a civilized society always require the cooperation and assistance of others.[97] We obtain what we value by providing others with what they value. This simple idea, which today we call mutually beneficial exchange, when widely practiced, has lifted much of the world's population out of poverty and subsistence.

Mutual Benefit is foundational to the role of business in society and Koch's Vision. We seek to understand and satisfy the needs of our constituencies, starting with providing products and services that our customers value more than their alternatives. When we do this while consuming fewer resources, our profit is a result of benefiting our customers and society.

Some people believe that exchange is zero-sum—for one side to win, the other side must lose. This can be the case, such as when one party benefits at the expense of the other party through involuntary extraction. Whether legal (government bailouts, subsidies, mandates, and tariffs) or illegal (fraud and theft), these win-lose approaches are always harmful to society.

Exchange is a positive-sum endeavor when it is voluntary and mutually beneficial. Both parties cooperate to get more of what they value and will only transact if both believe it will make them better off. This win-win approach respects each party's right to choose whether to transact. It is the only way to ensure value and good profit are created.

When companies are allowed to profit through extraction and exploitation, they avoid the constructive competitive pressure to innovate and create value for others. In contrast, when companies can only profit through voluntary cooperation, they have a strong incentive to innovate and anticipate ways of satisfying customers.

At Koch, we apply a win-win philosophy in all we do. We strive to build mutually beneficial relationships with all our core constituencies—employees, customers, suppliers, partners, communities, and governments. We seek to understand what they value and then cooperate with them to achieve mutually beneficial outcomes. Trust is the foundation for such relationships.

Contribution-motivated employees are essential to applying a philosophy of Mutual Benefit. They are collaborative, build trusted relationships, and make those they work with better.

OPENNESS

Openness is a simple concept reliant on a system of equal rights that respects the dignity of each person and their right to live as they choose—as long as they do not violate the rights of others. When people are respected, free to choose their own path, and rewarded for the value of their work, they can improve their own circumstances as they contribute to the well-being of others. An open society encourages honest exchanges of knowledge, opinions, and ideas while protecting individuals from the threats or force of those who disagree.

Unfortunately, today's trend is against Openness. Differences have become dividing lines, with those who disagree being demonized or "canceled." More broadly, nationalism and tribalism pit one group against another. Closed-minded people retreat into insular and protectionist groups, reinforcing their own biases and preventing the exploration of different perspectives through civil discourse.

The ancient philosopher Confucius taught that it is "a pleasure to learn," and that even in a group as small as three, there will always be one from whom we can learn.[98] By embracing Openness, we accelerate our rate of learning and improve relationships. Differences become opportunities for productive discussions even in the face of passionate disagreement.

Openness should extend to all interactions with others, including trade. Voluntary exchange—based on Mutual Benefit—fosters Division of Labor by Comparative Advantage and entrepreneurship that lead to a greater diversity of art, music, food, and other goods and services that enrich people's lives. Protectionist barriers to exchange, whether within or among nations, create closed systems that stifle innovation and value creation. As attributed to Frederic Bastiat: "When goods don't cross borders, soldiers will."

At Koch, we recognize the vital role of Openness in bringing about progress. Innovation flourishes when we encourage the free flow of ideas, well-designed experiments, challenge, and the building of knowledge networks. Employees learn more and make better decisions when they seek out diverse points of view and are open to feedback about how they can improve. They help others do the same when they share their ideas and suggest different approaches. If we are open, we recognize that no matter how well we have been doing, we can always do better. Openness helps us overcome entropy in society, our organizations, and our lives.

OPTIONS

The future is uncertain, yet the decisions we make today can greatly affect our ability to succeed in the future. This is why Options and optionality play a crucial role in decision-making. Possessing an option provides the ability or right, but not the obligation, to take an alternative course of action.

At Koch, we encourage everyone to understand what options are available and the benefits, costs, and risks of each. To determine whether acquiring, granting, or building an option would be profitable, we need to apply Marginal Analysis in estimating whether its future risk-adjusted value would be greater than its cost.

There are three types of options: exchange, contractual, and operational.

Those traded on an exchange—such as puts, calls, and swaps for stocks and commodities—are regularly used by employees involved in trading or risk optimization.

Contractual options are much more widely used, varied, and nuanced. They involve negotiations with counterparties and are embedded in contracts. Examples include:

- In a sale or purchase agreement, the right to change (within a range) the duration, volume, specifications, or other terms.
- The ability to sell an investment or other asset when most beneficial.
- On long-term contracts, the right to extend or exit early.
- When investing in another company, the right to increase participation or control, or convert the asset from one form to another: equity, preferred equity, debt, or other.
- The right of first refusal (ROFR) or right of first offer (ROFO).
- Getting profit participation when selling an asset that might become more valuable than anticipated.

When we grant or sell a contractual option, it is most important that we limit our obligations to avoid a disastrous loss, even if we believe the probability is low. This includes ensuring the document is clear, reflects the commercial agreement, and does not grant implicit or unintended options. It is also important to recognize that:

- Options we provide to customers in contracts on volume, quality, type of products, or duration can be very expensive, so we need to be fully compensated for the risk.

- Giving ROFR, ROFO, or other last-look options can chill bidders and significantly reduce the market value of an asset and need to be limited.
- When counterparties have the option to cash us out of an investment early, we need to structure it to ensure we still have a sufficient return.
- Granting someone an option to buy a Koch asset prevents us from selling it to others during the term of the option. Thus, we need to keep the term short.

Operational options create flexibility in an asset or organization. Examples include:

- Building assets so they can be expanded efficiently, produce different products, or use a variety of feedstocks, energy, or other inputs.
- Having the ability and the right to change the organization's structure and optimize people's roles as conditions change.
- When selling a collection of assets, keeping those that are not valuable to the buyer but may be to others.
- Innovating to create different products or ways of doing things.

All of us need to seek profitable opportunities to acquire, sell, and build Options that can create significant value for Koch. It is an important way we differentiate ourselves and is critical to our long-term success.

OUR VALUES

Of all the proven Principles of Human Progress, these eight are the foundational values of our culture and thus are among the most important for all of us to exemplify daily. They are an essential aspect of our Virtue and Talents dimension. They define who we are as an organization and are necessary for the long-term success of Koch and each of us.

1. Integrity

Have the courage to always act with integrity.

2. Stewardship and Compliance

Act with proper regard for the rights of others, especially regarding safety and the environment. Comply with all laws and regulations. Stop, Think, and Ask.

3. Principled Entrepreneurship

Create Virtuous Cycles of Mutual Benefit by becoming a preferred partner of customers, employees, suppliers, communities, and other core constituencies. Continually seek to identify and close the gaps between what you are and what you could be accomplishing if you were fully applying Principle Based Management.

4. Transformation

Transform yourself and help the company and others to do the same. Develop the visions, strategies, capabilities, products, and services that will enable us to satisfy unmet needs and create superior value.

5. Knowledge

Seek and acquire the best knowledge from any and all sources that will enable you to innovate and improve results. Share your knowledge proactively. Provide and solicit challenges consistently and respectfully.

6. Humility

Be humble, intellectually honest, and deal with reality constructively. Develop an accurate sense of self-worth based on your strengths, limitations, and contributions. Hold yourself and others accountable to these standards.

7. Respect

Treat everyone with honesty, dignity, respect, and sensitivity. Include and embrace different perspectives, experiences, aptitudes, knowledge, and skills in order to leverage the power of diversity.

8. Self-actualize

Be all you can be. Identify, develop, and apply your gifts and passions so you can best contribute in ways that are most meaningful to you. Be a lifelong learner.

OVERCOMING ENTROPY AND BUREAUCRACY

The second law of thermodynamics states that entropy (disorder or uselessness) always increases in a closed system because there are far more ways in which matter can be arranged that are disordered and useless than are ordered and useful. Otherwise known as the law of entropy, it is considered by many scientists to be the most fundamental law of nature.

Disorder increases spontaneously with time. Our challenge is to overcome entropy by continually striving for an open and beneficial order, which can only be created through the application of energy and knowledge.

Ever-increasing entropy afflicts human affairs just as it does the physical world. For individuals, organizations, and society, there are always more ways for things to go wrong than for them to go right. In other words, whatever *can* go wrong *will* go wrong.

At Koch, our approach to overcoming entropy is to create and deploy energy and knowledge through our principle-based framework. This requires energizing all employees to apply these principles, continually transforming themselves and their organizations. We seek to create and maintain a culture in which everyone is open to learning and recognizes that no matter how well we are doing, we can always do better. We learn what is possible and work to achieve it. This is our way of creating an order that is beneficial to us and others.

In organizations, the most common manifestation of entropy is bureaucracy. Bureaucracy results from fixed, detailed rules and procedures, rigid hierarchies, and perverse incentives. These bring about loss of the knowledge, ideas, and motivation of employees throughout the organization. The effect is entitlement, unaccountability, cynicism, form over substance, slow and poor decision-making, risk aversion, resistance to change, short-term focus, and lack of openness, knowledge sharing, and innovation.

To avoid this tendency toward stagnation and decline that is driven by entropy and bureaucracy, we strive to continually transform ourselves and our organizations. By daily renewing our dedication to understanding and applying Principles of Human Progress, we give ourselves and others the opportunity to realize our potential and live lives of meaning.

PARTNERSHIPS

Good partnerships are essential for long-term business success. They are necessary for building the culture and capabilities that enable superior value creation that is mutually beneficial.

No one can do this alone. It requires joining with others who have a wide variety of complementary capabilities. The more people with different and advantaged capabilities join together, the more successful they and their organizations will be.

Partners are those who join with us in any form, manner, or endeavor. Beneficial, lasting partnerships have three requirements:

- **Shared Vision:** The breadth of the necessary shared vision depends on the nature of the endeavor and each party's role in it. For those responsible for a business's success, such as its employees and co-investors, it is the full vision. For transactional relationships, as with customers and suppliers, it would be to make those transactions mutually beneficial. As trust develops, the transactional relationship can evolve into a true, quality partnership where each partner is motivated to help the other succeed and grow. For every type of endeavor and relationship, there must be an understanding and agreement on the vision—what they are jointly trying to accomplish and the best way to accomplish it.

- **Shared Values:** Partners share the values necessary for making the joint undertaking successful long term. At a minimum, these include honesty, mutual respect, Humility, knowledge sharing, and a commitment to continual Transformation.

- **Complementary Capabilities:** Each partner brings something different and important to the success of the endeavor. When both parties are intellectually honest and open about their strengths and weaknesses, they can apply comparative advantage to determine the division of labor that will generate the greatest results. Together, they will achieve more than they could individually.

To maximize Koch's long-term success, we strive to become the preferred partner of our core constituencies—all those who are important to that goal. The following are the types of partnerships that we consider most important:

- **Employees** who are contribution motivated and have a talent that will enable them to contribute. We help them find the role for which they have the greatest comparative advantage and reward them for the value they create.

- **Co-investors** who satisfy the three requirements for beneficial, lasting partnerships—shared vision, shared values, and complementary capabilities—with whom we can create a mutually beneficial relationship.
- **Customers** for whom we can create the greatest value who will reward us accordingly—particularly those we believe will succeed and grow.
- **Suppliers** who create the most value for us and for whom we can become a preferred customer by enabling and rewarding them.
- **Communities** where we are able to have the greatest long-term success due to their laws, culture, and location. By contributing to the well-being of the community, we become a preferred partner.
- **Lawmakers and regulators** with whom we can work in the spirit of Mutual Benefit so that laws enable, rather than hinder, people's ability to succeed by helping others.
- **People throughout society** will support us to the extent we consistently practice good stewardship and only earn good profit while striving to remove barriers holding people back and motivating others to do the same.

Developing mutually beneficial partnerships takes effort and time. Our relationships with our core constituencies are a top priority as they are vital to our long-term success.

PERSONAL KNOWLEDGE

Philosopher of science Michael Polanyi taught that we only truly know something—that is, have Personal Knowledge—when we can automatically apply it to get results. We develop personal knowledge by converting conceptual understanding into an effective tool for solving problems, addressing new opportunities, and discovering what does and doesn't work. Developing personal knowledge involves a personal transformation—what Polanyi called "a self-modifying act of conversion."[99] Reading a book or watching a video on how to ride a bike can be helpful, but developing personal knowledge requires riding one. Because practice makes permanent, not perfect, you must engage in correct, frequent, and prolonged practice.

When you're just learning how to do something, a template or operating procedure can be necessary and useful. As you study and practice in a particular field, you absorb increasing amounts of specific knowledge, including rules, facts, and relationships. This encourages a type of conformity, but at some point, you know these details well enough that you can begin to focus on the whole and innovate, recognizing the limitations of templates and processes.

Discoveries are more likely when you understand the meaning of things because you sense what and when something is wrong, even though you may not always be able to articulate your understanding. You are able to perceive patterns, problems, and opportunities—whether researching a new technology or market, operating equipment, interviewing a candidate, screening an acquisition, or doing anything with the goal of delivering value to both customers and the company.

Personal Knowledge helps you identify gaps between what is and what could be. Even without quantitative data, your intuition might tell you that something is wrong or something better is possible. This is why we encourage the passionate pursuit of hunches based on personal knowledge. Hunches and intuition can be tough to explain, but that doesn't make them incorrect. As Polanyi said: "We can know more than we can tell."[100] Hunches help you develop hypotheses that can be challenged and tested. This can lead to insights, discoveries, and new ways of doing things.

Our principle-based framework recognizes that many individuals have deep personal knowledge about how to produce the product(s) or deliver the service(s) of the organization, but the total knowledge is dispersed. This is why we believe it is impossible for a top-down approach to determine all the necessary activities, methods, and changes needed to be successful. Instead, we rely on a shared vision, superior cooperation, and a culture where the knowledge of all employees is valued and leveraged to create the greatest long-term value for Koch.

PRINCIPLE-BASED VS. RULE-BASED

For decades, Koch has emphasized the importance of understanding and applying Principles of Human Progress. Nobel laureate F. A. Hayek concluded that uncovering these principles was "perhaps the greatest discovery mankind ever made."[101] When practiced correctly, they promote peace, civility, Mutual Benefit, opportunity, success, and enable people to live a life of meaning.

Before this discovery, rulers throughout human history enforced a top-down and arbitrary rule-based system of control that made the human experience miserable. Nearly everyone was born in poverty, lived in poverty, and died in poverty. The average life expectancy hovered between thirty and forty years.

It was only when Principles of Human Progress began to be applied shortly before 1800 that people's lives dramatically improved. As millions of people gained the opportunity to live more fully as they saw fit, they began applying their abilities and knowledge to improve their lives by helping others improve theirs. While there will always be room for improvement, most people are healthier, wealthier, and happier than ever before.

The application of these principles in societies has greatly improved well-being, but there has not been a similar transformation in organizational management. Whether intentional or not, leaders who use prescribed, detailed rules and directives behave as though they don't need to motivate their employees or benefit from their knowledge and ideas. Those who think they have all the answers push only their own ideas and require standardization because they assume most people don't have much to offer.

At Koch, Principles of Human Progress guide everything, including visions, strategies, policies, practices, Partnerships, investments, and performance evaluations. These principles encourage entrepreneurship, discovery, and Transformation. They apply universally, whereas detailed rules and methods only work in specific applications under certain conditions, and even then tend to stifle motivation and creativity.

A principle-based approach is not an absence of rules. But when policies, processes, or procedures are necessary, they must be judged against general principles. We expect them to be continually challenged and improved—or eliminated when they undermine progress.

In keeping with Our Values, we comply with all laws and regulations. If, however, we find any of these rules to be counterproductive, we advocate for principle-based policies and try to persuade authorities to adopt them. Regardless, we fully comply with existing laws.

Internal audits are an important example of how the same activity can look quite different depending on the approach. Rule-based audits focus on enforcing conformity and finding violations. When principle-based, the focus is on learning what works and what doesn't, so that both employees and the business can improve.

The transformation of Koch began by applying principles that gave our employees the opportunity to transform themselves. We recognize, as Hayek did, that when we empower and motivate employees rather than try to control them, they are better able to contribute and transform Koch. We believe everyone, regardless of education or background, has the ability and knowledge to contribute, each in their own way.

Setting expectations according to general principles without prescribed, detailed directives or rules is core to our culture and long-term success. It frees everyone to think and innovate—to develop different methods and solutions—rather than mindlessly follow instructions. It creates an environment where every employee has the opportunity to find the right role, knows what to do to maximize value creation, and is motivated to do it without being told. This is a primary responsibility of every supervisor at every level.

PRINCIPLED ENTREPRENEURSHIP

Entrepreneurship is the innovative, experimental act of identifying and pursuing an opportunity. It can take any number of forms, such as creating a new business, product, service, process, method, or type of organization. It involves Risk because the future is always changing in unpredictable ways.

Principled Entrepreneurship is the discipline of always practicing entrepreneurship in a principled manner. Our Vision is to create good profit long term by providing products and services that customers value more than their alternatives, while consuming fewer resources and always acting lawfully and with Integrity. Good profit is earned by making a contribution in society—not from corporate welfare or other ways of profiting by taking advantage of people.

Corporate welfare is a form of *political* entrepreneurship, not Principled Entrepreneurship. Rather than profiting by creating value for others, it involves profiting by taking from others, which corrupts the political system. It also corrupts the country's culture by leading people to believe that success comes from harming rather than benefiting others.

Since Creative Destruction is a driving force in a market system, we continually strive to improve the value we create for customers and society faster than our most effective competitors. This entails not only a better understanding of what customers want now, but what they will want in the future. It is especially difficult because very few customers are aware of what they would prefer until they are shown a better alternative. Identifying and satisfying these unmet needs is essential to successful entrepreneurship.

We depend on the entrepreneurial contributions of our employees. If it is easier or more beneficial for employees to practice entrepreneurship elsewhere, we will inevitably fall behind. This is why we are dedicated to empowering employees to become principled entrepreneurs.

Independent entrepreneurs seek to create new and better products or services and ways of doing things. However, they rarely have the necessary resources, which requires them to develop their ideas sufficiently to access capital. The same is true inside Koch. To be a principled entrepreneur, you cannot let the need for approval stifle your initiative. Our principled entrepreneurs develop their ideas by seeking the knowledge and challenge that will lead to proposals that will earn approval.

A top-down, bureaucratic approach crushes entrepreneurship. We strive to create a Bottom-Up environment of Empowerment that unleashes the entrepreneurial spirit and initiative of contribution-motivated employees. Such employees continually identify and close the gaps between their current capabilities and what they could be accomplishing.

Supervisors at every level are responsible for building an environment that encourages and supports Principled Entrepreneurship. This includes establishing a clear understanding of what Principled Entrepreneurship looks like; enhancing the pursuit of knowledge through Experimental Discovery and knowledge sharing; eliminating waste and bureaucracy; and establishing an appropriate risk tolerance for trying something new. We expect supervisors to fight the complacency and inertia that develop over time, particularly when we have been successful; build a commitment to Stewardship and Compliance; and align the interests of employees with the interests of the company.

PROPERTY RIGHTS

Property Rights are a fundamental human right. As economist Alberto Benegas Lynch observed, property rights go far beyond ownership of land, buildings, or other physical assets: "Every individual freedom depends on private property." He realized that property rights are the "basis of civilization" and secure every individual's freedom of expression and the right to choose how they will use their time and talents.[102]

The concept of Property Rights has been around for centuries, but only recently has it been recognized as essential to a civil, peaceful, and prosperous society. Clear and protected property rights stimulate beneficial investment. Thus, more resources flow to those who produce the products, services, and innovations that people value, and away from those who do not—making possible the benefits of specialization and exchange through well-functioning markets. When the government respects these rights, disputes are solved peacefully and beneficially rather than in ways that are destructive. To the extent property rights are not defined and secure, we lose the capability and efforts of many who would be the greatest contributors to general well-being.

As Aristotle observed: "[People] pay most attention to what is their own; they care less for what is common . . . [they] are more prone to neglect their duty when they think that another is attending to it."[103] The incentive to be good stewards comes about as owners benefit from the value they create and bear costs from value they destroy. If owners are liable for injuries to people or property, they are motivated to prevent such injuries. When a business is losing money, its owners have a strong incentive to improve the business or sell it to someone who can make it profitable.

At Koch, we attempt to replicate some of the beneficial aspects of Property Rights using clear responsibilities, expectations, and decision rights. Decision rights define the degree of freedom an employee possesses to act or to make and implement decisions without approval. Rather than being centralized or decentralized, these rights need to follow the Division of Labor by Comparative Advantage. They flow to and from individuals based on whether and how they use them to create "good profit" for the company. In other words, they are earned and can expand or contract. Having decision rights does not mean you can do whatever you want; you have the obligation to seek input from those with beneficial knowledge and perspectives before deciding on a course of action.

In a completely free society, individuals can use their property as they choose, so long as they do not violate the rights of others. Decision rights in a company are different because it is the company, rather than individual employees, that owns the property and benefits or suffers most from its profits or losses.

To encourage a strong sense of ownership and entrepreneurship, employees are held accountable for a set of responsibilities and their results. (See Accountability.) Being responsible for something does not mean you have all the associated decision rights. For example, if you do not have full authority on a project, you are required to obtain the needed approvals, just as entrepreneurs without sufficient capital need to do. (See Principled Entrepreneurship.)

The allocation of private property in a market economy is continually changing, as should the allocation of responsibilities and decision rights within an organization. At Koch, supervisors work with employees to foster a clear, shared understanding of responsibilities, expectations, and decision rights. They regularly review and adjust them as needed, set standards for the appropriate use of property, and hold employees accountable for results and behavior consistent with Our Values. When all this is done well, employees are motivated to be good stewards and maximize their contributions to the company's long-term success. (See Alignment of Incentives.)

REPUBLIC OF SCIENCE

Superior knowledge and a culture that empowers everyone to realize their potential and fully contribute are essential for long-term business success. Knowledge is more than data, facts, or information; it's understanding, know-how, and all other value-adding capabilities.

Michael Polanyi's Republic of Science principle is a valuable guide for organizing to ensure knowledge is generated and shared freely, leading to beneficial innovations.[104] When scientists are free to work on problems that fit their abilities and interests and are well-informed about the work of others, they learn, adjust their efforts, and make discoveries.

Just as science advances through the extension and application of general principles, improving our application of Principles of Human Progress enables us to discover new approaches that lead to continual innovation and transformation.

We are able to create superior value for others and ourselves when we apply these principles. Rather than settling for what we've done in the past or what others are doing, we constantly share knowledge and ideas, test hypotheses, experiment, identify and close gaps, challenge, and adjust according to what works.

Progress starts by recognizing that there is always a better way. To discover that better way, we build multiple knowledge networks: inside our business and capability groups, throughout Koch, within our industries and fields of expertise, and anywhere else that may help us discover how to create more value. This is critical because no isolated individual or group can match the world's rapid innovation and improvement.

Our knowledge advances as we use these networks to help initiate individual efforts to improve results, which we subject to the tests of evidence and criticism. When a culture of respect and trust exists, employees share their ideas and seek the best knowledge to anticipate and solve problems. Open, honest exchanges lead to the discovery of new and better ways to create value. Such exchanges occur only when we eliminate stifling hierarchies, dictates, taboos, procedures, or fears, and properly apply our principles and incentives instead.

REQUIREMENTS FOR HUMAN ACTION

For Koch to succeed long term, we must enable employees to understand what we are trying to achieve and empower them to achieve it in a principled manner. Bringing about this beneficial result requires an understanding of what causes people to act.

In his book *Human Action*, noted economist and philosopher Ludwig von Mises provides that understanding. He posits that three requirements must be met for individuals to take action:

1. Unease or dissatisfaction with the present state of affairs
2. A vision of a better state
3. A belief that they can reach the better state[105]

For example, we mow our lawns only when we are dissatisfied with their present condition, believe they will look better, and know how to mow them. Customers switch to Koch when they become dissatisfied with their current supplier, believe we will serve them better, and are able to switch.

Organizations that fail to meet these three requirements develop a culture that stifles progress. In contrast, successful organizations:

1. Create dissatisfaction with the status quo
2. Provide a vision of long-term success and fulfillment
3. Empower employees to contribute by building a culture of Principled Entrepreneurship

We strive to create dissatisfaction with the current state by helping employees recognize that no matter how well they and the company are doing, unless they continually improve and transform themselves, Creative Destruction will ultimately cause us to become obsolete.

We help employees develop a vision of a better state, first by understanding their organization's and Koch's vision and our principle-based framework, then by demonstrating that they will be better off if they more fully apply this framework to advance these visions.

The most difficult requirement is helping employees believe they have a path to a better state. For many companies, satisfying this requirement becomes impossible because they have developed a bureaucracy-based framework and culture that stifles employees' ability to fully contribute.

We learned of one such situation directly from an officer at a major company. He said it was hopeless. They were stymied by bureaucracy, red tape, and resistance to change. When asked what he was doing about it, he responded: "After a while, you just paint your ass white and run with the antelope!" He and most others had given up. This happens when once-successful companies rest on their laurels and become complacent, self-protective, and stagnant. When they do, employees have no path to a better state, and decline sets in.

To overcome this tendency, our principle-based framework empowers our employees to reach a better state by motivating them to maximize their contribution to their organization's and Koch's long-term success. This entails ensuring they have meaningful work that fits their talents and passions, have appropriate control over their activities, are able to develop and grow, have the opportunity to be creative, and receive meaningful rewards.

RESPECT

For most of human history, people have been valued or devalued based on their ethnicity, gender, religion, nationality, politics, and social or economic status. Judging people on as little as one characteristic has led to unequal rights. When this devolves into viewing a group as less than human, it often results in slavery, genocide, and other atrocities. Totalitarian regimes, such as the Nazis in Germany and Communists in the Soviet Union, typically began by demonizing and vilifying those who were different or were believed to be a threat. Unfortunately, there are still many examples where such people are being fired, silenced, belittled, or otherwise attacked and treated as enemies.

Wherever a paradigm of respecting each person as an individual is embraced, there are much greater levels of freedom, peace, civility, trust, and human progress. Treating everyone with dignity and respect not only leads to better outcomes, but it is the right thing to do. It is disrespectful to believe you can know everything about a person and to judge an individual—positively or negatively—based on group identity or other characteristics. It is natural and appropriate for people to be proud of their heritage and other personal attributes, but there is no excuse for an "I'm better than you" attitude.

We naturally want to associate with people who are like us in some way; however, we all need to make an effort to build relationships with people outside our normal circles or comfort zones. This expands our knowledge and perspective, enriches our experience, and enhances our ability to learn and contribute.

People are more likely to share their opinions and ideas and engage in effective challenge when a culture of Respect and trust is promoted. We leverage the power of diversity by seeking and embracing different perspectives, experiences, aptitudes, knowledge, and skills to innovate and capture opportunities. With more than a hundred thousand employees and a presence in dozens of countries around the world, we rely on diversity—and respect for differences—to better understand and relate to customers and all other constituencies.

Respect is more than treating others kindly. It includes being honest. We must be truthful and sincere, especially when dealing with challenging situations or having difficult conversations. We show Respect by believing others can handle the truth and providing feedback that will help them deal with reality and improve. Avoiding or sugarcoating a tough message is a disservice to the person and the company. It lacks integrity and usually leads to a bad outcome.

RISK

Risk and reward are inseparable and a basic fact of business, as well as life. But not all risks are equal. We approach risk involving human safety and the environment differently from those that are purely financial. Our goal is to make risk decisions in a manner consistent with our principles. This encompasses eliminating catastrophic risks—especially those that could lead to a potential loss of life or a major environmental issue—and optimizing other risks.

Before pursuing opportunities, we seek to understand their risks and potential rewards and then determine whether to absorb, mitigate, or avoid those risks. As employees, we are expected to apply Koch's risk philosophy, not our own.

Applying the company's risk philosophy can be especially difficult when you are making financial decisions. Koch's substantial resources enable it to undertake far greater and larger financial risks than you would yourself. Suppose you have two opportunities that require the same investment. One has a 90 percent chance of making $100,000 and a 10 percent chance of making nothing. The other has a 50 percent chance of making $1 million and a 50 percent chance of making nothing. On a risk-adjusted basis, the expected value of the first opportunity is $90,000, and the second is $500,000; therefore, you should pursue the second opportunity. Although you only get a positive result for Koch 50 percent of the time, it is the right decision. It is natural to settle for the safer alternative, but doing so leads to an unsatisfactory return on capital and makes Koch less profitable over time.

One challenge in motivating good decision-making is the principal/agent problem. This tends to be created whenever a principal (owner) hires an agent (employee, consultant, or broker). The principal wants the agent to act in the best interest of the principal, while the agent usually wants what is best for the agent.

Consider what can happen when the principal and the agent have different risk profiles or incentives. Sometimes agents play it safe because there is no personal upside to taking appropriate risks. Incentives discourage prudent risk-taking when they fail to reward optimal outcomes and excessively penalize losses. Conversely, agents may take unauthorized or imprudent risks when there is not much personal downside. In such situations, agents "go for broke." Entire companies have been destroyed as a result of this problem. Even so, we don't want to create a rule-based, overly cautious culture. We seek to align the interests of all employees and agents so they will make decisions that maximize the long-term success of the company.

Good risk-adjusted decision-making also involves avoiding various decision traps. These predictable, systematic failings in judgment affect us all. One of the most serious and frequent is confirmation bias, which occurs when we preferentially look for evidence that supports what we want to believe and ignore or discount evidence to the contrary. This particular trap led to our disastrous acquisition of Purina Mills in 1998.

To help us avoid decision traps and appropriately address risks in our decisions and actions, our approach includes:

- Building a strong culture and capabilities to avoid catastrophic risks and minimize disruptions from incidents (Stewardship and Compliance).
- Engaging others with diverse experiences to challenge our assumptions.

- Developing realistic scenarios for a sufficiently wide range of potential outcomes, recognizing that we cannot perfectly predict the future.
- Establishing measures to monitor progress and creating options so adjustments can be made as needed.
- Experimenting on an appropriate scale rather than diving in without proper analysis (plunging).
- Not letting prior losses or a leader's initial rejection prevent consideration of a good opportunity.
- Recognizing the uncertainty in our investment assumptions, which is greatest for those farthest out, such as the large risks in long-term price and terminal value assumptions.
- Accounting for the improvements our competitors will probably make when projecting our own improvements.

Risk and reward cannot be our only criteria for evaluating opportunities. We apply our principle-based framework to ensure that we have the capabilities to make an opportunity successful long term. This includes considering its opportunity cost—not just whether it will be profitable, but whether it will provide a higher return on capital and other resources than alternative opportunities.

SCIENTIFIC METHOD AND CHALLENGE

Our approach to challenge utilizes Karl Popper's view of the scientific method which he called "Science as Falsification": After developing a theory, strive to disprove or find flaws in it, rather than trying to defend or justify it. As Popper said: "Every genuine test of a theory is an attempt to falsify it, or to refute it. It is easy to obtain confirmations, or verifications, for nearly every theory—if we look for confirmations."[106]

Truth is not what an expert or someone in the hierarchy declares is true. Truth is what stands the tests of evidence and criticism. To discover the truth, we encourage challenge—continual questioning and brainstorming to find a better way. Challenge is an opportunity to learn, not a chance to kill another person's idea or show off.

A quality challenge requires having the courage and willingness to respectfully question anyone's (especially a leader's) decisions, actions, proposals, or ideas. Challengers need to participate with intellectual honesty in the spirit of constructive improvement and solutions, rather than opposing something because it was "not invented here." They also need to make clear that they are challenging the idea, not the person.

Challenge is essential for good decision-making. This may occur at a formal meeting where people with different aptitudes and expertise—those with knowledge about the key drivers of success—discuss, brainstorm, and improve outcomes. But knowledge sharing and challenge can and should also happen in informal settings, such as one-on-one discussions, casual conversations, or small group meetings.

To drive Creative Destruction internally, nothing and no one can be immune to challenge. Supervisors at every level must both challenge their employees and foster an open environment that invites challenge and embraces change. They can solicit challenge by asking open-ended questions such as, "What are we missing here?" or "Is there a better way to do this?" or "What is possible if we fully applied our principles?"

If you find that your views are rarely challenged, perhaps you are giving the impression that challenge is not welcome. If that's the case, you are holding back progress—yours and your organization's.

SELF-ACTUALIZE

Self-actualizing employees are essential to Koch for us to succeed by creating value for others and creating virtuous cycles of mutual benefit. Self-actualizing employees are motivated to contribute, create, face reality, take on new challenges, cooperate, and help others succeed.

Abraham Maslow defined this as realizing one's potential—what he described as "everything that one is capable of becoming."[107] It is a deeply personal and unique journey of discovering your aptitudes, developing skills, and using them in productive ways. Self-actualizing is not about reaching the peak of a mountain, but rather a series of peaks that you continue to climb that give your life meaning. It is creating your own virtuous cycles on a personal level.

Self-actualizing goes beyond your basic physical and communal needs. It requires deliberately and persistently striving to improve, developing your aptitudes in ways that are beneficial to others. As Maslow put it: "Every person is, in part, his own project and makes himself." We must constantly learn "about our own strengths and limits and extend them by overcoming difficulties."[108] Maslow also warned that, "If you deliberately plan to be less than you are capable of being…you'll be deeply unhappy the rest of your life. You will be evading your own capacities, your own possibilities."[109]

This journey is all about experimenting to discover the work in which you can make the greatest contribution and have a passion for, while being a lifelong learner so you can continually transform yourself.

Helping each employee along this path is a critical responsibility of supervisors at every level. They must respect employees as unique individuals, continually evaluate and adjust their roles and responsibilities so they can best contribute, provide meaningful work that fits their talents and passions, and give ongoing coaching and feedback to promote learning, development, and growth.

In sum, our goal is for you to be all that you can be. That is not only the secret to success; it's the secret to a life of meaning.

STEWARDSHIP AND COMPLIANCE

The essence of Stewardship is recognizing our obligation to always act in a manner that respects the rights of others. By rights, we refer to the universal right for everyone to live as they choose, so long as they don't violate the rights of others. This includes everyone's right to their own property, along with the obligation to manage it responsibly and do the same for all other resources for which they are stewards.

Throughout history, the role of business in society has been to provide goods and services that help people improve their lives, and to do so responsibly. Likewise, our experience has been that we only succeed when we benefit others. Good stewardship is vital to mutual benefit, which, in addition to our moral and legal obligations, is why we all have stewardship obligations.

Nothing is more important than human life. Thus, the safety of all those with whom we interact—such as employees, contractors, and communities—is our top priority. To create the conditions for a safe workplace, all employees need to take personal responsibility for their own safety and the safety of those around them, and to ask questions and challenge practices whenever they have concerns.

Similarly, proper regard for the environment starts by understanding and giving priority to the highest-consequence risks. We proactively use technology, data, sound science, good judgment, and economic thinking to implement responsible environmental practices—even if not required by law. We seek to identify and apply bene-ficial technologies and practices that use fewer resources and improve the environmental performance of our products and processes. This benefits our customers, employees, investors, communities, and people throughout society.

Compliance with all laws and regulations is a requirement of every employee. Each of us is expected to know and understand the legal and regulatory requirements for our roles, identify anything that might lead to noncompliance, and discuss with our supervisors and others who are knowledgeable how best to comply. When unsure about how to respect the rights of others, work safely, be environmentally responsible, or comply with legal and regulatory requirements. Stop, Think, and Ask before proceeding.

Our words and commitments matter. Success depends on our having the courage to stand up for what we believe and not make commitments or act in ways that are inconsistent with our principles. This is central to what makes our approach to Environmental, Social, and Governance (ESG) different than most. We focus on helping people improve their lives and communities by motivating and empowering them rather than controlling and coercing them. We all need to be responsible for our actions, thoughtful about resources entrusted to our care, and always respectful of the rights of others.

See Koch's Stewardship Framework on kochind.com for more information.

TALENTS

The most important factor when selecting and retaining employees is whether they have virtue—including being contribution motivated. But it is critical that they also have a talent that will help us succeed long term. Employees who lack virtue can do far more damage than those who lack the right talent. Both factors are needed for any of us to create value.

A person's ability to excel in a given role mostly depends on their aptitudes or intelligences. In psychologist Howard Gardner's multiple intelligences theory, there are a number of independent forms of intelligence, and none of us is equally gifted in all of them. When someone is strong in an intelligence, such as logical-mathematical or interpersonal, they have the capacity to excel at activities requiring that intelligence. Whether Gardner is correct about the number or kinds of intelligences, it is clear that major differences exist among individuals and the roles they can perform well.

Talent alone does not guarantee success. Because the world is rapidly changing, continual learning and development are critical. We must work to develop our gifts into valued skills by trying new things to determine what we are and are not good at and by seeking feedback from those who will tell us the truth.

Because many organizations emphasize hierarchy, people often chase promotions or prestigious roles. Instead of fixating on some predetermined career path, Koch strives to create an environment where employees seek roles where they can maximize their contribution. This leads to greater opportunities and rewards for the employee.

At Koch, we strive to apply the Division of Labor by Comparative Advantage instead of forcing employees into one-size-fits-all roles they aren't good at or don't care about. Good supervisors work with their employees to help each develop a role with the responsibilities that will enable them to self-actualize by contributing. An employee's role, responsibilities, and expectations (RREs) describe how they need to utilize their talents to maximize overall results.

It is critical that everyone is in a role that fits their talents. If an employee is contribution motivated but not performing well, we probably have them in the wrong role. We need to help them find a more suitable role in their group or elsewhere in Koch. This requires that employees be honest with themselves and their supervisors about where their talent will enable them to fully contribute. Good supervisors guide these efforts and remove barriers that prevent employees from realizing their potential.

TIME PREFERENCE AND LONG-TERM FOCUS

Other things being equal, people prefer the satisfaction of a given value now, rather than later. This time preference varies from person to person and for the same person at different periods. The higher your time preference, the more willing you are to sacrifice a benefit in the future to get what you want now. The lower your time preference, the more you are willing to forgo a benefit now to bring about a better future.

The degree of your time preference is the amount of additional satisfaction required in the future for you to give up a unit of satisfaction now. The ratio of these differing valuations represents the price of time to you. When property rights are clearly defined and respected, time preference decreases, individuals are more willing to save, and businesses are more willing to invest long term.

Our long-term focus has been essential to Koch's success. It is why our owners reinvest 90 percent of earnings and seek employees who are contribution motivated and have a talent that will help us create long-term value. These, invariably, are employees who have lower time preferences.

This focus has caused us to develop many capabilities, such as becoming better able to select from diverse investment opportunities with different risks, returns, and time horizons. To help us do this, we estimate the ratio of the risk-adjusted net present value (NPV) of different opportunities to the capital consumed. When done properly, this helps us compare the benefit of a short-term profit opportunity to one that is longer term. It also provides a sense of urgency to quickly address problems and opportunities that can affect our future.

This emphasis keeps us from unduly penalizing earnings volatility, as public companies often feel forced to do, and to stay with an underperforming business when—and only when—we have hard evidence it has sufficient risk-adjusted potential. When it truly does, it can lead to a Virtuous Cycle of Mutual Benefit, which furthers our long-term success.

TRANSFORMATION

Not only is our world rapidly changing, but the rate of change is accelerating. We have long emphasized the importance of continuous improvement; however, today we need more than that. We need continual transformation, which requires a heightened sense of urgency. If we do not continually transform, Creative Destruction and entropy will overwhelm us, and we will fail.

Transformation doesn't mean doing what we've been doing a little better or a little faster. It means finding ways to do things much better or much faster or doing entirely new things. These include creating new and better products and services, using new technology, combining existing methods and technologies in new ways, significantly reducing the resources consumed, and eliminating unprofitable activities. None of this happens without employees who are contribution motivated. For every innovation, there is an innovator—and likely many contributors. For every improvement, there are employees with the initiative, ideas, and skills to make it happen.

Business transformation also requires building knowledge networks to inform us of methods, technologies, and trends from anywhere in the world that might improve, disrupt, or revolutionize what we do today. These knowledge-sharing networks, both internal and external, along with reality-based measures and well-designed experiments, are critical to achieving the necessary rate of transformation. If we are protectionist and close ourselves off from competition or innovation, we will become obsolete.

Transformations only come about if we transform ourselves. This starts with a willingness to undergo the most difficult and painful of all changes: changing our paradigms and habits, which involves focused and prolonged effort. Consider what's required for a bodybuilder to transform into a marathon runner. Long-term success also entails continually seeking help to acquire new knowledge and skills. Being a lifelong learner is essential.

Our organization is transformed when we continually develop and update its vision, strategies, capabilities, products, and services to create superior value and satisfy unmet needs. This is only possible in an entrepreneurial culture where employees are eager and willing to drive transformation from the bottom up rather than waiting for a top-down grand plan. While some transformations are big leaps forward, many are the cumulative result of employees continually challenging and pushing themselves and their teams to find new ways to create value.

Koch's transformations have always depended on employees who are contribution motivated—who know that no matter how well we (as a company or individuals) are performing today, we can always do better. If we dedicate ourselves to understanding and applying Principles of Human Progress to continually transform ourselves and our organizations, we can accomplish more and have better lives than we ever imagined.

VIRTUOUS CYCLES OF MUTUAL BENEFIT

Virtuous Cycles of Mutual Benefit (VCMB) are the processes by which we continually build capabilities that create value for others. VCMBs are a never-ending, mutually beneficial process of opportunity generation. We create these cycles when, *and only when*, we have the capabilities to become a preferred partner of those who are important to our success. Equally important is developing our ability to continually transform our capabilities.

Koch's growth and success is a result of applying Principles of Human Progress to build the capabilities that enable these cycles. Continuing to succeed in a rapidly changing world, where Creative Destruction is happening at a faster and faster pace, demands an even greater sense of urgency for creating these cycles.

We become a preferred partner when someone prefers working with us rather than their alternatives. Typically, this happens when we differentiate ourselves in providing what they value. In turn, we prefer them when they help us maximize our long-term success in harmony with our principle-based framework.

Virtuous cycles start with *employees*. An organization must have people who create their own virtuous cycles—employees who are committed to Our Values, enabling them to self-actualize. They are contribution motivated and have a talent that will help us succeed. Such employees take the initiative to discover their aptitudes, apply them to maximize their contributions, and then transform themselves by doing it again and again.

Koch becomes the preferred partner for these employees when we help them find work for which they have a passion and can make the greatest contribution—by actualizing their potential. This is the essential responsibility of every supervisor. It is realized by knowing and building trust with employees, helping find roles for which they have a comparative advantage, and motivating them to maximize the value they create.

The primary focus of all of us as employees is our customers, providing them with products and services they prefer over their alternatives. We seek those customers for whom we can create the greatest value and who appropriately compensate us. When this happens, we become their preferred supplier and they become a preferred customer, resulting in Mutual Benefit.

Others we need as mutually preferred partners are:

- **Suppliers** who create the most value for us and for whom we can become a preferred customer by enabling and rewarding them.
- **Communities** that enable our long-term success by valuing our presence as we help improve the quality of life they offer.
- **Investment partners** with aligned vision and values with whom we can develop a mutually beneficial relationship.
- **Lawmakers and regulators** with whom we can work in the spirit of Mutual Benefit so that laws enable, rather than hinder, people's ability to succeed by helping others.

- **People throughout society** by practicing good stewardship, consuming fewer resources, and removing barriers to having a life of meaning.

For a deeper dive, read Charles Koch's *Continually Transforming Koch Industries Through Virtuous Cycles of Mutual Benefit.*

SUPERVISOR RESPONSIBILITIES AND EXPECTATIONS

Throughout the book, we emphasized the important role of supervisors. Below is a letter shared with Koch employees in August 2023, followed by an outline of responsibilities given our principles. We hope this guidance is as useful to your organization as it was to ours.

A MESSAGE TO ALL SUPERVISORS:

If you have direct reports, then no matter what your title or role, you're a supervisor. That means your primary responsibility is to help your employees develop and maximize their contributions by applying Principle Based Management.

You are to develop trusted relationships and know your employees well enough to help them self-actualize. This includes providing honest, direct, and timely feedback, helping employees understand their strengths and weaknesses, and dealing with poor performance.

While we don't expect perfection, continually improving your effectiveness is essential for your—and the company's—success.

If, after reviewing these responsibilities, you realize that supervising isn't for you, that's okay. Explore with your supervisor and others what roles may be a better fit. It is critically important that everyone, including you, be in the right role.

Charles Koch
Chairman & Co-CEO

Dave Robertson
Vice Chairman & Co-CEO

Jim Hannan
KII President & COO

Vision: Help each employee better understand and embrace the team/business vision (and associated strategies and priorities) so they can make the greatest contribution to Koch.

- Work with your team to close gaps between today's performance and what is possible. Continually seek to transform.
- Engage with your team and your own supervisor to better identify and stop or modify activities that are not profitable.
- Think long term. Build, acquire, or develop the team capabilities needed to make the greatest contribution.

Virtue and Talents: Hire, develop, and retain contribution-motivated employees with a diversity of aptitudes so your team's culture more fully exemplifies Our Values. Work with your employees so each is in the right role with the right responsibilities and opportunities to self-actualize.

- Treat your team members as individuals. Personalize your coaching of each, including high performers, to help them learn what they are and aren't good at so they can self-actualize and increase their contribution.
- Continually make changes so your team has the right combination of perspectives, experiences, aptitudes, knowledge, and skills to drive profitable transformation.
- Lead by example. Use and ensure your team uses our principle-based framework to guide what everyone does.

Knowledge: Enable every team member to learn and improve so they can better help us succeed in a rapidly changing world.

- Create an inclusive team environment where decision-making is improved by soliciting and providing challenge, seeking and sharing knowledge, and identifying and closing gaps.

- Help your team experiment effectively, take profitable risks, and develop good economic thinking skills.
- Develop and modify your team's measures so they provide the information required for marginal analysis and insights that improve stewardship and profitability.

> **Comparative Advantage:** Maximize what your team and Koch can accomplish by applying Division of Labor by Comparative Advantage so each employee makes the greatest contribution relative to the contributions of others.

- Seek mutual benefit. Help each team member pursue work they are good at and care about in a way that maximizes the team's overall results. Proactively revisit comparative advantage as team members and conditions change.
- Foster a clear, shared understanding of responsibilities, expectations, and decision rights with each employee. Hold yourself and team members accountable for results and behavior consistent with Our Values.
- Remove barriers that stifle good decision-making, collaboration, and employees being in roles where they can best contribute.

> **Motivation:** Motivate each employee to make the maximum contribution to the team and Koch's long-term success by realizing their potential.

- Know your employees well enough to motivate each based on what is important to them, such as pay, meaningful work they have some control over and care about, and opportunities to develop and be creative.
- Encourage employees through your actions as well as words so they proactively create value in new ways.
- Recognize and reward value creation, not activities. Communicate with each team member so they understand how they earned their compensation and can increase it by contributing more.

ACKNOWLEDGMENTS

Most of all, we thank our editorial team: Steve Daley, Stephen Ford, Brian Hooks, Rod Learned, Dave Robertson, and Jodie Stutzman. Without their contributions, this book would not have been possible.

We also thank the many employees and other reviewers, including Liz and Elizabeth, for their invaluable suggestions and guidance.

NOTES

1   Cited in Zach Cutler, "Failure Is the Seed of Growth and Success," *Entrepreneur*, November 6, 2014.

2   F. L. Dyer and T. C. Martin, *Edison: His Life and Inventions* (1910)

3   This quote is based on the idea by Deming in his video series (1988–90); see also Cedric Chin, "Making Sense of Deming," Commoncog.com, updated August 19, 2024, https://commoncog.com/making-sense-of-deming/.

4   Deirdre Nansen McCloskey, *Bourgeois Equality: How Ideas, Not Capital or Institutions, Enriched the World* (University of Chicago Press, 2016), 5–29.

5   Eurostat, OECD, and World Bank (2025); Bolt and van Zanden, Maddison Project Database 2023; Maddison Database 2010—with major processing by Our World in Data. These historical estimates of GDP per capita are adjusted for inflation. We combine three sources to create this time series: the Maddison Database (before 1820), the Maddison Project Database (1820-1989), and the World Bank (1990 onward). Data source: Eurostat, OECD, and World Bank (2025); Bolt and van Zanden - Maddison Project Database 2023; Maddison Database 2010. Learn more about this data. Note: This data is expressed in international-S at 2021 prices. https://ourworldindata.org/economic-growth.

6   Child and Infant Mortality—Our World in Data, https://ourworldindata.org/child-mortality; Life Expectancy—Our World in Data, https://ourworldindata.org/life-expectancy; Poverty—Our World in Data, https://ourworldindata.org/poverty.

7   Thomas Hobbes, *Leviathan* (Cambridge University Press, 1904), 84.

8   Friedrich A. Hayek, *Law, Legislation and Liberty, vol. 2, The Mirage of Social Justice* (University of Chicago Press, 1976), 136.

9   Abraham Maslow, "A Theory of Human Motivation," *Psychological Review* 50 (1943), 370–96.

10 Cited by Scott Thorpe, *How to Think Like Einstein: Simple Ways to Break the Rules and Discover Your Hidden Genius*, 149.

11 Abraham Maslow, *The Farther Reaches of Human Nature* (Viking Press, 1971), 35.

12 Abraham Maslow, *Maslow on Management* (Wiley, 1998), 22.

13 Abraham Maslow, *Toward a Psychology of Being*, 3rd ed. (John Wiley & Sons, 1998), 221.

14 Maslow, *Maslow on Management*, 23.

15 John Stuart Mill, *On Liberty*, 2nd ed. (John W. Parker and Son, 1859), 67.

16 Hayek, *Law, Legislation and Liberty*, 136.

17 Maslow, *The Farther Reaches of Human Nature*, 35.

18 Joseph A. Schumpeter, *Capitalism, Socialism and Democracy*, 84.

19 Schumpeter, *Capitalism, Socialism and Democracy*, 84.

20 Adam Lashinsky, "Amazon's Jeff Bezos: The Ultimate Disrupter," *Fortune*,

November 16, 2012, https://fortune.com/2012/11/16/amazons-jeff-bezos-the-ultimate-disrupter/.

21 Schumpeter, *Capitalism, Socialism and Democracy*, 83.

22 Schumpeter, *Capitalism, Socialism and Democracy*, 84.

23 Letter from Charles Koch dated November 24, 1965.

24 Science as Falsification excerpt was originally published in Karl Popper, *Conjectures and Refutations* (Routledge, 1963), 33–39; Theodore Schick, ed., *Readings in the Philosophy of Science* (Mayfield Publishing Company, 2000), 9–13.

25 Ludwig von Mises, *Human Action: A Treatise on Economics* (Ludwig von Mises Institute, 1998), 13–14.

26 Cited by Scott Thorpe, *How to Think Like Einstein: Simple Ways to Break the Rules and Discover Your Hidden Genius*, 3.

27 Tony Hsieh, "Your Culture Is Your Brand," HuffPost, updated December 6, 2017, https://www.huffpost.com/entry/zappos-founder-tony-hsieh_b_783333.

28 Michael Polanyi, "The Republic of Science: Its Political and Economic Theory," Minerva 1 (1962), 54–73.

29 "Jack Clark's 8 Points of Team Culture," *Hoop Thoughts* (blog), June 11, 2015, https://hoopthoughts.blogspot.com/2015/06/jack-clarks-8-points-of-team-culture.html.

30 Chad Wesley Smith, "Grateful for Everything, Entitled to Nothing," Juggernaut, October 15, 2013, https://www.jtsstrength.com/grateful-everything-entitled-nothing/; "Transcript of Jack Clark—Grateful for Everything, Entitled to Nothing," *Invest Like the Best*, episode 215, https://podcasts.happyscribe.com/invest-like-the-best/jack-clark-grateful-for-everything-entitled-to-nothing-invest-like-the-best-ep.

31 Maslow, *Maslow on Management*, 22.

32 Polanyi, *Personal Knowledge: Towards a Post-Critical Philosophy*, 159.

33 Ludwig von Mises, *Bureaucracy* (Yale University Press, 1944), 13.

34 Robert Brelsford, "Flint Hills' Pine Bend Refinery Commissions Solar Project," *Oil & Gas Journal*, November 13, 2023, https://www.ogj.com/energy-transition/article/14301415/flint-hills-pine-bend-refinery-commissions-solar-project.

35 fred.stlouisfed.org (Downloadable data: https://fred.stlouisfed.org/graph/?g=1CA3x).

36 Viktor Frankl, *Man's Search for Meaning* (Beacon Press, 2006), 112.

37 Abraham Maslow, *Motivation and Personality*, 3rd ed. (Longman, 1987), 22.

38 "Success Index," Populace, Gallup, 2019, https://static1.squarespace.com/static/59153bc0e6f2e109b2a85cbc/t/5d939cc86670c5214abe4b50/1569955251457/Populace+Success+Index.pdf.

39 "Success Index," Populace.

40 de Tocqueville, *Democracy in America: Historical-Critical Edition of De la démocratie en Amérique*, 595.

41 The US Chamber of Commerce reported in 2024 that unemployment for individuals with criminal records tends to be around 30 percent. Stephanie Ferguson Melhorn et al., "The Workforce Impact of Second Chance Hiring," US Chamber of Commerce, September 18, 2024, https://www.uschamber.com/workforce/data-deep-dive-the-workforce-impact-of-second-chance-hiring-3.

42 Adam Smith, *The Theory of Moral Sentiments* (Dover Publications, 2006), 3.

43 Hope King and Eleanor Hawkins, "Fewer Americans want companies to take stance on politics," *Axios*, August 13, 2024, https://www.axios.com/2024/08/13/companies-politics-public-stances-election.

44 "Living Within Our Means," Richard Heffner's Open Mind Archive, December 7, 1975, https://www.thirteen.org/openmind-archive/public-affairs/living-within-our-means/.

45 TRI National Analysis 2015, EPA, January 2017, pages 29, 31, https://www.epa.gov/sites/default/files/2017-01/documents/tri_na_2015_complete_english.pdf.

46 Lily Zheng, "The Failure of the DEI-Industrial Complex," *Harvard Business Review*, December 1, 2022.

47 Shankar Vedantam, "Most Diversity Training Ineffective, Study Finds," *The Washington Post*, January 2008.

48 Maslow, *Maslow on Management*, 281.

49 Gad Levanon, "U.S. Labor Market Outlook," Static1, November 2022, https://static1.squarespace.com/static/6197797102be715f55c0e0a1/t/63865c667d4e5637c709dfae/1669749863982/BGI_LaborMarketOutlook_Nov2022_Final.pdf.

50 Lauren Weber, "62% of Americans Lack a College Degree. Can They Solve the Labor Shortage?," *The Wall Street Journal*, February 16, 2024, https://www.wsj.com/lifestyle/careers/employers-open-more-doors-to-workers-without-degrees-but-few-are-getting-in-732f1098.

51 Veera Korhonen, "U.S. Population by Sex and Age 2023," Statista, August 20, 2024, https://www.statista.com/statistics/241488/population-of-the-us-by-sex-and-age/.

52 Anthony P. Carnevale et al., "After Everything: Projections of Jobs, Education, and Training Requirements Through 2031," Center on Education and the Workforce, 2023, https://cew.georgetown.edu/cew-reports/projections2031/.

53 Gary Fields and John R. Emshwiller, "As Arrest Records Rise, Americans Find Consequences Can Last a Lifetime," *The Wall Street Journal*, August 18, 2014, https://www.wsj.com/articles/as-arrest-records-rise-americans-find-consequences-can-last-a-lifetime-1408415402?mod=article_inline.

54 The State of Skills-Based Hiring in 2023, Test Gorilla, 2023, https://assets.ctfassets.net/vztl6s0hp3ro/5B8Km5VxEDgdx0VhLQTjdX/c27d9e5af3209bf6580e0b52813a7d23/TestGorilla-The-state-of-skills-based-hiring-report-2023.pdf#.

55 Thomas Jefferson, Inaugural Address, March 4, 1801, The American Presidency Project, https://www.presidency.ucsb.edu/people/president/thomas-jefferson.

56 Max Weber, "Politics as a Vocation," *Essays in Sociology*, edited and translated by H.H. Gerth and C. Wright Mills (Routledge, 1946), 77–128.

57 https://www.mercatus.org/research/working-papers/cumulative-cost-regulations

58 Chris Edwards, "Occupational Licensing: Empowering the New American Worker," CATO Institute, December 15, 2022, https://www.cato.org/publications/facilitating-personal-improvement-occupational-licensing.

59 Frederick Douglass, *The Anti-Slavery Movement, A Lecture by Frederick Douglass before the Rochester Ladies' Anti-Slavery Society* (Lee, Mann & Company, 1855), 33.

60 Richard Cornuelle, "De-Nationalizing Community," Philanthropy Roundtable, Spring 1996, https://www.philanthropyroundtable.org/magazine/de-nationalizing-community/.

61 "Charitable Giving Statistics," National Philanthropic Trust, accessed September 24, 2025, https://www.nptrust.org/philanthropic-resources/charitable-giving-statistics/.

62 Douglass, *The Anti-Slavery Movement, A Lecture by Frederick Douglass before the Rochester Ladies' Anti-Slavery Society*, 33.

63 Alexis de Tocqueville, *Democracy in America: Historical-Critical Edition of De la démocratie en Amérique*, ed. Eduardo Nolla, translated from the French by Henry Reeve, Vol. 2, (Pennsylvania State University, 2002), 584.

64 Stand Together, "Adversaries Unite to Achieve Historic Criminal Justice Reform," YouTube, May 20, 2019, https://www.youtube.com/watch?v=BWjLCu41_ps.

65 "NEAP Report Card: Reading, Grade 8, as of 2022," The Nation's Report Card, accessed September 25, 2025, https://www.nationsreportcard.gov/reading/nation/achievement/?grade=8 ; "NEAP Report Card: Mathematics, Grade 8, as of 2022," The Nation's Report Card, accessed September 25, 2025, https://www.nationsreportcard.gov/mathematics/states/achievement/?grade=8.

66 Valerie J. Calderon and Daniela Yu, "Student Enthusiasm Falls as High School Graduation Nears," Gallup, June 1, 2017, https://news.gallup.com/opinion/gallup/211631/student-enthusiasm-falls-high-school-graduation-nears.aspx.

67 Summit Christian Academy, https://castlerockclassical.com/.

68 Path of Life Learning, https://www.pathoflifelearning.com/.

69 Barefoot University, https://barefootuniversity.org/.

70 Ray Ravaglia, "Alpha School: Using AI to Unleash Students and Transform Teaching," *Forbes*, February 10, 2025, https://www.forbes.com/sites/rayravaglia/2025/02/10/alpha-school-using-ai-to-unleash-students-and-transform-teaching/.

71 Editorial Staff, "Alcohol and Drug Abuse Statistics (Facts About Addiction)," American Addiction Centers, March 26, 2025, https://americanaddictioncenters.org/rehab-guide/addiction-statistics-demographics.

72 Owen Dyer, "US Life Expectancy Falls for Third Year in a Row," *British Medical Journal* (December 2018), 363, https://www.bmj.com/content/363/bmj.k5118.

73 Viktor Frankl, *The Unheard Cry for Meaning: Psychotherapy and Humanism* (Simon & Schuster, 1978), 21.

74 Aaron Earls, "Americans' View of Life's Meaning and Purpose Are Changing," Lifeway Research, April 6, 2021, https://research.lifeway.com/2021/04/06/americans-views-of-lifes-meaning-and-purpose-are-changing/.

75 Milton Quintanilla, "75 Percent of Millennials Say They Lack Purpose in Life, Survey Finds," Crosswalk, November 11, 2021, https://www.crosswalk.com/headlines/contributors/milton-quintanilla/75-percent-of-millennials-say-they-lack-purpose-in-life-survey-finds.html.

76 Bob Dylan, "It's Alright, Ma (I'm Only Bleeding)," *Bringing It All Back Home*, 1965, Warner Bros. Inc.

77 Maslow, *Toward a Psychology of Being*, 3rd ed. , 244–45.

78 Thomas Sowell, "Random Thoughts for July 2023," *Capitalism Magazine*, July

25, 2023, https://capitalismmagazine.com/2003/07/random-thoughts-for-july-2003/.

79 Charles Koch, *Good Profit* (Crown Business, 2015), 129.

80 Maslow, *Toward a Psychology of Being*, 245.

81 Von Hayek, Friedrich A., *The Fatal Conceit* (Routledge, 2017).

82 Thomas S. Kuhn, *The Structure of Scientific Revolutions* (Third edition), (University of Chicago Press, 1996), chapters 7 and 8.

83 Alexis de Tocqueville, *Democracy in America* (Harper and Row Publishers, 1969), 526.

84 Schumpeter, *Capitalism, Socialism and Democracy*, 84.

85 "Thomas Sowell: There Are No Solutions, Only Trade-offs," YouTube, Levan Ramishvilli, August 10, 2013, https://www.youtube.com/watch?v=3_EtIWmja-4.

86 Maslow, *Toward a Psychology of Being*, 214.

87 George Will, "How Houston Slipped on the Oil Patch," *The Washington Post*, January 17, 1988.

88 Cited by Scott Thorpe, *How to Think Like Einstein: Simple Ways to Break the Rules and Discover Your Hidden Genius* (Sourcebooks, 2000), 149.

89 Cited in Zach Cutler, "Failure Is the Seed of Growth and Success," *Entrepreneur*, November 6, 2014.

90 Saint Gregory the Great, "Moralia in Job" (Morals on the Book of Job); Vol. III, Part 6, Book XXXI, xlv, paragraph 87; p. 453. (Ex Fontibus Company, 2012).

91 "Isaac Newton Letter to Robert Hooke, 1675," Historical Society of Pennsylvania, accessed September 25, 2025, https://discover.hsp.org/Record/dc-9792/Description#tabnav.

92 Viktor Frankl, *Man's Search for Meaning* (Beacon Press, 2006), 110–11.

93 Frankl, *Man's Search for Meaning*, 65–66.

94 Maslow, *Maslow on Management*, 22.

95 Abraham H. Maslow, *Eupsychian Management: A Journal* (R. D. Irwin, 1965), 27.

96 Thorpe, *How to Think Like Einstein*, 3.

97 Adam Smith, *An Inquiry Into the Nature and Causes of the Wealth of Nations* (Regnery Publishing, Inc., 1998), 156.

98 The phrase opens Book I of The Analects (also called Lunyu), a collection of Confucius' teachings and sayings compiled by his disciples.

99 Polanyi, *Personal Knowledge: Towards a Post-Critical Philosophy* (University of Chicago Press, 1974), 159.

100 Polanyi, *Personal Knowledge*, 95.

101 F. A. Hayek, *Law, Legislation and Liberty* vol. 2 (University of Chicago, 1976), 136.

102 Toward Liberty, Institute for Human Studies, Inc., 1971, 2 and 9.

103 Aristotle, *Politics*, http://classics.mit.edu/Aristotle/politics, accessed December 1, 2008.

104 Michael Polanyi, "Problem Solving," *British Journal for the Philosophy of Science* 8, no. 30 (August 1957): 89–103.

105 Ludwig von Mises, *Human Action: A Treatise on Economics* (Ludwig von Mises Institute, 1998), 13–14.

106 Science as Falsification excerpt was originally published in Karl Popper, *Conjectures and Refutations* (Routledge, 1963), 33–39; Theodore Schick, ed., *Readings in the Philosophy of Science* (Mayfield Publishing Company, 2000), 9–13.

107 Maslow, *Motivation and Personality,* 22.
108 Maslow, *Toward a Psychology of Being,* 214 and 221.
109 Maslow, *The Farther Reaches of Human Nature* (Viking Press, 1971), 35.